BUSHWALKS IN THE SYDNEY REGION

VOLUME 2

Second Edition

Edited by

Stephen Lord and George Daniel

NATIONAL PARKS ASSOCIATION OF NSW INC, 1995

CONTENTS

Introduction - Page 4
The NPA - Page 5
Key Map - Pages 6-7
Index - Page 161

WALK

WALK

INTRODUCTION

This is the second volume of "Bushwalks In The Sydney Region" published by the National Parks Association of New South Wales. Like the first volume, this is a collaborative work, with many NPA members contributing walk suggestions. All those who contributed did so on a voluntary basis, so that the proceeds of this book can support NPA conservation projects and activities.

Eighty-two walks are described, adding to the 73 published in "Bushwalks In The Sydney Region Volume 1". They include walks on newly marked and constructed tracks, little known routes and some of the classic walks in the region. In all, there are 64 one-day walks, 15 two-day walks, 2 three-day walks and 1 six-day walk. Many walks are accessible by public transport and all are accessible by conventional (2WD) vehicles. Although all walks have been edited, an attempt has been made to retain the individuality of each contributor.

GRADES

Most walks in this book are intended for walkers with some experience, however some of the walks would provide a good introduction to bushwalking for beginners. The walks have been graded for people with bushwalking experience as easy (E), easy medium (EM), medium (M), medium-hard (MH) and hard (H). Some beginners may find the easy walks quite difficult. Total ascents (in metres) are provided for each walk.

TRACK DISTANCES & WALK RATE GUIDE

Because of the circuitous and undulating nature of walking tracks, most distances in this book which have been measured on maps are less than the actual distance (perambulated). As a guide, allow 20% more for the track sections than the map wheel distances for more accurate distances. Allow an average of 3-5 km/hour on a fairly level track or fire trail with a 5kg day pack and 3 km/hour with a 12kg (two day) pack. Add 10 minutes for every 300m ascent with a 5kg pack and 15 minutes with a 12kg pack.

MAPS

Spot heights on the maps indicate metres above sea level. Most of the maps are constant scale, 1:25,000, the same as the CMA topographic maps, and are 'true north up'. Magnetic variation for the Sydney region (1995) is 12.2° East.

To use the compass variation diagram: 1) place your compass over the diagram with its dial north aligned with true north, 2) rotate the map till the compass pointer is aligned with the magnetic north of the diagram, 3) the map is now oriented for your position, and by relocating the compass to your position (or where you think you are) read off bearings to features, landmarks from the dial clockwise from true north.

The diagram below indicates how to use topographic map grid references.

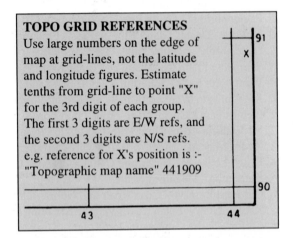

TOPO GRID REFERENCES
Use large numbers on the edge of map at grid-lines, not the latitude and longitude figures. Estimate tenths from grid-line to point "X" for the 3rd digit of each group. The first 3 digits are E/W refs, and the second 3 digits are N/S refs. e.g. reference for X's position is :- "Topographic map name" 441909

Central Mapping Authority (CMA) National Park maps of Blue Mountains, Wollemi, Royal & Heathcote and Ku-ring-gai Chase are useful for showing the way to and from walks and for overall views of the areas. It is also recommended that CMA Topographic Maps be taken on walks into remote parts of Wollemi, Blue Mountains, Kanangra Boyd, Morton and Nattai National Parks. Walkers in these areas should be in parties of at least four, as a safety precaution.

FIRST AID, FOOD AND HYGIENE

The areas of first aid, safety, food, hygiene, equipment and navigation have not been covered in this book, as there are several books devoted to these subjects. Two are: "Australian First Aid" by St John Ambulance of Australia, and "Stay Alive" by Maurice Dunlevy, issued by the Australian Government Publishing Service.

CORRESPONDENCE

Every care has been taken in ensuring the track notes and maps are correct, but no responsibility is taken for any inaccuracies. Constructive criticism, comments and notification of errors are welcome, address to NPA (Sydney Branch), PO BOX A81, Sydney South, NSW, 2000.

THE NATIONAL PARKS ASSOCIATION OF NSW

The National Parks Association of New South Wales Inc (NPA) is a non-government community organisation. Although it often works closely with the National Parks and Wildlife Service, the NPA is a separate organisation largely funded by its members.

The NPA works for the establishment of a system of national parks and reserves which will sample and protect every major vegetation community in New South Wales. NPA also has a particular interest in the protection of wildlife and is working for endangered species legislation. The other major area of activity is monitoring the management of national parks to ensure that the values of each area are not compromised by inappropriate and destructive activities. NPA also aims to promote environmental education and the conservation of the natural environment outside the national park system.

Since its inception in 1957, NPA has been involved in thousands of conservation issues. Its first major activity was to develop and lobby for an act to establish the National Parks and Wildlife Service, a goal finally achieved in 1967. Since then, NPA has submitted many national park proposals to the State government. A number of our present parks, including Barrington Tops, Mount Kaputar, Brisbane Water, Myall Lakes, Seven Mile Beach and Nangar National Parks, are the result of carefully researched submissions prepared by NPA. One of NPA's current projects is to promote "Greenbelt" reserves around the periphery of Sydney and the protection of the remaining small pockets of natural vegetation on the Cumberland Plain in western Sydney.

NPA provides a regular walks program for its members. Over 400 walks are available in the Sydney region each year. They range from easy one day strolls to week-long wilderness walks. Canyoning, canoeing, cycling, abseiling, base camping and overseas trekking are also available. Many activities are suitable for family groups.

Membership of NPA also gives you:
1. The bi-monthly National Parks Journal with articles on conservation issues, the walks program, notices of meetings and activities, book reviews, branch news, photographs and letters.
2. Monthly meetings with guest speakers, slide shows and discussions, a lecture series on National Parks, environmental issues and the natural sciences (extra fee payable) and social functions.

3. The opportunity to join a working committee to help influence the outcome of conservation issues.

NPA has recently published a definitive guide to the 49 National Parks and State Recreation Areas in the northern half of New South Wales. As well as outlining the parks' walking tracks, the Guide comprehensively describes landform, history, vegetation, wildlife, visitor facilities and other recreational opportunities of the areas. The Guide is available from NPA branches and selected book shops.

NPA BRANCHES

NPA has 19 branches located throughout the state. Each has a walking program and committees and working groups which tackle regional conservation issues.

NPA branches are located at Armidale, Berrima (Southern Highlands), Blue Mountains, Central Coast, Central West, Clarence Valley, Far North Coast, Far South Coast, Hawkesbury-Cumberland, Hunter, Illawarra, Lachlan Valley, Macarthur, Mid North Coast, Milton, Southern Sydney, Sydney, Tamworth (Namoi Valley) and Three Valleys (Nambucca).

If you are interested in joining NPA, either to participate in our walks program or to help with the group's conservation work, please contact the NPA at the address below..

NPA State Council Head Office,
Room 12, Level 4,
Imperial Arcade,
83-87 Castlereagh Street, Sydney
PO Box A96, Sydney South, 2000.
Phone (02)233-4660.
Fax (02)233-4880

Membership fees (1995) are:-
Adult	$38
Family/Household	$45
Concession	$19
Schools/Libraries	$50
Corporate	$100

Donations of $2.00 or over to NPA are tax deductible.

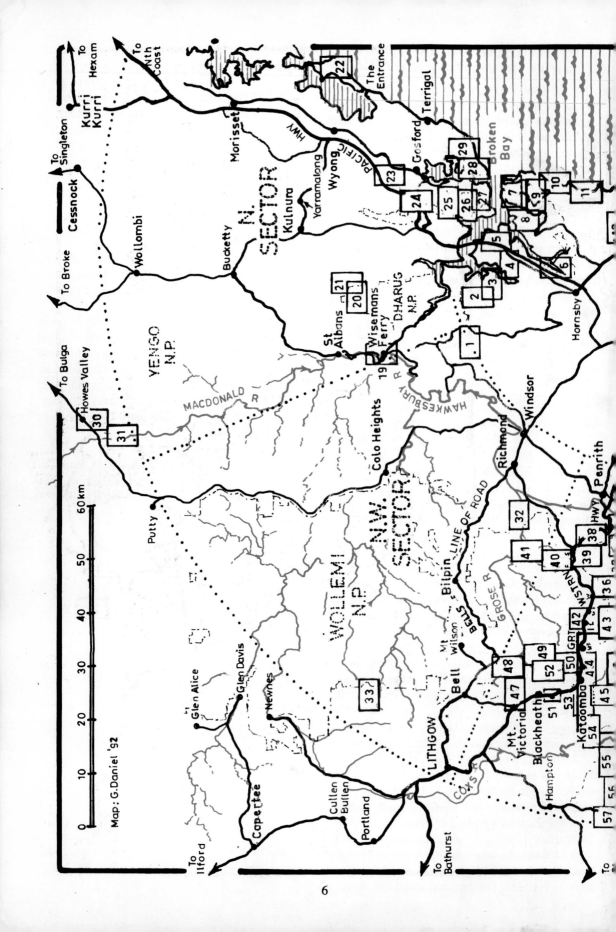

Map: G.Daniel '92

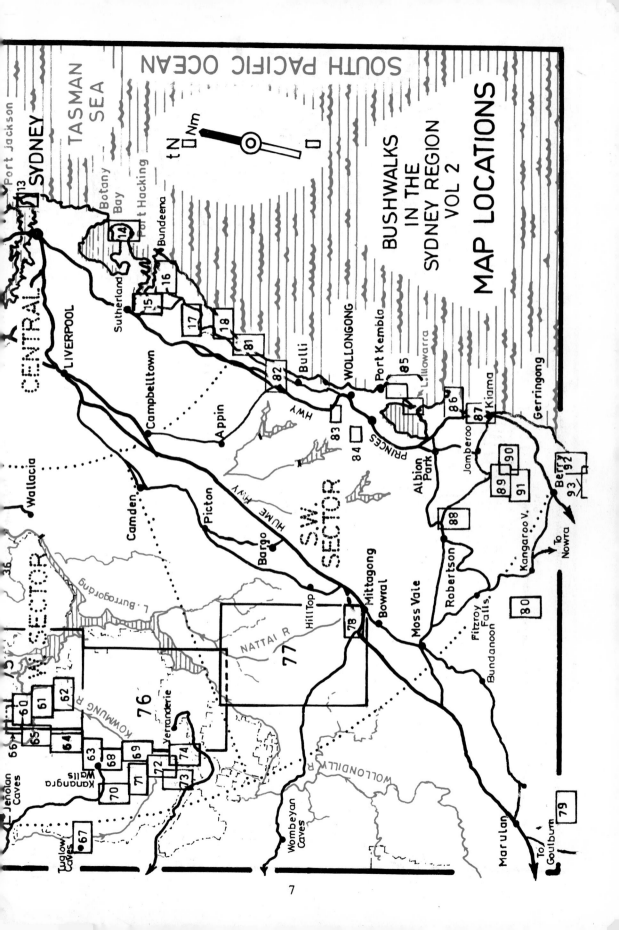

BUSHWALKS
IN THE
SYDNEY REGION
VOL 2

MAP LOCATIONS

SOUTH PACIFIC OCEAN

TASMAN SEA

SYDNEY

Port Jackson

Botany Bay

Port Hacking

Bundeena

Sutherland

Liverpool

Campbelltown

Appin

Bulli

WOLLONGONG

Port Kembla

Dapto

Lake Illawarra

Kiama

Jamberoo

Gerringong

Albion Park

Kangaroo V.

Robertson

To Nowra

Berry

Moss Vale

Bowral

Mittagong

Hill Top

Bundanoon

Fitzroy Falls

Camden

Picton

Bargo

S.W. SECTOR

NATTAI R.

HUME HWY

PRINCES HWY

L. Burragorang

KOWMUNG R.

Yerranderie

Kanangra Walls

Jenolan Caves

Tuglow Caves

WOLLONDILLY R.

Wombeyan Caves

Marulan

To Goulburn

Wallacia

N.W. SECTOR

7

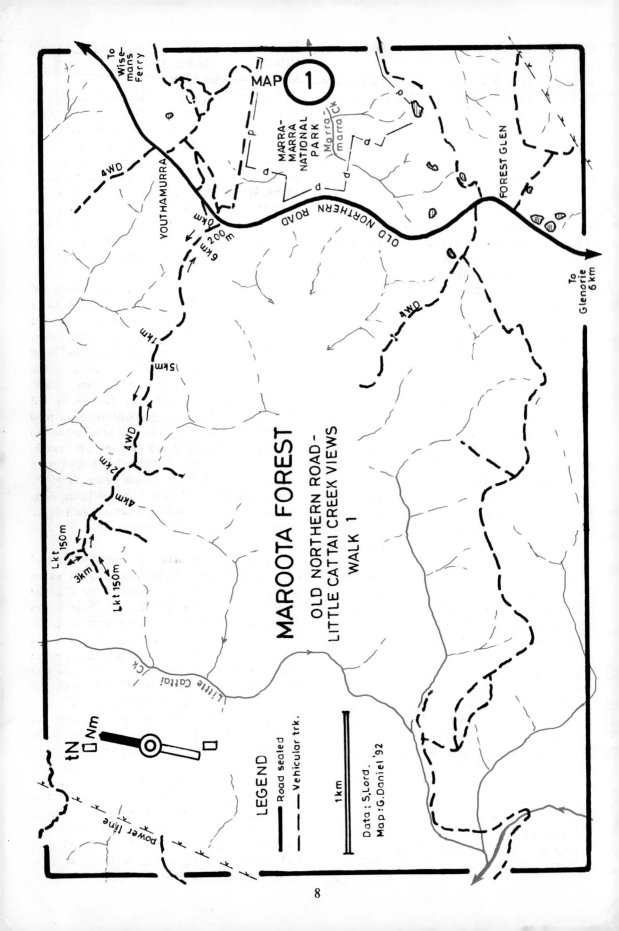

MAP (1)

MAROOTA FOREST

OLD NORTHERN ROAD –
LITTLE CATTAI CREEK VIEWS

WALK 1

MARRA-MARRA NATIONAL PARK

OLD NORTHERN ROAD

FOREST GLEN

To Wisemans Ferry

To Glenorie 6km

YOUTHAMURRA

Marra-marra Ck

Little Cattai Ck

LEGEND
Road sealed
Vehicular trk.

1km

Data: S. Lord.
Map: G. Daniel '92

Power line

tN
Nm

4WD
6km
200m
1km
5km
4WD
2km
4km
Lkt 150m
3km
Lkt 150m
4WD

CENTRAL AREA

1. MAROOTA FOREST: OLD NORTHERN ROAD - LITTLE CATTAI CREEK VIEWS

The Maroota Forest, a long standing National Park proposal of both NPA and the NP&WS, is located approximately 28km NW of Sydney west of the Old Northern Road, between Glenorie and Maroota. It contains most of the upper catchment of Little Cattai Creek.

The proposed park has fine samples of Hawkesbury sandstone vegetation communities, rare plant and animal species, and unpolluted, weed-free creeks. The area supports a wide range of wildlife, including the Platypus, Koalas, Wombats, Grey Kangaroos, Wedge Tailed Eagles, Lyrebirds and Gang Gang cockatoos. The area also provides catchment protection to Little Cattai and Kellys Creeks, both of which drain into the Broadwater Swamp - a valuable waterbird breeding and feeding area. Unfortunately, due to Government inaction in dedicating this forest as National Park, the subsequent lack of management has resulted in the area suffering damage in the forms of illegal rubbish dumping and bush rock theft. However, the recently elected Carr Government has stated it will dedicate the area as a National Park within its first year - lets hope they keep their promise.

This walk, which provides a sample of the Maroota Forest, starts from a bend in the Old Northern Road 9km north of Glenorie (1km south of the Yoothamurra Kiosk). Leave the car just south of the fire trail junction.

Walk along the fire trail which leads NW along the ridge top. At 2km and 2.2km there are trail junctions; veer right at both. In late Winter and early Spring there are fine displays of wildflowers along the way. Towards the end of the bluff the trail forks again. Take the right fork a short distance to where the trail ends at a large rock shelf. From here and a little way down the ridge there are views of the Little Cattai Creek valley and the valley of one of its major eastern tributaries. The lush vegetation which can be seen on the valley floors contain huge Deanes Gums. Return the short distance to the trail junction and turn right along the other branch trail for 250m to another rocky outcrop where there are more views into the valleys to the west and south. After a break, return the same way.

Grade: Easy, 50m asc. **Distance:** 7km.
Best in Spring. No Public Transport.
Map 1 and CMA Cowan and Wilberforce.

Stephen Lord

2. MARRAMARRA N.P.: SMUGGLERS RIDGE - MARRAMARRA CREEK - MARRAMARRA RIDGE

Smugglers Ridge in Marramarra National Park is said to be named after the practice of smuggling rum into the infant colony of NSW along this northern route. One wonders how the early colonists found this negotiable ridge so far from Sydney Town - perhaps they followed aboriginal routes. This pleasant 13km walk, which is mostly on fire trails, is best in late winter and early spring when the Eriostamon, Boronia and other wildflowers are in bloom. The impact of early farming and later urban settlement can also be observed.

To reach the walk starting point, turn off Arcadia Road into Cobah Road at Arcadia. Drive along Cobah Rd for 3.3km (Cobah Rd has a number of unusual turns, so follow the street signs carefully). Cobah Road becomes Bloodwood Road where Nollands Road crosses it. At this point set your tripmeter to zero. Follow Bloodwood Road north and NNE disregarding fire trails on the left and right. At 4.7km along, you will come to a road fork where Cobah Ridge fire trail branches off to your right. Disregard it and take the left branch, which veers westward. A National Park sign is on your right. The trail then passes under electricity transmission lines. At 6km from Nollands Road intersection, there is parking space on the left for several cars. A fire trail branches off to the west here.

Start the walk by taking this westward fire trail for 2km. Once past a locked gate, you are within Marramarra National Park. Continue on the trail which follows Smugglers Ridge. There is an Aboriginal rock carving of a kangaroo on a flat rock by this road. Just under 2.5km from the locked gate you come to an extensive rock platform which overlooks Marramarra Creek. This is a pleasant spot for morning tea. Search for the commencement of a narrow foot track, initially leading off NE, then turning NNE and descending. Near the creek the remains of fences can be seen on the hillside. Below you on the flat by the water is an untended orange orchard. The orchard and fences are reminders that small patches of arable land along the tributaries of the Hawkesbury were cultivated at a time when river transport was used to take the crops to buyers. At low tide, Marramarra Creek is very shallow. It is interesting to speculate on the effect of cultivation, both beside the creek and in its head-waters, in reducing the navigability of this creek.

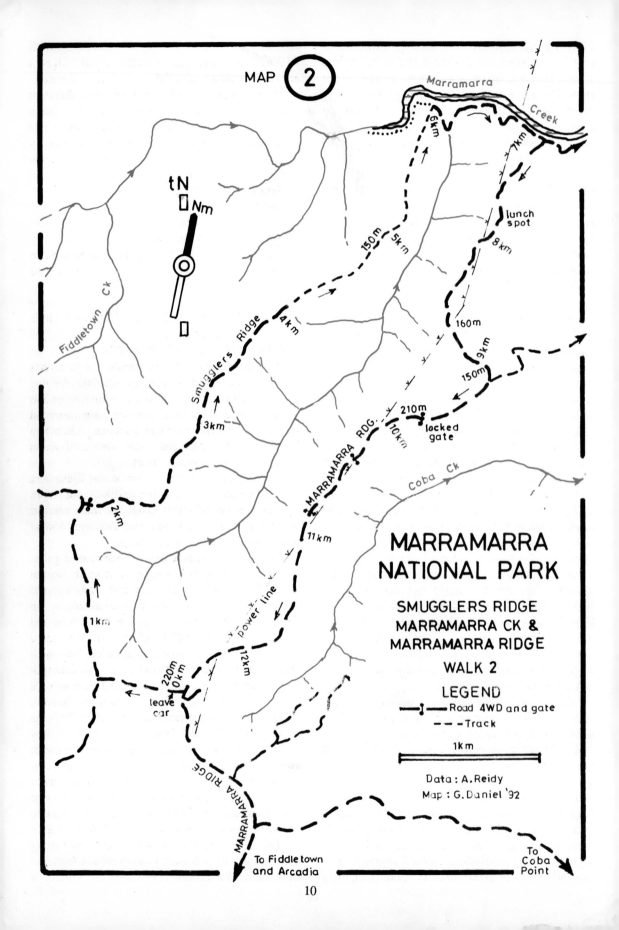

MAP ②

Marramarra Creek

tN ☐ Nm ☐

6km

7km

lunch spot

Fiddletown Ck

150m 5km

8km

Smugglers Ridge 4km

160m

3km

9km

150m

210m

MARRAMARRA RDG. 10km

locked gate

Coba Ck

2km

11km

MARRAMARRA NATIONAL PARK

SMUGGLERS RIDGE
MARRAMARRA CK &
MARRAMARRA RIDGE

WALK 2

LEGEND

power line

1km

220m 0km

12km

leave car

├──┤ Road 4WD and gate
- - - Track

1km

Data : A. Reidy
Map : G. Daniel '92

MARRAMARRA RIDGE

To Fiddletown
and Arcadia

To Coba Point

10

A fire trail follows Marramarra Ck downstream near its southern bank. Follow it and in 1.2km you meet a fire trail coming down the steep hill on your right. This gives access to Marramarra Ridge, your return route. If you continue by the creek you will find that the grassy verge narrows and thicker vegetation bars further progress downstream.

The steep ascent to Marramarra Ridge will give you an appetite for lunch which is best enjoyed atop one of the rocky outcrops bordering the fire trail. Continue on the trail to the locked gate which marks the Marramarra Ridge entry to the National Park. Beyond this (3km) you will find the place where you left your car.

Grade: Easy/Medium, 250m asc.

Distance: 13km.

Best in late Winter and early Spring.

No public transport.

Map 2 and CMA Cowan and Hawkesbury River (Tourist). Anita Reidy

3. MARRAMARRA NP.:
COBA RIDGE - COBA POINT

From the bluff above Coba Point within Marramarra National Park there are panoramic views of Berowra Creek and the Hawkesbury River. The only access is by walking along a disued fire trail along Coba Ridge.

From Arcadia Road, turn into Cobah Road and travel 3.3km to Bloodwood Road (Cobah Rd has a number of unusual turns, so follow the street signs carefully). Travel north along Bloodwood Rd for 4.7km to a distinctive "Y" road junction - left branch to "Marramarra Creek" and right branch to "Cobah Ridge". Take the right (eastern) road along Coba Ridge. Drive along the fire trail for 2.8km to a trail junction and a sign "Marramarra National Park" and park the car. Depending on road conditions, it might only be possible to drive for 1km along this trail.

Walk down the right hand trail. After 1.7km there is the first of a series of SE turn offs. Continue left (north-east) at all junctions. After 3.1km the fire trail is barred by a locked gate, and the fire trail beyond has reverted to a walking track. This track, which passes through areas of Red Bloodwood, Scribbly Gum, Stringybarks with understories of Banksia, Grevillia, Geebung and Mountain Devil, leads all the way to the bluff over Coba Point. A large rock shelf on the right of the track 2.8km beyond the gate (just before the track makes a steep descent), provides good views up Berowra Creek,

and into Coba Bay.

There are open grassy areas on the ridgetop above Coba point and a little further down the ridge there are panoramic views of Coba Bay, Berowra Creek, Bar island and the Hawkesbury. This is the suggested site for lunch and a long break. Coba point bluff is in excellent condition - no litter or ugly fireplace rings. Make sure you help keep it that way. Return by the same route.

Grade: Easy/Medium, 220m asc.

Distance: 14km.

No Public Transport.

Best Season: Autumn, Winter and Spring.

Map 3 and CMA Cowan & Hawkesbury River (Tourist). Stephen Lord

4. BEROWRA VALLEY BUSHLAND PARK: BEROWRA TO COWAN VIA THE GREAT NORTH WALK

The Great North Walk (constructed in 1988) has provided some excellent new opportunities for day walks close to Sydney that can be reached by public transport. The walk from Berowra to Cowan via Berowra Creek passes through a section of Berowra Valley Bushland Park and offers wonderful views from a number of vantage points.

From Berowra station, cross at the lights and walk south along the Pacific Highway, then turn right into Berowra Waters Road. The track starts at the intersection of Crowley and Berowra Waters Roads (near the telephone exchange).

Follow the track as it winds steeply into a gully. After 750 metres, take a signposted track (to the Great North Walk) on the right and cross a creek. After 1.3km there is a track junction where the Great North Walk enters from the south. Keep on the fire trail heading NNW. After about 500m there is an excellent view from a rock ledge. The view encompasses a reach of Berowra Ck, with Sams Ck Inlet directly below, and the Calna Ck/Berowra Ck confluence further to the south. Mangroves line the western shore and waterbirds can often be seen soaring above Berowra Creek.

After a break continue along the fire trail as it swings north. After 400m, leave the fire trail and take a signposted track on the left. Follow this track down to a creek, over two wooden bridges, then up some steps and on to a ridge, where there are more excellent views of Berowra Ck from rock outcrops.

The track then steeply descends. At one point there is a set of well-made stone steps that lead to a small cave. The cave is a good spot for a break, it

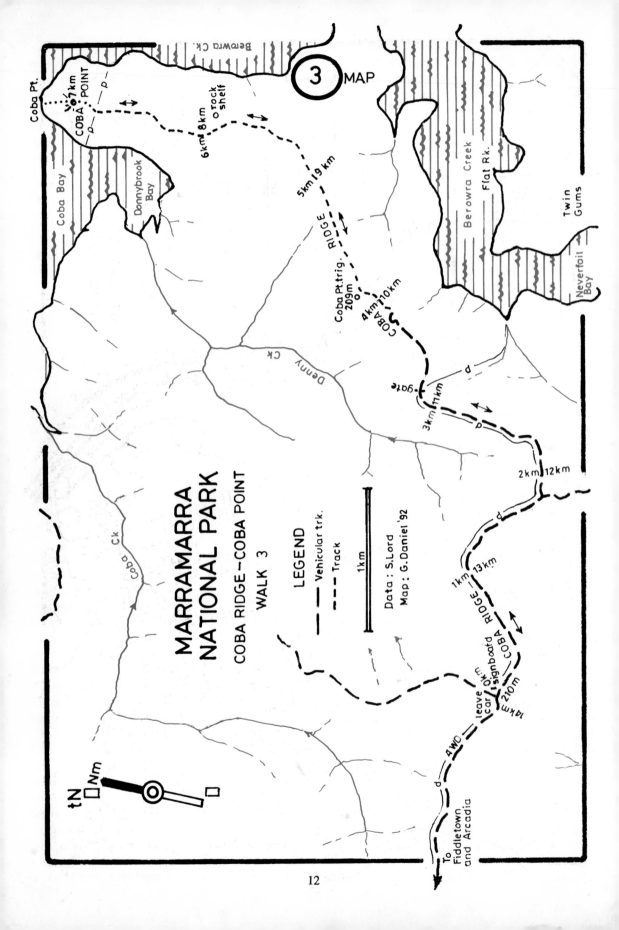

MARRAMARRA NATIONAL PARK

COBA RIDGE – COBA POINT

WALK 3

LEGEND

— · — Vehicular trk.
– – – Track

Data : S. Lord
Map : G. Daniel '92

1km

Coba Pt.
Coba Pt.
COBA POINT
COBA POINT
1·7 km

Berowra Ck.

③ MAP

6km 8km
rock shelf

5km 19 km

RIDGE

Coba Pt. trig.
209m

4km 10km
COBA

Coba Bay

Donnybrook Bay

Denny Ck

Coba Ck

Berowra Creek

Flat Rk.

Twin Gums

Neverfail Bay

gate
3km 11km

2km 12km

1km 13km

COBA RIDGE

leave car 0km
signboard
210m
14km

4WD

To Fiddletown and Arcadia

N
Nm

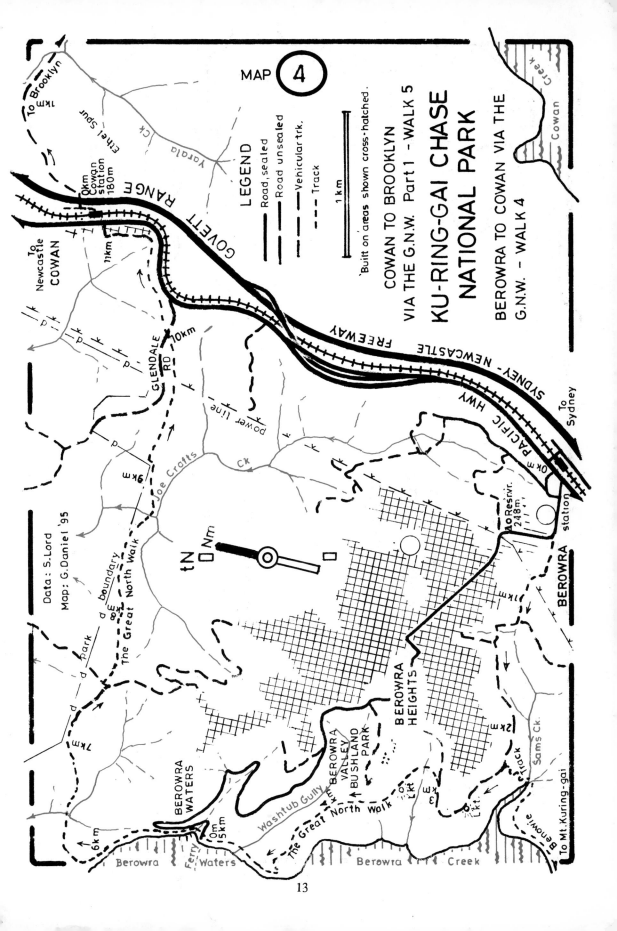

MAP 4

KU-RING-GAI CHASE NATIONAL PARK

COWAN TO BROOKLYN VIA THE G.N.W. Part1 – WALK 5

BEROWRA TO COWAN VIA THE G.N.W. – WALK 4

LEGEND
Road, sealed
Road unsealed
Vehicular trk.
Track

1 km

'Built on areas shown cross-hatched.'

Data: S.Lord
Map: G.Daniel '95

tN   Nm

GOVETT RANGE

To Brooklyn
1km

Ethel Spur

Cowan station 180m
9km

Yarala Ck

To Newcastle
COWAN

11km

GLENDALE RD
10km

power line

Joe Crafts

9km

Ck

The Great North Walk

park boundary

7km

6km

BEROWRA WATERS

0m 5km

Washtub Gully

The Great North Walk

Berowra Waters

BEROWRA VALLEY BUSHLAND PARK

BEROWRA HEIGHTS

Berowra Creek

Lkt.

3km

2km

Sams Ck.

Benowie Track

To Mt.Kuring-gai

Reservr. 248m

1km

BEROWRA station

To Sydney

PACIFIC HWY

SYDNEY - NEWCASTLE FREEWAY

0km

Cowan Creek

13

even contains a bench seat. The track continues down to the waters edge, then follows the eastern shore of Berowra Creek, past Washtub Gully Ck, to Berowra Waters.

At Berowra Waters, there are Tea Rooms and Boat-sheds where you can buy a meal and refreshments. Where a creek flows under Berowra Waters Rd and near the toilets, there is a stand of riverine gallery rainforest - a restricted and important vegetation community.

Head north along the road that follows the eastern shore of Berowra Ck, past a fenced car-park, and onto a track that continues north. After 900m, the track leads east away from Berowra Creek and climbs steeply up the ridge. In a short distance you ascend 100m. On top of the ridge there is a large rock from which there are panoramic views of Berowra Waters and further south - including some of the country you have traversed. This rock outcrop makes an excellent spot for lunch.

After lunch, follow the track as it leads east down off the ridge and into the upper catchment of Deep Bay Ck. The track sidles down into the gully, and crosses the creek which contains clear water-holes. The track then contours SE, before leading up and along a ridge. There is one more great view, this time to the north, of Joe Crafts Bay and Berowra Ck, with the ridges of Marramarra N.P. and Muogamarra Nature Reserve in the distance.

The track continues to where it meets a fire trail. Follow this fire trail for about 400m, then take a fire trail on the left. After a short distance, take the signposted walking track on the right which follows a ridge in an easterly direction. Berowra and upper Joe Crafts Ck valley can be seen to the south. The track follows a spur down to Joe Crafts Ck, then continues east up a spur. Once on the ridge top, the track crosses a fire trail, passes under a power-line, then crosses a second trail. You then continue on through some Casuarinas to meet Glendale Rd. Cross over and follow the track as it sidles around a gully quite close to the Pacific Highway. The track then joins a fire trail west of Cowan village. Follow the fire trail for 350m, then turn right and up to the Pacific Highway. Immediately opposite is Cowan railway station.

Grade: Medium, 200m asc.

Distance: 14km.

Public Transport: Train to Berowra and Cowan stations.   Suits Autumn, Winter and Spring.

Map 4 and CMA Cowan.

Stephen Lord

5. KU-RING-GAI CHASE N.P.:
COWAN TO BROOKLYN
VIA THE GREAT NORTH WALK

Until recently, the NW section of Ku-ring-gai Chase National Park remained an undeveloped secret. The Great North Walk now provides access to this scenic area. The track leads to spectacular view points over the Hawkesbury River and Cowan Creek and to an historic railway dam.

From Cowan railway station, cross to the eastern platform and descend some steps. Turn left and walk north for 75 metres beside the railway line. Take the track on the right which leads through the bush, then across the F3 freeway via a concrete bridge. The track then descends from Ethel Spur to cross Yarala Creek which flows into Jerusalem Bay. It then follows the northern side of the creek. At low tide you can walk along the sandy flats of the Jerusalem Bay inlet. There are mangroves and water birds, and armies of soldier crabs. Follow the track or the sandy flats around to the head of the north-west arm of the bay.

For the next 3km the track is rudimentary but is clearly marked with red trail blazes. The track leads past a cave just above the water-line, then directly up a ridge to the north. From vantage points there are views of Jerusalem Bay and ridges to the south. The track then crosses Govett Ridge and Ten Bob Ridge then down to Campbells Creek.

Continue on NNW gradually ascending to the top of a major N-S ridge. Along the way, the track passes by a beautiful sandstone cave and there are views into pristine valleys to the east. Where the track meets a fire trail, there are views of the F3 freeway and the northern railway line.

Follow the fire trail north where there are fine views of Porto Bay, the Hawkesbury River, Sandbrook Inlet and Long Island - a good spot for a lunch break. The trail descends to Brooklyn Dam which was built as a water supply for steam trains. Take the track which passes just downstream of the dam, then rejoins the fire trail. Follow the main fire trail as it leads east, ignoring branches on both sides that lead to power-line pylons. Finally, take the signposted walking track on the left down via some steps to the Brooklyn Road, just east of the railway bridge. Continue east along Brooklyn Rd to the Brooklyn shops and railway station.

Grade: Medium, 300m asc.   **Distance:** 10km.

Public Transport: Train to Cowan and from Hawkesbury River railway stations.

Best in Autumn, winter and Spring.

Maps 4,5 and CMA Cowan   Stephen Lord

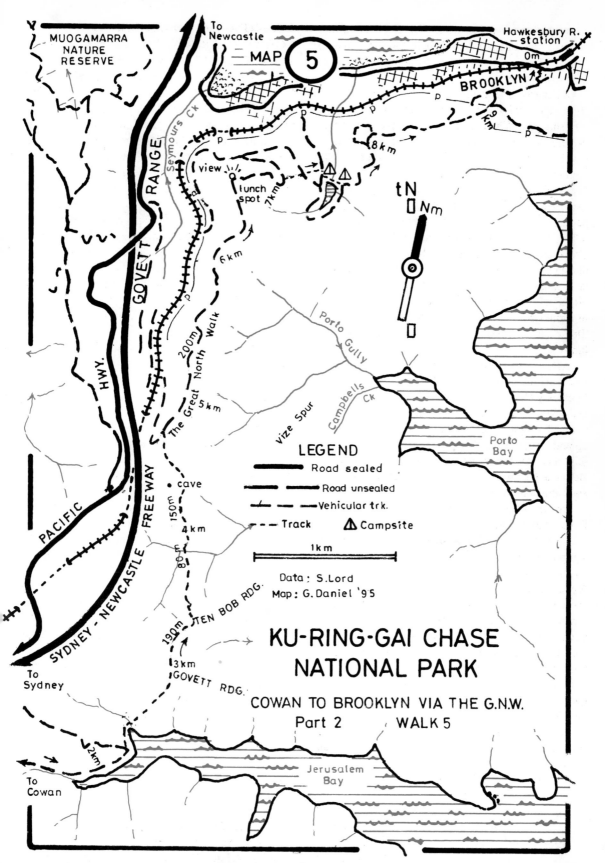

MUOGAMARRA NATURE RESERVE

To Newcastle

MAP 5

To Newcastle

Hawkesbury R. station

BROOKLYN

0m

9 km

8 km

view

lunch spot

7 km

tN

Nm

6 km

Seymours Ck

GOVETT RANGE

Porto Gully

Campbells Ck

200m

The Great North Walk

5 km

Vize Spur

Porto Bay

PACIFIC HWY.

SYDNEY - NEWCASTLE FREEWAY

cave

150m

4 km

80m

LEGEND

Road sealed

Road unsealed

Vehicular trk.

Track ⚠ Campsite

1 km

Data: S. Lord
Map: G. Daniel '95

TEN BOB RDG.

190m

3km

GOVETT RDG.

KU-RING-GAI CHASE NATIONAL PARK

COWAN TO BROOKLYN VIA THE G.N.W.

Part 2 WALK 5

2km

To Sydney

To Cowan

Jerusalem Bay

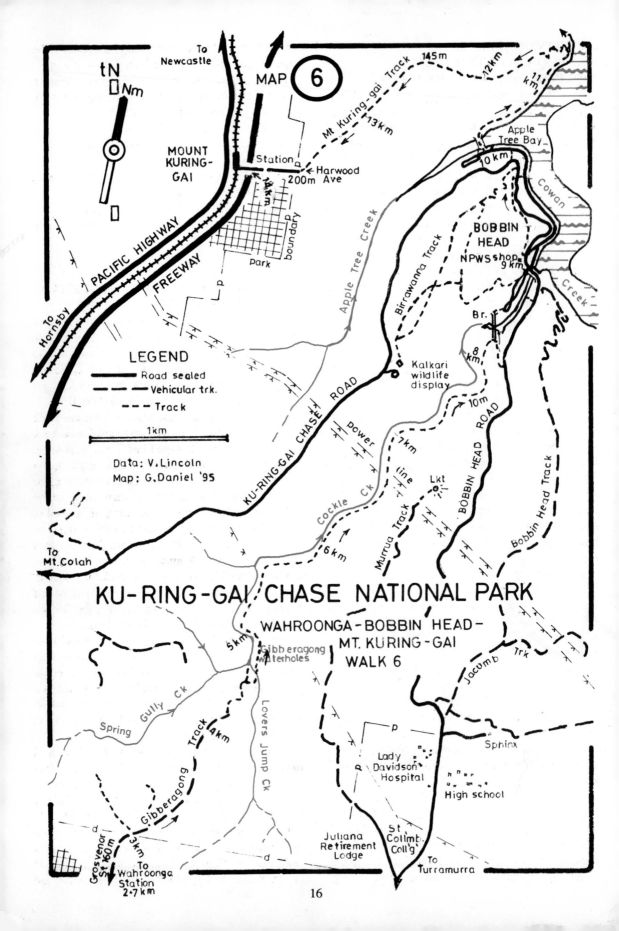

MAP ⑥

To Newcastle

tN
Nm

MOUNT KURING-GAI

PACIFIC HIGHWAY

FREEWAY

To Hornsby

Mt Kuring-gai Track   145m   12km   11km

13km

Apple Tree Bay

Station
Harwood 200m Ave

10km

boundary

park

Apple Tree Creek

Birrawanna Track

BOBBIN HEAD
NPWS shop
9km

Cowan

Creek

Br.

8km

LEGEND

Road sealed
Vehicular trk.
Track

1km

Data: V. Lincoln
Map: G. Daniel '95

KU-RING-GAI CHASE ROAD

Kalkari wildlife display

power line   7km

10m

BOBBIN HEAD ROAD

Bobbin Head Track

Cockle Ck

6km

Murrua Track

Lkt

To Mt. Colah

KU-RING-GAI CHASE NATIONAL PARK

WAHROONGA - BOBBIN HEAD - MT. KURING-GAI
WALK 6

5km
Gibberagong Waterholes

Jacomb Trk

Spring Gully Ck

Lovers Jump Ck

Gibberagong Track   4km

p

Sphinx

Lady Davidson Hospital

High school

Grosvenor St 160 m   3km

To Wahroonga Station 2·7 km

Juliana Retirement Lodge

St Columb. Coll'g

To Turramurra

d

6. KU-RING-GAI CHASE N.P.: WAHROONGA - BOBBIN HEAD - APPLETREE BAY - MT KURING-GAI

The Bobbin Head section of Ku-ring-gai Chase National Park has an excellent network of walking tracks. It is possible to walk from Wahroonga to Mt Kuring-gai following the Gibberagong (Grovenor), Birrawanna and Mt Kuring-gai Tracks. Features along the way include the Gibberagong water-holes, mangroves, and lookouts over Cowan Water.

This walk starts from the northern end of Grovenor Street. The shortest route to the trackhead from Wahroonga station (2.7km) is via Illoura Avenue, Stuart Street and Cleveland Street.

The fire trail leads directly on from the end of Grovenor Street. After 100m take the right hand trail. At a small cliff-line the fire trail ends and a track, which continues directly ahead, winds downhill to the Gibberagong Water Holes.

Immediately before the Gibberagong Water Holes the track forks. Take the right branch and cross Lovers Jump Creek. Follow the track as it bears around the eastern side of the water holes. There are a couple of large rocks which serve as vantage points for views over the water holes.

Continue on down the track as it follows Cockle Creek. This is a beautiful gully, especially in Spring. Further downstream you will see mangroves in the estuarine section of the creek. The track veers away from the creek up onto a low ridge. At a track junction, take the left branch which leads down to a newly constructed boardwalk through a fine stand of Mangroves and a bridge over Cockle Creek.

Once across the bridge, walk through the Bobbin Head picnic areas to the Bobbin Inn. At the NP&WS Wildlife Shop, take the signposted Birrawanna Track up a gully via a number of steps, then uphill to Ku-ring-gai Chase Road near the NP&WS district office. Cross the road and have lunch overlooking Cowan Water.

After lunch, locate the rough track which commences at the western end of the picnic area, and follow it down to Apple Tree Bay. Cross the wooden footbridge and set off NE along the track round the waters edge for 1km to a signposted track junction. Take the left hand "Mount Kuring-gai" track which takes you to Mt Kuring-gai station. This track is quite steep at first and contains two zigzags. Further on (at about the 10.5 km "mark") you will come to a magnificent rock section on the right. If you have time, it is a great place to explore. There are chasms, clefts and a large orange coloured cave. Return to the track, up some stone steps around the rocks and then follow the level track to the eastern end of Harwood Avenue. Follow Harwood Avenue to a footbridge over the F3 Freeway to Mt Kuring-gai station.

Grade: Easy/Medium, 210m asc.
Distance: 11km, (14 km station to station).
Best Season: Spring.
Public Transport. Train to Wahroonga and from Mt Kuring-gai stations.
Map 6 and CMA Hornsby and Cowan.

Val Lincoln

7. KU-RING-GAI CHASE N.P.: GREAT MACKEREL BEACH - WEST HEAD - WHITE HORSE BEACH

The West Head area offers excellent views of Pittwater and the Hawkesbury River. The area is also of historical interest, in that some of the landmarks are associated with one of Governor Phillip's early expeditions. There are also some gun emplacement ruins dating from World War II.

From the jetty at Great Mackerel Beach, walk north along the beach, cross a small creek to a track at a sloping diamond-shaped large rock near some Cabbage Tree palms. Follow this track as it contours past Resolute Beach, then around a point to near West Head Beach, a small cove where Governor Phillip and his exploration party stayed in 1788. The track then goes past numerous steps on your left. Signs on short posts mark the way up a steep slope to a track junction (1.6km from Great Mackerel Beach). Turn right and walk for 300m to the picnic area at West Head. West Head has one of Sydney's finest lookouts with views over Broken Bay, Barrenjoey, Pittwater and Palm Beach.

From West Head walk up the West Head road for 750m to the eastern arm of the Koolewong track. Take this track to another great lookout where there is a very fine gnarled Sydney Redgum on the clifftop. There are views over Lion Island and Brisbane Water National Park. Return to the road via the western arm.

Walk westward for 1.2km along the West Head road to a car-park on the right of the road. Walk through the car-park and take the track which heads off in a NW direction. At a junction, turn right at the sign to White Horse Beach. On the way down to this beach you will see a saddle on your left with a faint foot track. Take this track for 200m to a rocky clifftop above Flint and Steel Beach for more great views. Return to the White Horse Beach track and

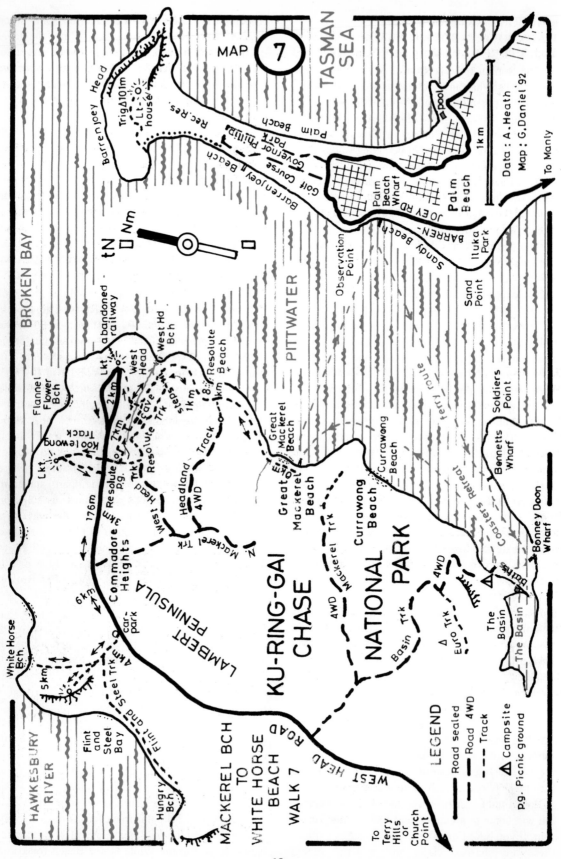

walk down to White Horse Beach.

Take a break here, before returning to the West Head Road and then walk back along the road towards West Head to the Resolute Picnic area. Walk through the picnic area to its southern corner and follow the Resolute track southward. After about 100m turn left at the Red Hand track, past a rock overhang with hand stencils, to a track junction (600m). Turn right and follow this track until you reach a track junction encountered earlier (straight ahead leads to West Head). Turn right and follow the track back to Great Mackerel Beach.

Grade: Medium, 360m asc.**Distance:** 11km.
Suits all seasons.
Public Transport: Bus from Wynyard to Palm Beach Wharf and ferry to Great Mackerel Beach.
Map 7 and CMA Ku-ring-gai N.P. (Tourist).
    Reference: "Sydney Cove 1788" by Dr. John
    Cobley.   Alan Heath

8. KU-RING-GAI CHASE N.P.: WILLUNGA, WALLAROO AND SALVATION TRACKS

The Lambert Peninsula in Ku-ring-gai Chase National Park offers wonderful views of Cowan Creek and Pittwater. Walks on the peninsula are especially good in the Springtime when the wildflowers are in bloom.

Park your car at the Willunga walk trackhead (footprint track 6) on the western side of West Head Road. Walk along this track for 1km to the highest point in the National Park - where there are extensive views of both Cowan Creek and Pittwater from near the trig. After a break, walk SW down the ridge on a narrow track for 150m to a large rock shelf - where there are more great views. Next, continue SW on a track for 250m to the Salvation track. Turn right (west) and walk for 300m to a track junction. Veer right (WNW) on the Wallaroo track. After 1.7km there is another track junction. Take the right branch and walk for 1.3km to a good lookout at the end of the track.

Return to the Salvation track junction. Turn left (ENE) and walk for 1.4km to the West Head Road. Turn left, and walk north 1km along West Head Road to the car.

Grade: Easy, 130m asc.   **Distance:** 10km.
Best in springtime   No Public transport.
Map 8 and CMA Ku-ring-gai N.P. (Tourist)
                                          Alan Heath

9. KU-RING-GAI CHASE N.P.: WARATAH TRACK

The Waratah track, on the Lambert Peninsula, leads to some delightful lookouts with extensive views of Coal and Candle Creek. The walk starting point is at Footprint track 2 on the western side of West Head Road.

The track undulates through heath and forest country. Wildflowers are a delight in Spring. After 2.5km, the track crosses a large bare rock patch. Look for some aboriginal rock engravings on the right here. About 700m further on, you will see a flat-topped hill with a rocky outcrop at its southern end on your left. Take a narrow track which leads 150m up the slope to near the centre of this hill. Walk south for 100m on a narrow track to the top of the rocky outcrop. This is a great spot for a break. The views of Coal and Candle Creek from near Akuna Bay to Cottage Point are excellent. Next walk north along the hill to a large cairn where there are views over Yeomans Bay.

Return to the Waratah track and continue north for 100m to a track junction. Take the left track and walk for 1km to a vantage point at the end of the track on a rock shelf. Some trees provide shade for a pleasant lunch break. After a break, walk back along the Waratah track to West Head Road.

Grade: Easy, 60m asc.   **Distance:** 9km.
Best in springtime for the wildflowers.
No Public transport.
Map 8 and CMA Ku-ring-gai N.P. (Tourist)
                                          Alan Heath

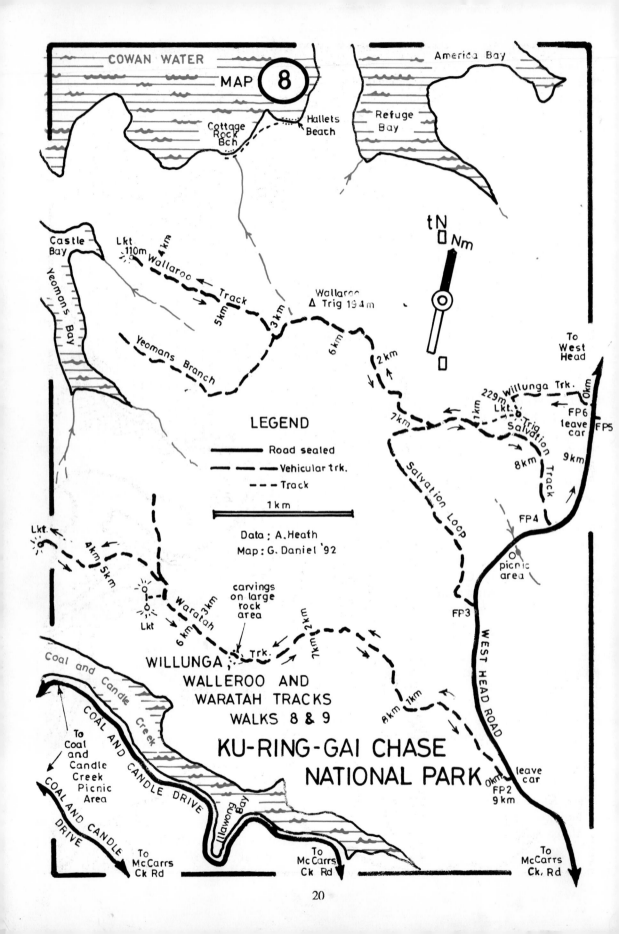

COWAN WATER

MAP (8)

America Bay

Refuge Bay

Cottage Rock Bch

Hallets Beach

Castle Bay

Yeomans Bay

Lkt 110m 4km
Wallaroo Track
5km
3km

Wallaroo △ Trig 194m

Yeomans Branch

6km

2km

tN
Nm

To West Head

229m Lkt. Willunga Trk. 0km
1km
Salvation Track
FP6 leave car
FP5

7km

Salvation Loop

8km

9km

FP4

LEGEND

Road sealed
Vehicular trk.
Track

1km

Data : A. Heath
Map : G. Daniel '92

picnic area

FP3

Lkt.
4km 5km

Waratah 3km
6km
Lkt.

carvings on large rock area

2km

1km

WEST HEAD ROAD

Trk.

1km

4km 1km

WILLUNGA,
WALLEROO AND
WARATAH TRACKS
WALKS 8 & 9

KU-RING-GAI CHASE
NATIONAL PARK

Coal and Candle Creek

COAL AND CANDLE DRIVE

To Coal and Candle Creek Picnic Area

COAL AND CANDLE DRIVE

Illawong Bay

0km leave car
FP2 9km

To McCarrs Ck Rd

To McCarrs Ck Rd

To McCarrs Ck Rd

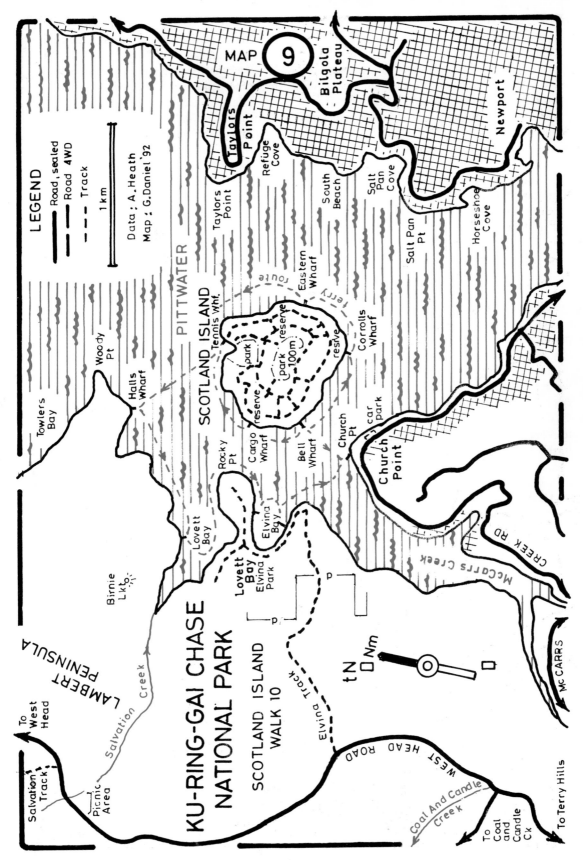

MAP 9

LEGEND
Road, sealed
Road 4WD
Track

1km

Data : A.Heath
Map : G.Daniel 92

PITTWATER

KU-RING-GAI CHASE
NATIONAL PARK

SCOTLAND ISLAND
WALK 10

SCOTLAND ISLAND

Bilgola Plateau

Newport

Taylors Point

Refuge Cove

Taylors Point

South Beach

Salt Pan Cove

Salt Pan Pt

Horseshoe Cove

Eastern Wharf

ferry route

Corrolls Wharf

Tennis Whf.

reserve

park

park
100m

reserve

reserve

Church Pt

car park

Church Point

Woody Pt

Halls Wharf

Towlers Bay

Rocky Pt

Cargo Wharf

Bell Wharf

Elvina Bay

Lovett Bay

McCarrs Creek

CREEK RD

McCARRS

Birnie Lkt.

Lovett Bay
Elvina Park

p

p

p

Elvina Track

tN

Nm

LAMBERT PENINSULA

To West Head

Salvation Track

Salvation Creek

Picnic Area

WEST HEAD ROAD

Coal And Candle Creek

To Coal and Candle Ck

To Terry Hills

21

10. SCOTLAND ISLAND

Scotland Island is set in the southern section of Pittwater. A trip to this scenic forested island (about 1km in diameter) makes a enjoyable days outing. Make your own way on the pleasant tracks and roads between the foreshore and the public parks.

Andrew Thompson received a land grant for Scotland Island in 1810, for courageous flood rescue work. He named it after his homeland, and had intentions of setting up a salt works. The island is covered with stands of tall Spotted Gums with Burrawang cycads as an understory.

Catch a ferry from Church Point and disembark at Bell Wharf - one of five public wharves on the island. Tracks lead from these wharves to gravel roads which run more or less parallel to the shoreline at different levels. Tracks and roads link these contour roads. It is a pleasant walk around these roads and tracks even though there are a lot of houses nestled amongst the trees. There are many places at the waters edge to explore - especially at low tide. A very pleasant park near Tennis Wharf on the northern side of the island is the suggested lunch spot. There is also a large park in the centre (top) of the island.

Catch a ferry, from any wharf for the trip back to Church Point. On the return route, the ferry travels to Halls Wharf, Lovett Bay, Elvina Bay on Western Pittwater for a relaxing cruise to round off the day.

Grade: Easy, 110m asc.　　**Distance:** 5km. Suits all seasons.

Public transport: Buses from Manly (or Wynyard to Mona Vale, then another to Church Point). Ferry (Church Point Ferries Pty Ltd) or water taxi from Church Point.

Map 9 and CMA Mona Vale or Sydney Street Directory.　　　　　　　　　　Alan Heath

11. BILGOLA TO LONG REEF BEACH VIA THE COASTLINE

Although this walk is not a true bushwalk, the spectacular coastal scenery with high cliffs and golden beaches make this walk one of the best coastal walks in the Sydney area. This walk, a Warringah Bicentennial project, takes you to fossil-rich rocks on the headland between Bilgola and Newport beaches, at Bungan Head and at the southern end of Bungan beach. The fossils are mostly of plant life. Marine life abounds in the rock pools encountered and there are numerous beaches for swimming in summer. The walk, follows some

of the route that Governor Phillip and his exploration parties travelled in 1788 on their way to Pittwater and Palm Beach.

Note: the routes around the cliff bases are not recommended other than at low tide and when seas are slight. Take extreme care near clifftops, particularly in windy weather.

If travelling by bus, the walk starts from The Serpentine (road) at a point 50m south of the junction of Plateau, Barrenjoey and Old Barrenjoey Roads at Avalon. Initially walk to the lookout on Bilgola Head to enjoy the views, then return to the steps which descend through trees to the northern end of Bilgola Beach (the starting point for car travellers).

The route generally follows the coastline, along the beaches and around or over the top of headlands. The first good lookout is from near the water tanks in Porter Reserve - a 200m deviation to the western end of Attunga Road, Bilgola (this involves crossing Barrenjoey Road).

The track descends to Newport Beach. Walk along the beach, past the rock pool and around the base of Bungan Head. Bungan Beach has limited car access, and is less crowded than most of the Northern Beaches. Next rock-hop below Mona Vale Headland Reserve to Basin Beach - a small protected cove. From its northern end, deviate to the top of Mona Vale Headland for more excellent coastal views.

Continue along Basin Beach, past a rock pool, then along the broad expanse (1km) of Mona Vale Beach. At the southern end of Mona Vale Beach, climb up the grassed headland to Coronation Parade. Between Nos. 101 and 103 Coronation Parade there is a path which will lead you down to the northern end of Warriewood Beach. [It is sometimes possible to walk on sand below the headland between Mona Vale and Warriewood beaches]. At the southern end of Warriewood Beach, the Bicentennial Walkway leads past the surf club and up some steps to the top of Turimetta Head. There are also good views from the extreme east end of this headland.

Drop down a very eroded wide track to Turimetta Beach and proceed to the rock pool at the northern end of Narrabeen Beach. Climb Narrabeen Head to a lookout via some steps 200m west of the rock pool. Return to Narrabeen Beach and cross the channel (which could be up to 0.5m deep) where Narrabeen lagoon empties into the ocean. Alternatively, walk over the Ocean Street bridge. Head south, along the long stretch of Narrabeen and

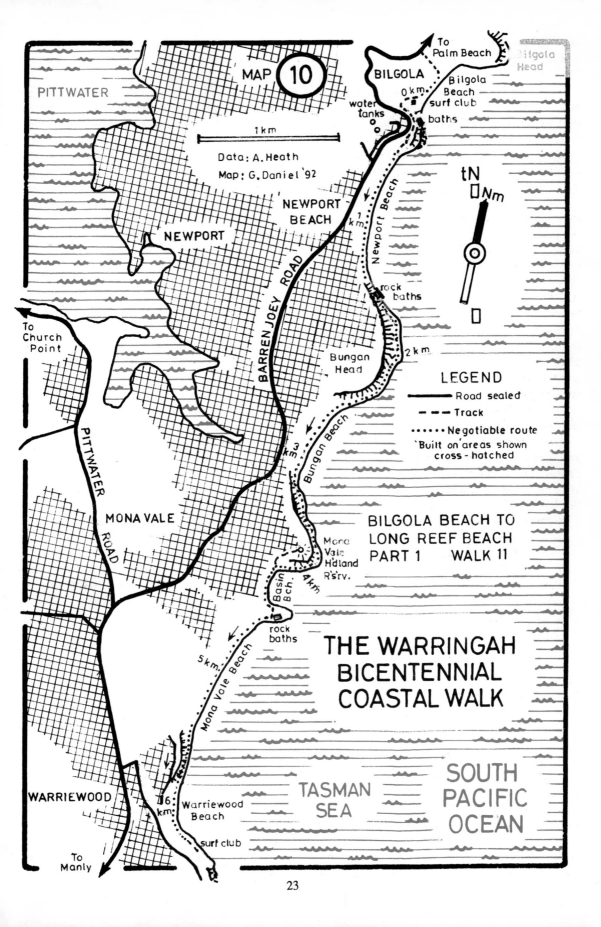

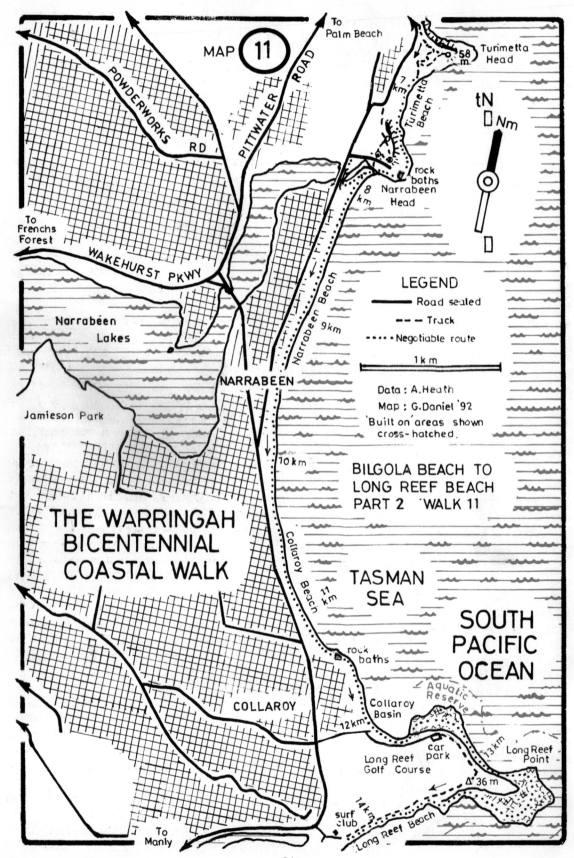

MAP 11

To Palm Beach

POWDERWORKS RD

PITTWATER ROAD

To Frenchs Forest

WAKEHURST PKWY

Narrabeen Lakes

Jamieson Park

NARRABEEN

Turimetta Head
58 m

7 km

Turimetta Beach

tN Nm

8 km
rock baths
Narrabeen Head

Narrabeen Beach

9 km

LEGEND
——— Road sealed
– – – Track
· · · · · Negotiable route

|————— 1 km —————|

Data : A. Heath
Map : G. Daniel '92
'Built on' areas shown
cross-hatched.

10 km

BILGOLA BEACH TO
LONG REEF BEACH
PART 2   WALK 11

THE WARRINGAH
BICENTENNIAL
COASTAL WALK

Collaroy Beach

11 km

TASMAN
SEA

SOUTH
PACIFIC
OCEAN

COLLAROY

rock baths

Collaroy Basin

12 km

Aquatic Reserve

13 km

Long Reef
Point

Long Reef
Golf Course

car park

Δ 36 m

14 km

surf club

Long Reef Beach

To Manly

24

Collaroy Beaches (3.5 km) to the rock baths.

The next section of coastal waters is protected in the Long Reef Aquatic Reserve. Continue past Collaroy Basin, then up to a helipad and car-park. Follow the vehicle track to the highest point on Long Reef Headland, marked by a geodetic station. There are more great views from here.

Finally, follow the cliff edge which leads to the surf club and car-park at Long Reef Beach, then walk up to Pittwater Rd to a bus stop.

Grade: Easy/Medium, 100m asc.

Distance: 16km.

Suits all seasons, great in clear weather.

Public Transport: Bus from Wynyard station.

Maps 10,11 and Sydney Street Directory.

Alan Heath

12. MANLY DAM RESERVE: MANLY DAM CIRCUIT

The Manly Dam Reserve preserves an important area of urban bushland. The dam and its main feeding watercourse - Curl Curl Creek - are very picturesque.

Start the walk from the car-park, adjacent to the Manly Dam wall (access by car is from Condamine and King Streets, Manly Vale). Walk back up along King Street (NE) 400m to where the road bends ESE, just opposite the Water Research Laboratory. Take the track on the left, cross a creek and continue past back fences of a few cottages and re-enter the Reserve.

Follow the Waterfall Track and cross a side creek flowing through reeds - a good area for viewing water birds. Next, turn up a track to the right and climb steadily for 800m to a fire trail. Follow the track for another 800m where another fire trail joins on the right. The track crosses a small creek, then swings around to the west to cross Curl Curl creek. Just beyond the creek, turn left (SE) and follow the track which follows Curl Curl Creek downstream, past some waterfalls back to the dam. Continue on the track, as it follows the dam foreshore back to the picnic areas. At the first picnic area, take the wildflower walk on the right, then the Nature Trail which leads to a track junction. Turn left back to the car-park.

Grade: Easy, 60m asc.　　**Distance:** 8km.

Best in Autumn and Spring.

Public Transport: Bus to corner of Campbell Parade and Condamine Street.

Map 12 and Sydney Street Directory.

Flora Graham

13. GARRIGAL N.P.: ROSEVILLE BRIDGE - BANTRY BAY - SEAFORTH OVAL

Within Garrigal National Park is the Bantry Bay Catchment - the largest forested pocket of bushland on the foreshores of Sydney Harbour. This walk offers delightful foreshore walking, an interesting natural rock arch and panoramic views of the harbour and the city skyline. The track also passes some disused explosives magazines at Bantry Bay, which date from 1915. Public transport is available to points near the walk start and finish (see below). Alternatively, a car shuttle is required between Roseville Bridge and Seaforth Oval.

The starting point is the car-park on the eastern foreshore of Middle Harbour. Access is from the NE end of the Roseville Bridge. The walk passes though a section of the newly dedicated Garrigal National Park (this section was formerly Davidson Park State Recreation Area).

From the car-park, head SE along the sign-posted Flat Rock Track. There are pleasant views of the harbour through the trees and a good display of wildflowers at most times of the year. At Flat Rock Beach, rock-hop across the creek below the waterfall and continue around to the Magazine Track which passes disused explosives magazines.

After leaving the magazines, the track rises steeply in parts to a fire trail to a three-way junction. Turn right and cross Bates Creek. Climb up and cross the Cook Street trail, and follow the trail opposite for 160m, then take the Natural Arch track on the right. It is unmarked and indistinct, but marked by white paint stripes on rocks. It leads down 300m to a natural rock bridge over Main Creek - a very interesting formation which could be suitable for a lunch stop. There is room to shelter under the rock bridge if it is raining.

After a break, continue along this track for 400m to a track junction. Turn right (SE) and walk 500m to Bluff Lookout, where there is a wonderful view over Bantry Bay, Middle Harbour and the distant city skyline.

From Bluff Lookout, descend to the Bay track by climbing down some narrow crevices between the rocks. The Bay Track heads south and follows the eastern shore of Bantry Bay. It crosses several small creeks, and comes eventually to a cleared grassy area where there are picnic tables, toilets, drinking water and a wharf.

Two tracks connect the picnic area with Seaforth Oval on Wakehurst Parkway - the Timbergetters Track which starts immediately behind the toilets, and the Old Bullock Track which

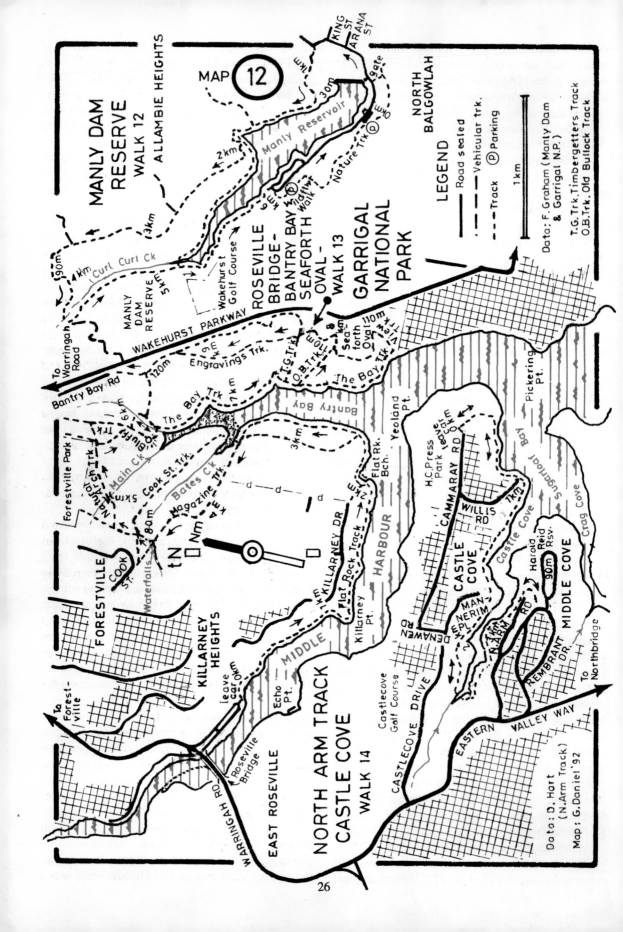

MAP 12

MANLY DAM RESERVE WALK 12
ALLAMBIE HEIGHTS

ROSEVILLE BRIDGE - BANTRY BAY & SEAFORTH OVAL - WALK 13

GARRIGAL NATIONAL PARK

NORTH BALGOWLAH

LEGEND
——— Road sealed
—·—·— Vehicular trk.
- - - - Track
(P) Parking
|———1km———|

Data: F. Graham (Manly Dam & Garrigal N.P.)
T.G.Trk.Timbergetters Track
O.B.Trk. Old Bullock Track

Manly Reservoir

Nature Trk.

Wakehurst Golf Course

WAKEHURST PARKWAY

MANLY DAM RESERVE

Curl Curl Ck

To Warringah Road

Bantry Bay Rd

Engravings Trk.

T.G.Trk.
O.B.Trk.

Seaforth Oval

Bantry Bay

The Bay Trk.

The Bay Trk.

Pickering Pt.

Yeoland Pt.

Flat Rk. Bch.

Main Ck Trk.

Monarch Trk.

Bluff Trk.

Cook St Trk.

Bates Ck

Magazine Trk.

Forestville Park

FORESTVILLE

COOK ST.

Waterfalls

KILLARNEY HEIGHTS

KILLARNEY DR.

Flat Rock Track

Killarney Pt.

MIDDLE HARBOUR

Echo Pt.

leave car

Castlecove Golf Course

CASTLECOVE DRIVE

H.C.Press Park leave car

CAMMARAY RD.

WILLIS RD.

CASTLE COVE

Castle Cove

Sugarloaf Bay

Crag Cove

MIDDLE COVE

Harold Reid Rsv.

MAN-NERIM EPL.

N.ARM RD.

REMBRANT DR.

DENAWEN RD.

EASTERN VALLEY WAY

To Northbridge

Roseville Bridge

WARRINGAH RD.

EAST ROSEVILLE

NORTH ARM TRACK CASTLE COVE WALK 14

To Forestville

Data: D. Hart (N.Arm Track)
Map: G.Daniel '92

N

26

commences 100m further around the shore from the wharf. Both are steep but not very long (about 600m). From Seaforth Oval, there are more marvellous views of the harbour and the city.

Grade: Easy/Medium, 200m asc. Natural Arch Track rudimentary only.

Distance: 10km.

Public Transport: 1) To the start: catch a Forest Coachlines bus from Chatswood station interchange. Alight at Malga Avenue, East Roseville. Cross Warringah Rd by an overhead bridge to Babbage Road, then follow a track down to the Middle Harbour shoreline. Cross under Roseville Bridge near the water's edge, then take the steep track which leads up to the footpath on the left hand side of Roseville Bridge. Cross the bridge over Middle Harbour, then go down a ramp. Cross back under the bridge to the car-park and the start of the track.

2) From the finish: catch Government bus No. 169 to Wynyard via North Sydney - an hourly service Mondays to Saturday. On Sundays, walk down Wakehurst Parkway to Lister Avenue from where buses run hourly to Manly Wharf or to Seaforth junction, where buses to Wynyard are available. Alternatively, take the Engravings Track from Seaforth Oval which runs parallel to the Wakehurst Parkway to Bantry Bay Rd, then walk 2km NNW up Wakehurst Parkway to Warringah Rd for buses to Chatswood.

Suits all seasons.

Map 12 and CMA Parramatta River.

Flora Graham

14. NORTH ARM WALKING TRACK, CASTLE COVE

The North Arm Walking Track was constructed in 1988 - a Willoughby Council bicentennial project. It follows the foreshore of the North Arm of Sugarloaf Bay, Middle Harbour. The track itself is 4.5km long, and passes through some of Sydney's most beautiful harbour-side bushland, with fine views over Middle Harbour. Tap water is available at the end of North Arm Road and Harold Reid Reserve.

The walk starts at the eastern end of Cammaray Rd, Castle Cove - access via Castlecove Drive, Deepwater Rd and Denawen Ave. Set off down a steep sealed track to near the foreshore. This was a favourite place of entertainment prior to the First World War. Many came by boat for picnics and dancing. There are still signs of buildings, a maze

of paths and steps, secluded nooks with remains of seats and concrete floor slabs. According to historical records, "On Sundays, ferries would bring the "Merchant Princes" from their mansions at Vaucluse with their nannies, cooks, butlers and waitresses for a "sausage sizzle" at the picnic grounds".

Just above the boat landing, pick up a track which leads west and follows the shoreline almost to the Willis Rd access point, where there is a large route map.

Look out for the rare and endangered Creeping Leucopogon, a small inconspicuous plant that grows in moist sites, especially on rock ledges and in creek lines. Just before Willis Road, there is a resting place below the track on the stone jetty.

Make a short diversion up Willis Road to view Innisfallen Castle. This sandstone castle with its imposing battlements was built in 1903. For more than 90 years, the Willis family occupied the castle. Originally it was surrounded by 21ha of bushland and the only means of access was by boat.

Return to the walking track, now a Sydney Water access way, for a short distance past a pumping station. Soon the track narrows and follows a delightful route over creek crossings and through Casuarina forest.

At about 1.8km from the start, ignore a track to the right which climbs through high rocks to Mannerim Place.

The next section passes through low woodland on a sandstone ridge well above the mangroves of North Arm. The track is wide and easy walking as it merges in to the Sydney Water access-way coming down from Deepwater Rd. Continue on the access-way, and after 300m take a track on the left which leads down to a creek crossing (the North Arm of Sugarloaf Bay, just above the tidal limit). This crossing may be impassable after heavy rain or unusually high water.

Once on the other side, the track leads across the sandy river flats before climbing onto the sandstone ridge above the mangroves. These grey mangroves form a forest on the mud flats and are vital in maintaining balanced estuarine life cycles. The track is well defined. It undulates, then climbs steeply up some steps to North Arm Road.

Turn left and road walk about 200m to where the road ends and two tracks commence. Take the right hand track which climbs to Harold Reid Reserve. Walk left up the loop road through the picnic area to a lookout that provides an outstanding view over Middle Harbour. This is the recommended lunch spot.

If travelling by car, walk back along the track to Cammaray Rd. If using public transport, catch a bus (route 275) from the front gates of Harold Reid Reserve to Chatswood station (limited service) or walk to Eastern Valley Way via Rembrandt Drive and Greenfield Ave and catch a bus (routes 207/8) to North Sydney station.

Grade: Easy, 100m asc.

Distance: 9km (return).

Public Transport: Forest Coach Lines buses run between Chatswood station and Castle Cove, Monday - Saturday.

Map 12 and CMA Parramatta River or Sydney Street Directory.

Dorothy Hart

PACK WEIGHT BREAKDOWN GUIDE

For 2-day walk (Autumn/Spring)

ITEM	WT(kg)
Backpack; internal frame 70 litre	2.40
Tent; 2 person, ridged, wall design with floor and insect screens	1.60
Sleeping bag; down -5deg to +13deg	1.60
Sleeping mat	0.50
Rain jacket; nylon outer, pvc inside	0.50
Culinary; billies, cup, plate, matches, knife, plastic spoon, soap, washing kit, 4 litre cask liner (water)	0.67
Clothes; long trousers, jumper, small towel, socks (spare)	0.93
Food; toasted muesli (breakfast)	0.23
cheese, crisp bread biscuits (lunch)	0.30
1 dried meal (dinner)	0.38
Beverages; water 1 litre plus containers	1.06
tea/coffee, dried milk, sugar	0.35
Sundries; First aid items, torch, sun screen, toilet paper, tooth brush, insect repellent, compass, whistle	0.50
TOTAL	11.02

Optional extras: maps, camera, cooker, fuel, gaiters, fresh food, fruit etc.

---

15. SYDNEY HARBOUR N.P.: HERMITAGE FORESHORE - NIELSEN PARK

The Hermitage Foreshore offers an opportunity for a quiet harbour-side walk. The four small beaches and secluded picnic areas are ideal for escaping from the bustle of the city. Nielsen Park, the walk destination, has a protected swimming area, shady grassed areas, historic Greycliffe House and an important bushland remnant.

The walk starts from the western end of Bay View Hill Road, Vaucluse. Follow the track that leads off NNE along the foreshore. The track passes Queens Beach, a picnic area near the Hermitage and Hermit Bay. Continue on, past Tingara Beach and Milk Beach to a pleasant lookout point over Shark Island and the harbour. This is also a good point to admire Strickland House, a grand mansion, now owned by the State Government.

After 1km there is a track junction (signposted Vaucluse Rd). Turn right here, and walk up to a roadway. Turn right and follow the road for 50m, then branch off to the left towards an NP&WS workshop. Walk around the workshop and branch left immediately onto the track to Mt Trefle - from which there are great views. This bushland remnant is very important as it is the only known location of a recently discovered Casuarina species.

Return down the Mt Trefle branch-track, turn left and walk down through tall Teatree heath to Greycliffe House. Greycliffe House and the Gardener's Cottage were built in the 1850s, by William Charles Wentworth's son-in-law.

Continue on down to the foreshore. You may like a swim in the netted swimming area or a picnic lunch on the open grassy areas. After a break, walk north past a small bushland patch to the wonderful rock platform at Bottle and Glass Point, where there are views towards Manly and North Head.

Return to the swimming area, then continue SW up some steps to Steel Point where there are fortifications which date from 1871. Walk south, around the Commonwealth land on a road, then take the track on the right which leads down to the foreshore. Follow this track, back to the Vaucluse Road track junction, and continue on along the Hermitage Foreshore Trail back to Bay View Hill Road.

Grade: Easy, 50m asc.   **Distance:** 5km.
Suits all seasons.

Public Transport: Govt Bus 324 from Circular Quay or Edgecliff station.

Map 13 and CMA Sydney Heads.

Stephen Lord

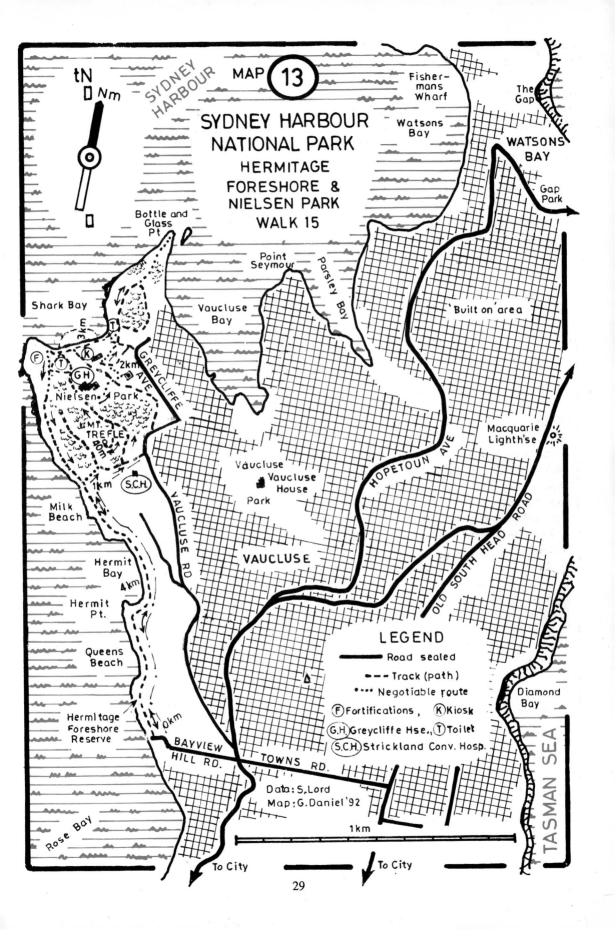

MAP 13

SYDNEY HARBOUR NATIONAL PARK
HERMITAGE FORESHORE & NIELSEN PARK
WALK 15

tN

Nm

SYDNEY HARBOUR

Fishermans Wharf

Watsons Bay

The Gap

WATSONS BAY

Gap Park

Bottle and Glass Pt

Point Seymour

Parsley Bay

Shark Bay

Vaucluse Bay

'Built on' area

3km

2km

GREYCLIFFE AVE

Nielsen Park

MT. TREFLE 80m

Macquarie Lighth'se

HOPETOUN AVE

Vaucluse House

Vaucluse Park

1km

S.C.H

VAUCLUSE

Milk Beach

VAUCLUSE RD

Hermit Bay

4km

OLD SOUTH HEAD ROAD

Hermit Pt.

Queens Beach

LEGEND
—————— Road sealed
- - - - Track (path)
• • • • Negotiable route
(F) Fortifications, (K) Kiosk
(G.H) Greycliffe Hse., (T) Toilet
(S.C.H) Strickland Conv. Hosp.

Diamond Bay

Hermitage Foreshore Reserve

0km

BAYVIEW HILL RD.

TOWNS RD.

Data: S. Lord
Map: G. Daniel '92

Rose Bay

1km

TASMAN SEA

To City

To City

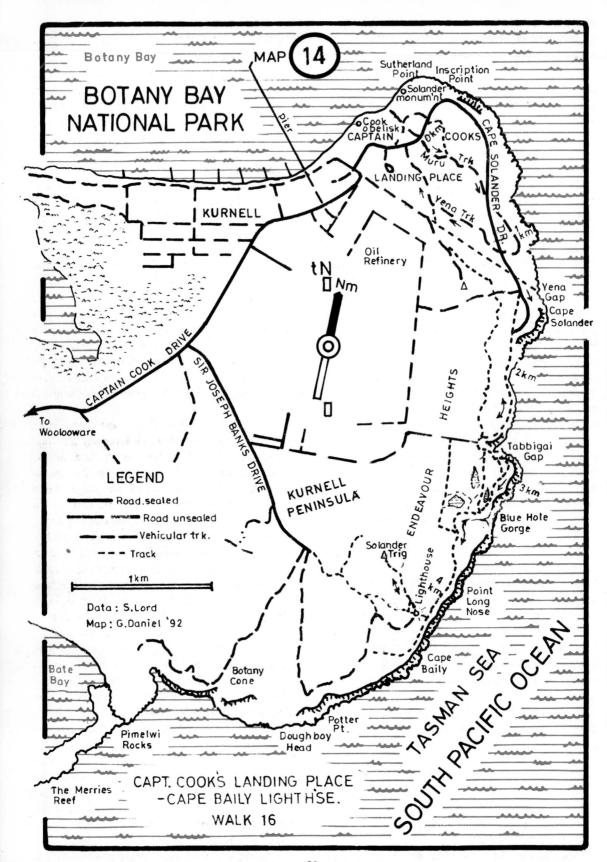

MAP (14)

BOTANY BAY
NATIONAL PARK

Botany Bay

Sutherland Point
Inscription Point
Solander monum'nt
Cook obelisk
CAPTAIN
pier
KURNELL
COOKS
Muru Trk
0km
LANDING PLACE
Yena Trk
CAPE SOLANDER DR.
1 km

Oil Refinery

Yena Gap
Cape Solander

tN
Nm

2 km

HEIGHTS

CAPTAIN COOK DRIVE

SIR JOSEPH BANKS DRIVE

To Woolooware

Tabbigai Gap

ENDEAVOUR

3 km

Blue Hole Gorge

LEGEND

———— Road, sealed
~~~~ Road unsealed
— — Vehicular trk.
- - - Track

KURNELL PENINSULA

Solander △Trig
Lighthouse
4 km

Point Long Nose

1km

Data: S.Lord
Map: G.Daniel '92

Cape Baily

Bate Bay

Botany Cone

Potter Pt.
Doughboy Head

TASMAN SEA

SOUTH PACIFIC OCEAN

Pimelwi Rocks

The Merries Reef

CAPT. COOK'S LANDING PLACE
-CAPE BAILY LIGHT H'SE.
WALK 16

30

16. BOTANY BAY N.P.:
CAPTAIN COOKS LANDING PLACE - CAPE BAILY LIGHTHOUSE

The coastal lands within Botany Bay National Park are bounded by high sea cliffs and contain coastal heath, sand dunes, freshwater swamps and historic military relics.

Start the walk by following the Muru track which leaves Solander Drive SE of the museum at Captain Cooks Landing Place, at Kurnell. The track leads through forest, with Teatree, Christmas Bush and Hakea shrubs. Where the track meets Solander Drive, cross over to the coast and walk along to the Yena picnic grounds and view Yena Gap.

Next, follow the Solander Drive south to Cape Solander, then take the track through dense stands of Casuarina, Banksia and Baeckea to Tabbigai Gap. Tabbigai Gap and other gorges along the coast are the result of volcanic activity about 50 million years ago. Dykes (long fingers of basaltic rock), forced their way up through the sandstone rock, then weathered more quickly than the surrounding sandstone, leaving narrow gorges. South of the gorge are fishermens' shack ruins occupied up until the 1960s. Unfortunately, the construction of an oil refinery effluent pipeline has degraded the area.

The coast south of Tabbigai Gap is more exposed to the salt winds. Coast Rosemary, Wild Fuchsia and Honey Myrtle are found here. The track passes by several freshwater swamps or swales. The Blue Hole Gorge, near the largest swale, provides shelter for mosses and ferns.

The track then continues past Point Long Nose to the Cape Baily Lighthouse. From the lighthouse there are views south along Bate Bay. The large bare sandhill behind the bay was covered in vegetation as late as 1971, but through a combination of illegal vehicle use and fires, it has become completely denuded. From the lighthouse, head NW to Solander Trig, which at 67m is the highest point in the National Park. At the trig, there are more views and the remains of concrete bunkers which date from World War II.

Return to the Cape Baily Lighthouse, then back along the track and Solander Drive to Yena Picnic area. Finally, take the Yena Track back to Captain Cooks Landing Place. Along the way, Grass Trees, Scribbly Gums and Burrawang Cycads can be seen.

Grade: Easy, 50m asc.   **Distance:** 10km.
Best in Autumn, Winter and Spring.
Public Transport: Kurnell Buses from Cronulla station, Ph 524-8977.
Map 14 and CMA Port Hacking.   Stephen Lord

17. ROYAL N.P.:
LOFTUS - WINIFRED FALLS - DEER POOL - LITTLE MARLEY - BUNDEENA

Royal National Park contains a great variety of scenery including plateau shrubland, valley forest, coastal heathland, attractive waterfalls and beaches.

It is possible to complete this walk in one day, however, because of the distance (20km), the temptation to linger at the attractive spots along the way, and in order not to not miss the last ferry from Bundeena, it is suggested that the walk be done as a two-day walk with an overnight stop at Winifred Falls. Camping permits and information on current restrictions must be obtained from the Audley Visitors Centre (ph 521-2230).

From Loftus railway station walk south past the Tramway Museum on the Princes Highway, cross the railway line at the level crossing and follow the branch line to the now disused Royal National Park railway station. Keep heading south along a signposted track which descends to Audley where you cross the Hacking River on the causeway to the Visitors Centre at the start of Lady Carrington Drive. Audley has extensive picnic grounds and a kiosk.

Call in to the Visitors Centre and then find a track directly opposite it which leads up the road bank to the east for 30m, turns north for 80m and then east again following an old pipeline on an overgrown track to the top of the ridge. Keep following this and avoid tracks to the garbage tip hidden on the right. The track makes a gradual descent through thick heath and shrubland, with a great variety of wildflowers in springtime, to cross the head of Muddy Creek before ascending to cross the gravel Warumbul Road. Follow the fire trail through the gate opposite and go down a steep section, where the shrubland changes to Eucalypt forest, to Winifred Falls (7km from Loftus).

Make this the camp-site - it is a pleasant spot with plenty of room. There is a good pool at the base of the falls for a swim. Follow the creek downstream for 10 minutes to deep water at the head of navigation of South West Arm.

Next day, cross at the top of Winifred Falls and follow the creek upstream on its eastern side for 150m until you find an eroded rocky track going straight up the hill SE through open forest. The track then turns to the north and again to the east at the ridge top where a track comes in from the south. Keep going east and descend to Anice Falls which has only limited camping space.

A short climb leads onto an overgrown fire trail

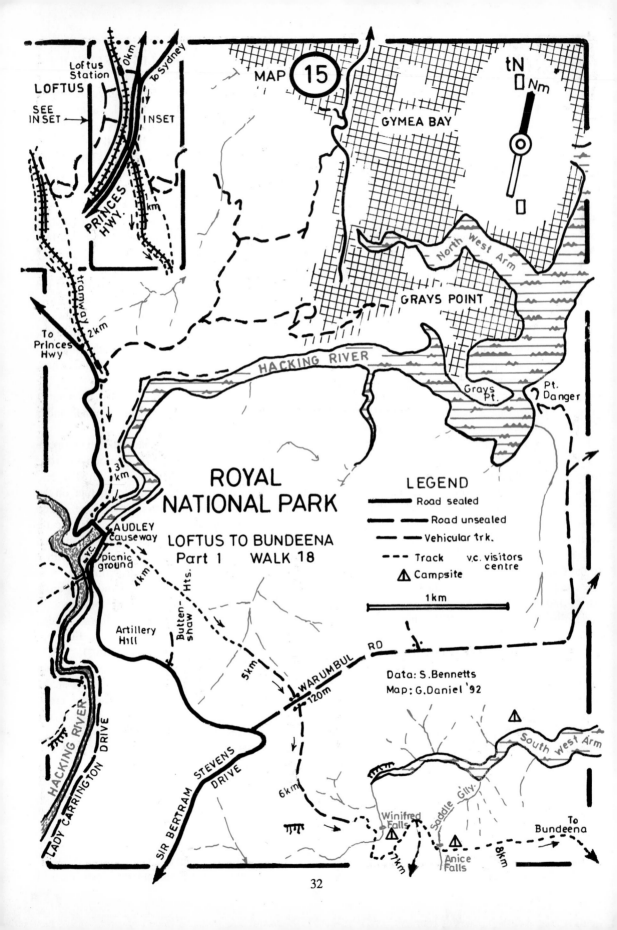

LOFTUS

Loftus
Station

SEE
IN SET

INSET

To Sydney

PRINCES HWY.

0km

1km

To Princes Hwy

tramway

2km

3½ km

AUDLEY
Causeway

v.c.

picnic
ground

4km

Artillery Hill

Buttenshaw Hts.

5km

LADY CARRINGTON DRIVE

HACKING RIVER

SIR BERTRAM STEVENS DRIVE

MAP ⑮

GYMEA BAY

tN
Nm

North West Arm

GRAYS POINT

HACKING RIVER

Grays Pt.

Pt. Danger

ROYAL
NATIONAL PARK

LOFTUS TO BUNDEENA
Part 1   WALK 18

LEGEND

────── Road sealed
── ── ── Road unsealed
─ ─ ─ ─ Vehicular trk.
- - - - - Track   v.c. visitors
⚠ Campsite   centre

├──────────┤ 1km

Data: S. Bennetts
Map: G. Daniel '92

WARUMBUL RD

120m

South west Arm

6km

⚠

Winifred Falls

⚠

Saddle Gully

7km

Anice Falls

⚠

8km

To Bundeena

32

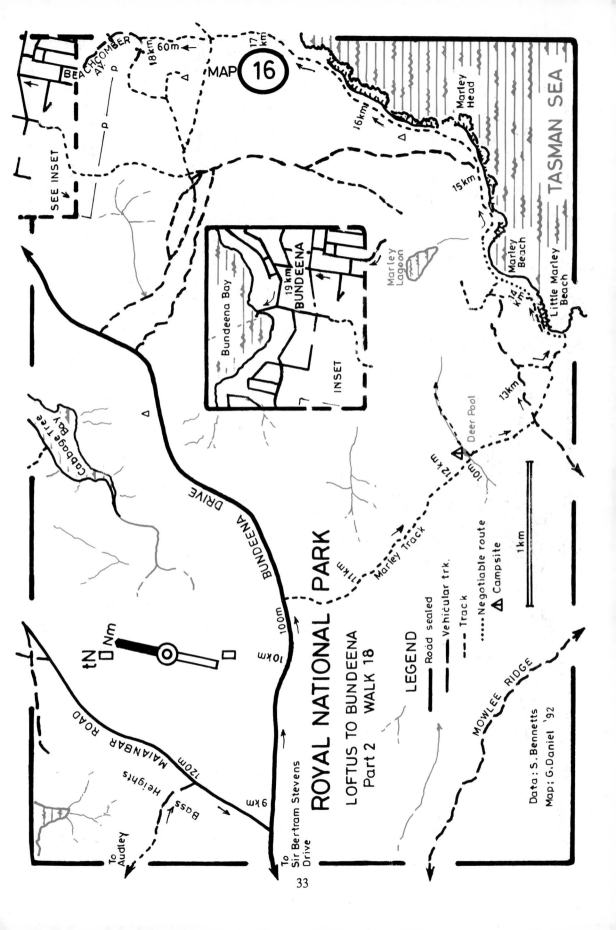

ROYAL NATIONAL PARK

LOFTUS TO BUNDEENA
Part 2   WALK 18

MAP (16)

TASMAN SEA

Marley Head

Marley Beach

Little Marley Beach

Marley Lagoon

BUNDEENA

Bundeena Bay

INSET

SEE INSET

BEACHCOMBER AV.

18km   60m
17km
16km
15km
14km
13km
12km
11km
10km

Deer Pool

10m

Marley Track

Cabbage Tree Bay

BUNDEENA DRIVE

Nm
N

100m

10km

120m

Bass Heights

MAIANBAR ROAD

9km

To Audley

To Sir Bertram Stevens Drive

MOWLEE RIDGE

LEGEND

Road sealed
Vehicular trk.
Track
Negotiable route
△ Campsite

1km

Data : S. Bennetts
Map ; G. Daniel '92

33

with views to Cronulla and the Sydney skyline before coming out onto the bitumen Maianbar Road. (This point could be difficult to find coming in the reverse direction but it is beside a pipe culvert as the road turns from a straight to curve further east). Head south along this road for 600m and turn east along Bundeena Drive for 1.7km to the car-park at the start of the Marley Track.

This popular track has views across the sandhills behind Marley Beach. The track descends into forest around the Deer Pool which has good camping and swimming but suffers from over use. The track leads out from the SE corner of the camp-site and after 500m (10 mins), turn left onto a fire trail running NE. After 500m you reach a rock shelf with good views over Little Marley. Take a well-used track on the right which leads south then SE, to emerge on the northern side of a small lagoon behind Little Marley Beach. This is an attractive spot with shady trees and grassed areas. Camping is not permitted in this area.

From the northern end of the beach the track crosses the headland through coastal heath onto Marley Beach. It is dangerous to swim here. Take care not to disturb the ecologically sensitive high sand dunes. Cross the lagoon entrance and follow the steps up onto the headland. From here on there are numerous eroded tracks to confuse you but generally keep fairly close to the top of the ocean cliffs with their fascinating range of sandstone colourings. Remember to turn around to see the view down the coast behind you.

Nearly 2km from Marley and as the track descends to a rocky flat headland keep watch for a marker post close to the cliff edge. Here the track drops down and crosses a gully where a creek cascades into the ocean. Walk up the steps on the other side and follow the deeply eroded tracks until the houses of Bundeena come into view. The track meets a bitumen road which leads to a gate at the end of Beachcomber Avenue. Head north then west through the Bundeena streets to reach the wharf at the end of Brighton Street. Rest your legs on the scenic ferry trip across to Cronulla. It is then a short walk to the railway station.

Grade: Day 1. Easy, 130 asc, 7km.
Day 2. Medium, 70m asc, 13km.
Total distance: 20km.
Suitable all year but best in spring.
Public Transport: Train to Loftus, ferry from Bundeena, (ph Cronulla Ferries 523-2990).
Maps 15,16 and CMA Port Hacking

Steve Bennetts

18. ROYAL N.P.: THE FOREST PATH

The Forest Path traverses the lower slopes of Forest Island, a hill that has almost been surrounded by the valleys of the Hacking River and Bola Creek. NPA members played the major role in the route planning, surveying and construction of this track.

Park the car on Lady Wakehurst Drive, near the southern end of Lady Carrington Drive. The Forest Path heads off Lady Wakehurst Drive 50m west of this junction. Walk west 600m to a track junction, where the Couranga track comes in from the west. Keep on the Forest Path as it meanders north, then east alongside the Hacking River.

The soils in this area were formed by the weathering of the Narrabeen group of sandstones, claystones and shales and have yielded a greater supply of nutrients than is found in the Hawkesbury sandstones that characterise the majority of Royal National Park. Consequently the vegetation along the Forest Path is mainly a mixture of lush, temperate/sub-tropical rainforest and wet sclerophyll forest.

These forests provide homes for a vast array of wildlife. The crowns of trees, such as Coachwood, Sassafras, Lillipilli and Crab-apple, interlock to form a dense canopy. Beneath the canopy, a variety of ferns, epiphytes, vines, fungi and lichens thrive. Possums, gliders, wallabies, Lyrebirds and Bowerbirds, leeches, other invertebrates and many other animals utilise the food and shelter found here.

Just before the Hacking River junction with Bola Creek the track swings south. After 3.5km (from the starting point) the Forest Path meets Lady Carrington Drive just south of Bola Creek, where there is a picnic area. After a break, walk south for 700m to Lady Wakehurst Drive and the car.

Grade: Easy, 20m asc. **Distance:** 4.5km.
Suits all seasons. No Public transport.
Map 17 and CMA Royal & Heathcote N.P. (Tourist). Stephen Lord and George Daniel

---

GAITERS
Gaiters help prevent scratches, scuffing and bruises and stop grass seeds, small sticks and gravel getting into your socks and boots. They also guard against snake bite. Stiff sided gaiters made from canvas or Gore-Tex are best. Velcro fasteners are an advantage.

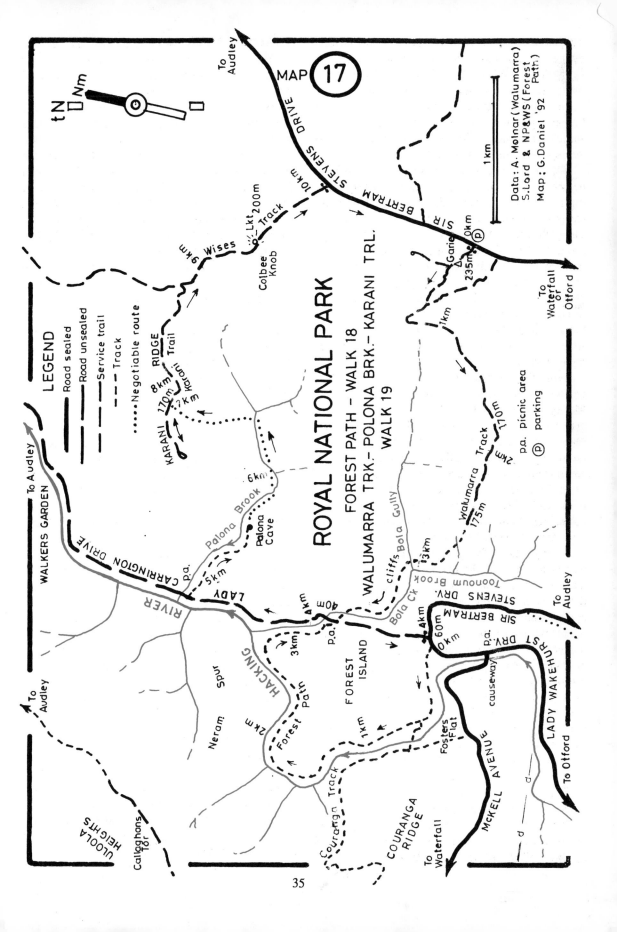

MAP 17

ROYAL NATIONAL PARK

FOREST PATH – WALK 18
WALUMARRA TRK.– POLONA BRK.– KARANI TRL.
WALK 19

LEGEND

━━━ Road sealed
──── Road unsealed
─ ─ ─ Service trail
- - - Track
· · · · Negotiable route

Data: A. Molnar (Walumarra)
S. Lord & NP&WS (Forest Path)
Map: G. Daniel '92

1 km

p.a. picnic area
Ⓟ parking

19. ROYAL N.P.: WALUMARRA TRACK - POLONA BROOK - KARANI RIDGE

The first half of this walk follows the lovely Walumarra Track through a good cross section of the flora of Royal National Park. Vegetation communities encountered include Mallee heath, woodland, dry and wet sclerophyll forest and even a temperate rainforest in Bola Creek. The second half of the walk is harder with some trackless sections. It includes the limestone area on Polona Brook - a deep gully with cliffs, waterfalls and a cave. The Geological Map for the Sydney Region shows quartz sandstone with shale in the Royal N.P., but there is limestone as well. Do not expect Jenolan Caves but it is limestone never-the-less.

From Audley, drive south along Sir Bertram Stevens Drive, then set your tripmeter to zero at the turn off to Wattamolla. At 2km, note the fire trail on your right - the walk exit point. Proceed another 1km to the signposted Walumarra Track on the right. There is ample parking on the left side of the road.

Walk down the Walumarra track for 200m to Garie trig. This is the highest spot in the area. The city and the Blue Mountains can be seen on clear days. A little further on at a trail fork, take the left branch. On this high wind-swept plateau, the vegetation is low, very thick and almost impenetrable. The pebbles on the road are naturally occurring laterite - sandstone containing iron oxide. There are exposed rock platforms everywhere. The soil is very shallow and of poor quality. The vegetation, although dwarfed, is very diverse. An interesting plant found in the wetter areas here is the carnivorous sundew.

At a sharp turn to the south, there is a rock ledge, under which there is shelter from strong winds. Small trees grow on the deeper soil here, where there is constant water seepage.

After 2.6km, the fire trail ends. A track zigzags down amid Gymea Lily, Sydney Redgum and Scribbly Gums towards Bola Creek. With the cliffs behind you and the forest canopy above and in front of you, it feels as if you are in a cathedral. It is a dramatic change indeed from the ridgetop. The deep, rich soil and the shelter provided by the cliffs support this magnificent forest. As you proceed down the slope the vegetation changes again. Wattles, Cabbage Tree Palms, ferns and mosses indicate that you are entering the rainforest. It gets darker and cooler. This is one of the prettiest parts of the Walumarra Track.

From here, the track crosses Bola Gully, then follows Bola Creek, through dark rainforest to Lady Carrington Drive.

Turn right and follow Lady Carrington Drive for 1km to Polona Brook and a good lunch spot. There is a good chance of seeing Lyrebirds along the way. There is a picnic table on the northern side of the creek away from the road. Retrace your steps 100m from the creek, and take the track on the left (SE) which goes steeply up a hill. It takes about 30 minutes to reach the waterfall and limestone formations which include Polona Cave. Take note of the impressive cliffline which Polona Brook has carved out of the sandstone. The cave was only found in 1925. It is a unique part of the park so do not picnic here - just admire and move on. This place is sensitive and should be treated with respect.

After leaving the cave, scramble up the waterfall (on the southern side) then follow the creek upstream along a rudimentary track. At some points the creek bed, whilst slippery, is easier going. In the Spring, there are Waratahs in this section.

Follow the creek to the upper waterfall about 700m above the first one. Do not mistake the small falls for the main one above - the height of the second falls is about 10m. Before scrambling up the fall on the right side, walk down under the waterfall to view the shale rock, mosses and ferns amid animal footprints in the soil.

Above the falls, is a broad flat valley, slightly below the plateau level. It is now harder to see the incoming creeks, and even the main one is just a depression in the soil. About 200m above the falls, but before the main creek divides, turn due north. Take a compass bearing and pick your way up the valley. About 500m of this trackless walking should get you to the Karani Ridge fire trail.

Turn left and walk to the end of this trail, where there are good views of the Hacking River Valley. After a pause, walk back along Karani Ridge fire trail (1.4km) to Wises fire trail. Turn right and walk 1.4km to Sir Bertram Stevens Drive. Turn right again and walk a final 1km back to the car.

Walumarra: coastal Aboriginal for "To Protect".

Grade: Medium, 160m asc.

Distance: 11km.

No public transport. Suits all seasons.

Map 17 and CMA Royal N.P. (Tourist).

Reference: Walumarra Track by NPA Sthn Sydney Branch, available from the Royal N.P. Visitors Centre.

Andrew Molnar

20. ROYAL N.P.:
OTFORD - FIGURE 8 POOL - BURNING PALMS - GARAWARRA - OTFORD

Set in Australia's oldest national park (dedicated in 1879), this walk features panoramic coastal views, littoral rainforest, a fascinating rock pool and a beautiful ocean beach.

The walk starts at Otford Gap. If coming by train, alight at Otford and take the track that leads off from the eastern side of the station and heads east uphill. Where the track meets a road, turn left and walk a short distance to Fanshawe Rd. Turn right up the hill, cross Lady Wakehurst Drive to Otford Gap.

After admiring the extensive views, head north along the track for 300m, where there is a track fork. Take the left branch - the right branch leads to Werong Beach. Continue on this track through delightful bush to a second track junction (2km from Otford Gap). Take the right fork here to Burning Palms via Palm Jungle. After 300m there is a lookout on the cliff edge which offers panoramic views of the coastline as far south as Port Kembla.

Continue on the track as it descends through the magnificent Palm Jungle - a large littoral rainforest area on the steep slopes above the ocean. Cabbage Tree Palms, vines, Birds Nest Ferns and Elkhorns are some of the beautiful rainforest plants found here in this unusual jungle community.

Where the track emerges from the rainforest onto grassland (1.5km from the lookout above Werong Beach) look for a small watercourse (often in a muddy patch). Take the faint track through the grass which follows this watercourse downstream towards the coast. After about 100m you come to a cliff edge where you can view the rock platform below. If there is water over the rock platform, do not descend to it but return to the track and continue on to Burning Palms. If the sea is low enough, with the platform exposed, scramble down the cliff-face and head to the left for about 25m to the Figure 8 pool. It is a perfect figure 8 about 3m long and is a nice pool for a dip. Take particular care on the rock platform, keeping an eye out for large waves.

Walk north along the rock platform for 1km around two headlands to Burning Palms - an unspoilt ocean beach, backed by lush vegetation and an imposing escarpment. This is the recommended spot for lunch, a swim and a break.

After lunch, walk to the northern end of the beach, and take the track that leads northwards among some huts for 600m to an open grassy area on the Burgh Ridge. From here, there are good views of Burning Palms to the south and South Era Beach to the north.

Head west up the Burgh Ridge Track for 900m to the top of the escarpment and Garawarra picnic area and car-park - an ascent of 220m from the beach. At Garawarra, take the signposted Cliff Track which heads off SSW. This is a pleasant level track, but offers few views, even though it runs close to the cliff-edge. Ignore branch tracks to the left and right. At 2.5km from Garawarra car-park you arrive at the track branch encountered earlier in the day that leads to Burning Palms. Continue ahead (west) back to Otford Gap.

Grade: Easy/Medium, 240m asc, with rock scramble and rock hopping at the Figure 8 pool.
Distance: 13km.
Suits all seasons.
Public Transport: Train to Otford.
Map 18 and CMA Royal and Heathcote N.Ps (Tourist).

Stephen Lord

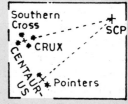

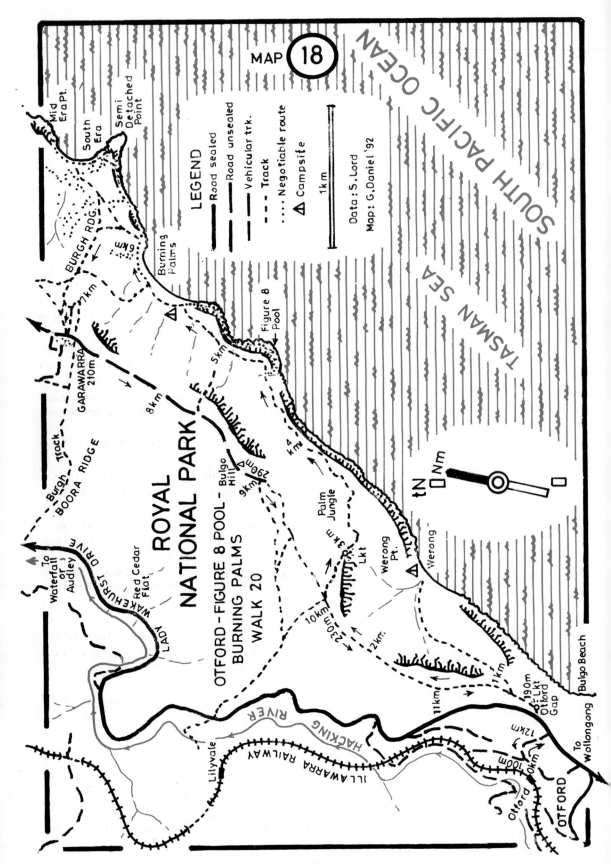

MAP **18**

SOUTH PACIFIC OCEAN

TASMAN SEA

LEGEND

Road sealed
Road unsealed
Vehicular trk.
Track
Negotiable route
△ Campsite

Data: S. Lord
Map: G. Daniel '92

1km

Mid Era Pt.
South Era
Semi Detached Point

Burning Palms

BURGH RDG.

6km

Figure 8 Pool

7km

GARAWARRA 210m

5km

8km

BURGH Track

BOORA RIDGE

4km

ROYAL NATIONAL PARK

Bulgo Hill
280m

9km

OTFORD–FIGURE 8 POOL–
BURNING PALMS
WALK 20

Palm Jungle

Lkt

3km

Werong Pt.

Werong

Waterfall or Audley

To

WAKEHURST DRIVE

Red Cedar Flat

LADY

Bulgo Beach

10km

230m

2km

1km

190m O.Lkt Otford Gap

11km

11km

Lilyvale

HACKING RIVER

ILLAWARRA RAILWAY

12km

Otford 10km

100m

To Wollongong

OTFORD

N

Nm

38

NORTHERN SECTOR

21. DHARUG AND YENGO N.Ps: GREAT NORTH ROAD - LOWER MACDONALD RIDGE

In 1825, Heneage Finch was instructed to survey a route from Sydney to the Hunter Valley. The most difficult part was the ascent of Devines Hill on the northern side of the Hawkesbury River from Wisemans Ferry. Gangs of convicts, some in chains, worked long and hard to build a road with retaining walls, ramps and drains which zigzagged to the top of the ridge. This walk follows this section of the Great North Road, and provides wonderful views of the Hawkesbury River and the Lower MacDonald Valley.

From Dural, travel to Wisemans Ferry. Cross the Hawkesbury River and turn left. Continue on for 500m to a "Settlers Road" sign post. The Great North Road branches to the north here. There is very limited parking.

Start the walk here, pass a locked gate and walk up the Great North Road. Note the extensive well-fitted sandstone ramparts and buttresses and the old stone-quarrying site. After 1km, note the "hangman's cave" with a hole in its roof. Have an early morning tea break looking back across the Hawkesbury River.

At the top of the hill there is a second locked gate and a trail junction. Here you pass from Dharug N.P. to Yengo N.P. Follow the left-hand road briefly, then veer left (west) along a lesser fire trail. Continue out along the ridgetop, first on the fire trail, then a walking track on a narrow ridge, and finally over a virtually trackless knoll. All along the right-hand side of the track are excellent views of the MacDonald Valley to the north and west, including the road to St Albans with the MacDonald wilderness beyond. After 4km (300m before the trail end) note a stone-walled rock pool. You finally reach a rocky escarpment looking SW over farmland and houses of Lower MacDonald - a superb spot for a break. Return to the trail junction at the locked gate.

Head east up the Great North Road. Pass one service trail on the right to a second "Service Trail - walkers only" sign on the right and a locked gate. This level fire trail leads to a rocky lookout (2km) perched high above Wisemans Ferry with spectacular views over the Hawkesbury River. This is the suggested lunch spot.

After a break, return to the Great North Road. The downhill return to the car is relaxing, and has glimpses of the Hawkesbury, and a different perspective on the historic roadway.

Grade: Easy/Medium, 230m asc.
Distance: 13km.
Suits all seasons, but avoid hot days.
No Public Transport.
Map 19 and CMA St Albans and Lower Portland.

Jeanette Blomfield and Val Lincoln

22. DHARUG N.P.: MANGROVE CREEK - TEN MILE HOLLOW VIA SIMPSONS TRACK

Lt Percy Simpson was a free settler, who selected land at Cooranbong, on the banks of Dora Creek on a bridle track halfway between Wisemans Ferry and Wallis Plains (Maitland). This bridle track route, which was discovered by J. McDonald, was advocated by Simpson as an alternative route to the Great North Road. However, this line was not adopted as a major route but became incorporated in a minor road system.

This walk follows a section of Simpsons Track from the pumping station on Mangrove Creek to The Great North Road at Ten Mile Hollow camping area, with an optional extension to Clares Bridge. The "Track" is still a clearly defined roadway with well-preserved stone embankments which follows the alluvial flats of Mangrove Creek as far as its tributary Ten Mile Hollow Creek, then gradually climbs up beside this creek to Ten Mile Hollow camping area. Note the weir at the pumping station may be impassable after heavy rains or after release of water from Mangrove Creek Dam (ring Gosford City Council Water Supply (043)25-8388 before 4pm weekdays for information on water level near the weir).

To get to the walk starting point, drive north along the F3 freeway and take the Peats Ridge exit to Central Mangrove. Turn left into Wisemans Ferry Road and drive for 11km. Branch right into Pembertons Hill Road and drive about 2km to a locked gate 200m uphill from the pumping station and weir.

After crossing near the weir, turn sharp right and follow a short walking track until it joins the

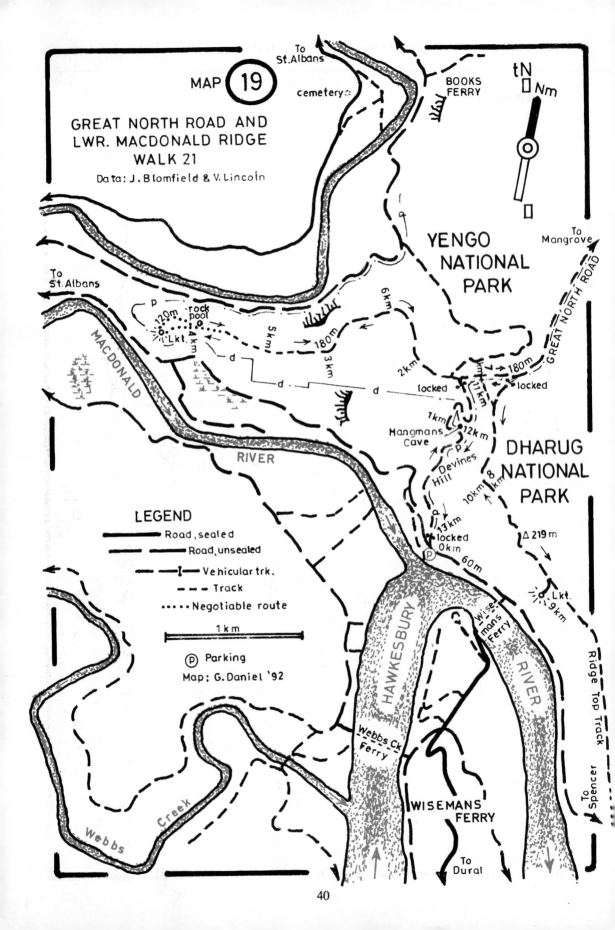

MAP ⑲

GREAT NORTH ROAD AND
LWR. MACDONALD RIDGE
WALK 21

Data: J. Blomfield & V. Lincoln

To St. Albans

cemetery

BOOKS
FERRY

tN
Nm

YENGO
NATIONAL
PARK

To
Mangrove

To
St. Albans

MACDONALD

p
rock
pool
120m
Lkt.
1km

6km

5km
180m
3km

2km
180m

GREAT NORTH ROAD

d
d
d
locked
11km
locked

1km
12km

Hangmans
Cave
p
Devines
Hill

RIVER

DHARUG
NATIONAL
PARK

10km 8km

LEGEND

Road, sealed
Road, unsealed
Vehicular trk.
Track
Negotiable route

1 km

Ⓟ Parking

Map: G. Daniel '92

a
13km
locked
0km

Ⓟ

60m

△ 219 m

Lkt.
9km

HAWKESBURY

Wisemans
Ferry

RIVER

Ridge Top Track

Webbs Ck
Ferry

Webbs   Creek

WISEMANS
FERRY

To
Spencer

To Dural

40

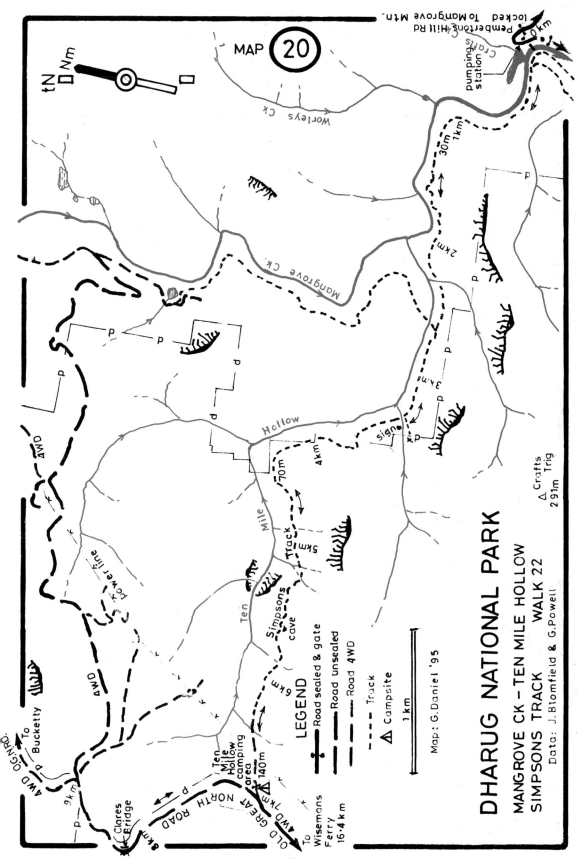

MAP 20

Nm
tN

To Mangrove Mtn.
Pembertons Hill Rd locked
Crafts
pumping station
0 km
1 km
30m
2km
3km
signs
P
P
P
P
P
P
P
Worleys Ck
Mangrove Ck
Hollow
70m
4km
5km
Mile
Ten
Track
Simpsons cave
6km
Powerline
4WD
4WD
4WD OLD GT NR OTH RD
To Bucketty
9km
Clares Bridge
8km
140m
7km
Ten Mile Hollow camping area
To Wisemans Ferry 16·4 km
OLD GREAT NORTH ROAD

△ Crafts
2·91m Trig

DHARUG NATIONAL PARK

MANGROVE CK – TEN MILE HOLLOW
SIMPSONS TRACK   WALK 22

LEGEND

Road sealed & gate
Road unsealed
Road 4WD
Track
△ Campsite

1 km

Map: G.Daniel '95

Data: J.Blomfield & G.Powell

41

old road (Simpsons Track). Follow the creek, noting the stone foundations of early settlers' homes. The roadway leads onto a grassy river flat at the junction of Mangrove and Ten Mile Hollow Creeks. About 500m past the grassy flat, note the track which crosses Ten Mile Hollow Creek. This track leads to Dubbo Valley via Mangrove Creek (see Walk 23).

Follow the old road along the southern side of the creek and select a suitable morning tea spot. At the next tributary do not take a well-defined walking track which continues in a westerly direction up the gully - it leads to a dead end. Instead, at the river flat, cross the small creek to the right (north). On the other side is an NP&WS sign "Service Trail - Walkers Only" where you enter Dharug N.P.

The road heads generally north at this point, but soon swings west. The old roadway follows the valley up to a level plateau. About 2km in from the park boundary there is a beautiful sandstone cave on the left a few metres above the track. Simpsons Track emerges at Ten Mile Hollow picnic and camping area at its junction with The Great North Road (now a 4WD road).

For an optional extra, turn right (north) and continue 1.2km to the old convict-built Clares Bridge (built about 1830). Have lunch here or at Ten Mile Hollow picnic area, then return to the car by the same route - downhill all the way.

Grade: Easy/Medium, 160m asc.
Distance: 14km plus 2.4km return to Clares Bridge.
Best in Autumn, Winter, Spring.
No Public Transport.
Map 20 and CMA Mangrove and NRMA Central Coast Holiday Map.

Jeanette Blomfield and Greg Powell

23. UPPER MANGROVE - DUBBO VALLEY - MANGROVE CREEK

Dubbo Valley was settled by Europeans not long after Governor Phillip and his party explored the Hawesbury River system. It is a delightful, quiet vale near Mangrove Creek.

Drive north along the F3 freeway and take the Calga exit to Central Mangrove. Turn left into Wisemans Ferry Road, then right into Waratah Road (4.5km past Central Mangrove). Drive 3.8km to the end of the sealed road at a three-way

junction and park the car.

Take the upgraded old logging road which winds down the steep valley side for 3.3km to a lovely grassy glade where Dubbo Creek meets Mangrove Creek. This is a good spot for a break. Cross the bridge and turn right and explore upstream a short way, then retrace your steps back to near the bridge.

Head south along a trail on the western side of Mangrove Creek. After 1km from the bridge, you come to an old graveyard, just past some power-lines, where some early pioneers are resting. About 1km further on, note the branch road on the right which leads to the Great North Road.

The trail leads to a cleared paddock. Cross a side creek here and once past the paddock turn left at a junction and follow the former road which is now a walking track through to Ten Mile Hollow Creek and Simpsons Track junction. Have lunch at the grassy flats near the junction of Mangrove Creek and Ten Mile Hollow Creek.

Return to the start by the same route, or if you can arrange a car shuttle, continue on another 2.7km along Mangrove Creek to the pumping station at the end of Pembertons Hill Road, then walk 200m up the road to a gate to complete the walk. (see Walk 22 for details).

Grade: Easy/Medium, 270m asc.
Distance: 18km (12km with car shuttle).
No Public Transport.   Suits all seasons
Map 21 and CMA Mangrove and NRMA Central Coast Holiday Map.

Jeanette Blomfield and Val Lincoln

24. NORAH HEAD WILDFLOWER WALK

The coastal country near Norah Head contains rock swimming pools, high dunes, good beaches and large swales that are a haven for water birds. The original vegetation on the sand dunes was a community of coastal plants including magnificent Angophoras, Banksias, Melaleucas and Burrawangs. Unfortunately these dunes were mined in the 60s and 70s and have now been partially overrun with the vigorous weed Bitou Bush. This walk is within an area in which there is a maze of tracks and trails. If at any time an incorrect track is taken, head east toward the coast.

Norah Head is 15km east of Wyong via Toukley or 12km north of the Entrance. Start at

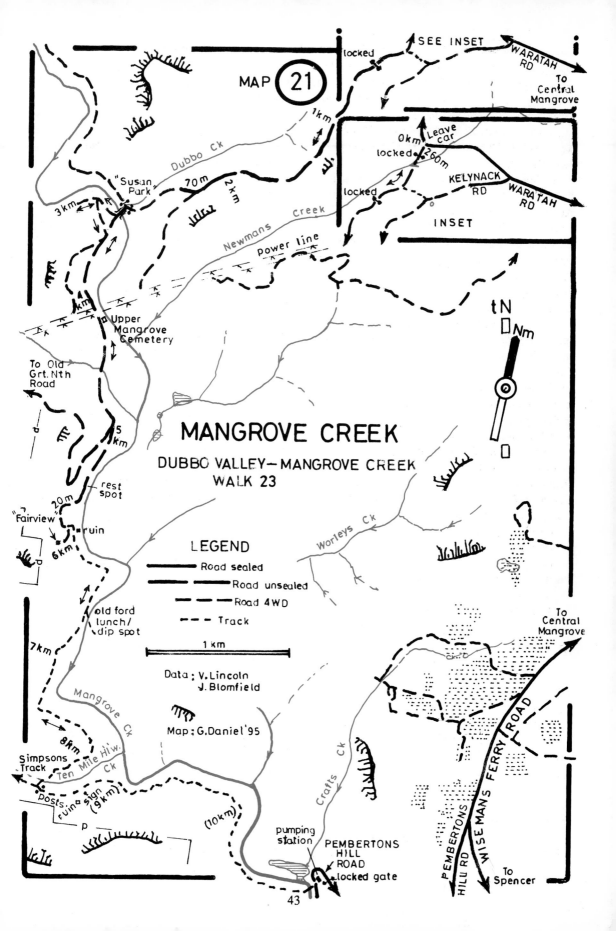

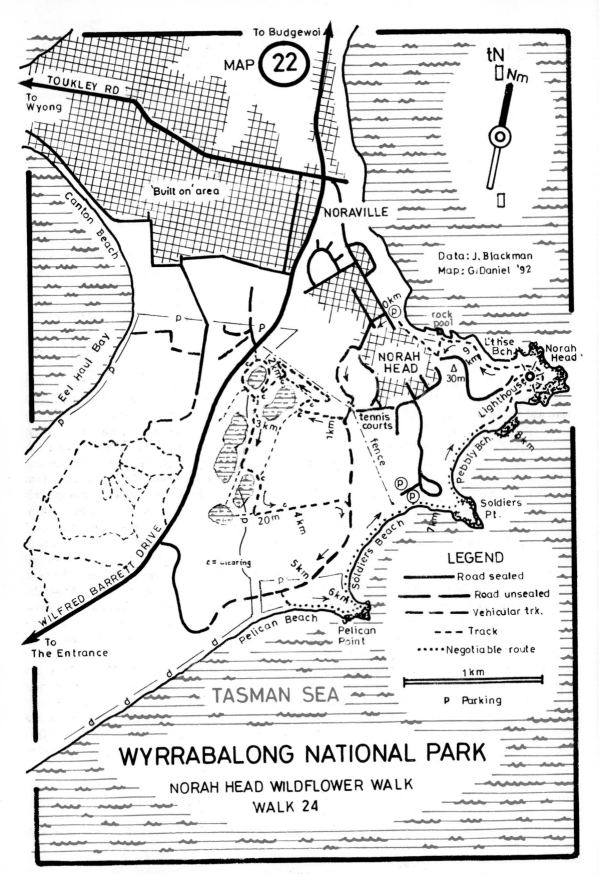

To Budgewoi

TOUKLEY RD

To Wyong

'Built on' area

NORAVILLE

Canton Beach

Eel Haul Bay

tN

Nm

Data: J. Blackman
Map: G. Daniel '92

rock pool

L'th'se Bch.

Norah Head

NORAH HEAD

0 km

9 km

Δ 30m

Lighthouse

tennis courts

fence

Pebbly Bch.

8 km

Soldiers Pt.

P

P

2 km

3 km

1 km

4 km

5 km

6 km

20m

c = clearing

Soldiers Beach

7 km

WILFRED BARRETT DRIVE

To The Entrance

Pelican Beach

Pelican Point

TASMAN SEA

LEGEND

——— Road sealed
— — — Road unsealed
– – – Vehicular trk.
- - - Track
······ Negotiable route

|—————| 1 km

P   Parking

WYRRABALONG NATIONAL PARK
NORAH HEAD WILDFLOWER WALK
WALK 24

the junction of Bungary Rd and View Street, Norah Head. Walk SW along View Street, cross Soldiers Point Drive then continue on to where a lane leads off on the right (immediately before View Street bends to the left). Turn into the lane and after 50m turn left onto a fire trail. Follow the main trail past turn-offs on each side. At the bottom of a dune the main trail curves to the left. Follow this to Victoria Street. At this point turn right and go through a large gate near a Tennis and Bowls Club. Take the fire trail on the right side of the car-park which leads to a fence. Go through the gate, turn left and about 200m further on you will find a trail on the right. This track is a little overgrown at the start but improves. It climbs to the top of a high dune and then leads down to a large sandy clearing. Here trails go off in several directions. Turn sharp right, then right again (after 3m) and follow an overgrown trail to the next clearing - often ablaze with wildflowers. Turn right to a fence and follow it to the left for 400m until it meets another trail coming in from the left. Take this trail (heading SE) to a clearing where there is a small creek on the right. Cross here and walk to the next clearing where there is an old gate and some wire fencing. Turn right and follow the fence through a small forest of red gums to a clearing with four large gums in the centre and blue metal covering the sand.

Next, turn left through an old gate and walk along the Angophora Ridge above the lakes. Walk past two turn-offs on the left and take the third one. If you go too far you will come to a lake full of dead trees and Bitou Bush - if so, retrace steps 250m to the turn off.

Follow the right hand track around the edge of the lake to the next clearing. Turn left onto an overgrown track. After 5 minutes the track improves and joins a trail coming in from the right. At this point, take an overgrown track on the left. After 250m of rough walking on this track it emerges onto a wide, sandy fire trail. Turn right and follow this trail to a very large clearing behind the coastal dunes. At the end of this clearing there are a number of trails. Take the one on the left over the dune to the beach.

Once on the beach, head NE. Walk over Pelican Point, along Soldiers Beach, across Soldiers Point, along Pebbly Beach then around the rocks, past the lighthouse on Norah Head to a rock pool. Finally walk up some steps to the shops and bus stop.

Grade: Easy, 30m asc.   **Distance:** 10km.
Public Transport: Buff Point bus to View St, Norah Head from Wyong station. Week days: 50 mins past the hour, Weekend 8.25am. and 10.25am. Busways (043)62-1030.
Best in Spring for viewing wildflowers and at low tide for exploring the rock platform.
Map 22 and CMA Toukley.   Jean Blackman

25. WEST GOSFORD RAILWAY DAMS

In a bygone era water was piped from two railway dams on Fountain Creek, west of Gosford, to Gosford station for the steam trains. This walk leads to these picturesque, disused dams which are great for swimming.

Take the Gosford turn-off from the F3 freeway. At West Gosford, turn left off the Pacific Highway into Manns Road. Drive 3.7km along Manns Road and turn left into Reeves Road. Drive 1.6km to its end and park the car.

Take the well-used track heading uphill (west). It leads past a huge rock outcrop with interesting weathering, whilst below are palms in a ferny valley. Continue uphill to a rough clearing. Cross over, and veer slightly to the left and uphill along a rough vehicle track. Follow this trail and at a fork take the left branch then continue downhill for about 100m to a large rock shelf which overlooks the first Railway Dam. Retrace your path a few metres up the rock shelf and on the left find a small rough track which leads down to the sandy beach at the western end of dam, where a creek feeds it. Clear reflections of trees can be seen from this beach. Cross the rock shelf over which Fountain Creek flows and take the track which follows the creek upstream for 200m to the base of a second dam wall. Climb the sloping rock on left side to view this dam.

Follow a track here for 120m along the southern side of the dam till the undergrowth becomes thick and difficult to penetrate. It leads to a rocky bridge across the creek. View the reflections then walk back to the beach at the first dam for lunch. After a break, and perhaps a swim, return the same way via the rock shelf to the car.

Grade: Easy, 50m asc.   **Distance:** 2km.
Best in Summer for swimming.
No Public Transport.
Map 23 and CMA Gosford.   Ann Hamilton

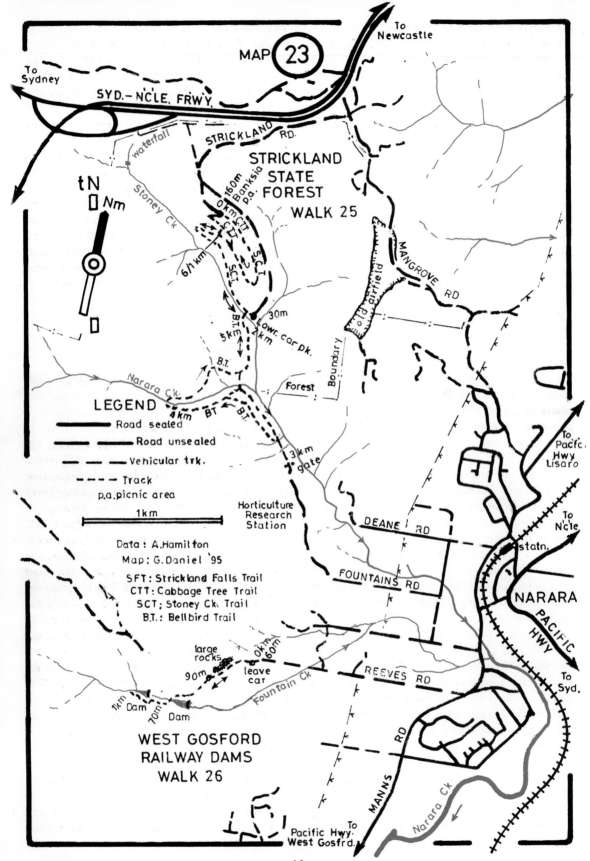

MAP 23

To Newcastle

To Sydney

SYD.-N'CLE. FRWY.

STRICKLAND RD.

STRICKLAND
STATE
FOREST
WALK 25

waterfall

Stoney Ck

tN
Nm

160m
Banksia p.a.
0km CTT
CTT
SCT
6/1 km
SCT

old airfield

MANGROVE RD

30m
Lowr. car pk.
B.T.
5km
2km
B.T.

Narara Ck.

LEGEND
4km BT
B.T.
B.T.

Forest
Boundary

3km
gate

_____ Road sealed
- - - - - Road unsealed
– – – Vehicular trk.
- - - Track
p.a. picnic area

Horticulture
Research
Station

DEANE RD

statn.

1km

FOUNTAINS RD

To Pacfic
Hwy
Lisaro

To
N'cle

Data: A. Hamilton
Map: G. Daniel '95

SFT: Strickland Falls Trail
CTT: Cabbage Tree Trail
SCT: Stoney Ck Trail
B.T.: Bellbird Trail

NARARA

PACIFIC HWY

large
rocks
0km
60m
90m
leave
car

Fountain Ck

REEVES RD

To Syd.

1km Dam
70m Dam

WEST GOSFORD
RAILWAY DAMS
WALK 26

MANNS RD

Narara Ck

To
Pacific Hwy.
West Gosfrd.

46

26. STRICKLAND STATE FOREST: BANKSIA PICNIC GROUND - NARARA CK

Strickland State Forest contains attractive stands of rainforest interspersed with many interesting tree species not native to the area. These trees were planted late last century when this forest was the site of Australia's first Forestry School. There is an optional walk to some Aboriginal rock engravings.

From West Gosford, drive along Manns Road, into Narara Valley Road, then left into Mangrove Road (gravel). Continue past an airfield on the left and turn left into a side road to Banksia Picnic Ground, Strickland State Forest (signposted). If you come to the expressway overpass you have travelled 150m too far.

Drive 1.3km down the Strickland Forest Road and take the right fork at a junction. Park at Banksia Point picnic area where there are toilets and barbecues. At the southern end of the car-park, the left branch of the Cabbage Tree Track heads downhill, passing magnificent rocky pinnacles. In Spring, there are Gymea Lilies in bloom. This well formed track crosses a delightful grassy saddle, then winds down through glorious palms and ferny hillsides for 900m to a track junction. Take the left-hand track for 1.1km to Stoney Creek (signposted).

Cross Stoney Creek via some stepping stones to the Bell Bird Track. After 400m veer left at a "Y" track junction (the right branch is the return route). Continue on for 120m to Narara Creek. Cross over on a log bridge, and follow the track as it follows Narara creek downstream for 600m to a gate at the southern boundary of the State Forest. On both sides of the track here, there are magnificent Bunya Pines which are native to southern Queensland.

Retrace steps 200m and take the track which branches off to the left (west) marked with an arrow on a low post. After 500m, at a track junction, take the left branch which undulates in a westerly direction through the rainforest roughly parallel to Narara Creek. It then descends via a few steps to the creek bed. Cross over to a pleasant spot for a rest and a snack (but watch out for leeches).

The track now swings back to the east. You pass through a palm jungle and cross a side creek before returning to the "Y" track junction (mentioned earlier). Turn left and return along the

Bellbird Track to the stepping stones over Stoney Creek. Walk back uphill on the Stoney Creek Track to the Cabbage Tree Track and turn left - signposted "Banksia Point Picnic Area". The track winds up through more palms below large rocks with interesting weathering, then switches back and ascends through dry sclerophyll forest to the walk starting point.

For an optional extra, drive back to Mangrove Road, then turn right and proceed for 180m and park the car. Take the track which starts behind the barrier (near a tall power pole with straining wires). It runs left almost parallel to the road for several hundred metres and then divides. Take the left branch, and look on the left side for a track and plaque indicating Aboriginal rock engravings. This short walk takes about 45 minutes return.

Grade: Easy, 180m asc.
Distance: 8km.
Suits all seasons.
No Public Transport.
Map 23 and CMA Gosford.

Ann Hamilton and Stephen Lord

27. BRISBANE WATER N.P.: GIRRAKOOL - MOONEY MOONEY CK

The Girrakool Circuit is a 6km loop track which provides a good overview of the vegetation communities of Brisbane Water National Park. Commencing in the dry plateau country at Girrakool Picnic Area, it follows Piles Creek downstream. Once below the cliffline, the track passes through gully rainforest where Coachwood and Water Gum dominate. A 1.6km extension track follows Piles Creek further downstream to Mooney Mooney Creek. Here, the valley opens out and large Deanes Gum and Turpentine grow, and on the lower reaches of Piles Creek, there are mud flats with stands of mangroves.

To reach the walk starting point, leave the F3 Freeway by the Gosford/Woy Woy exit - the first exit north of the Mooney Mooney Bridge. Follow the Wisemans Ferry and Old Sydney Town signs, then turn left at a roundabout, 800m from the Gosford Road. Drive SW down the Pacific Highway, past the Old Sydney Town entrance, to the Girrakool turn-off on the left. Leave the car in the Girrakool car-park.

Take the left hand (eastern) track. After 150m there are some aboriginal engravings on a rock

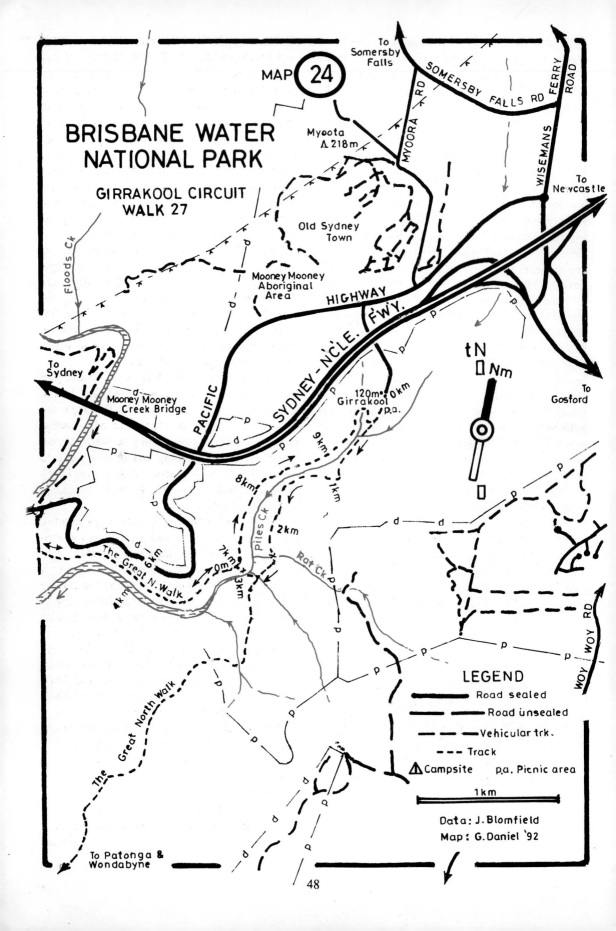

MAP (24)

BRISBANE WATER NATIONAL PARK

GIRRAKOOL CIRCUIT
WALK 27

To Somersby Falls

SOMERSBY FALLS RD

MYOORA RD

WISEMANS FERRY ROAD

To Newcastle

Myoota Δ 218m

Old Sydney Town

Mooney Mooney Aboriginal Area

HIGHWAY

SYDNEY – N'CLE. FWY.

PACIFIC

Floods Ck

To Sydney

Mooney Mooney Creek Bridge

To Gosford

tN

Nm

120m
Girrakool p.a.
0km
9km
1km
2km
8km
Piles Ck
Rat Ck
7km
0m
3km
6km
The Great N. Walk
4km

The Great North Walk

WOY WOY RD

LEGEND

Road sealed
Road unsealed
Vehicular trk.
Track
△ Campsite   p.a. Picnic area

1km

Data: J. Blomfield
Map: G. Daniel '92

To Patonga & Wondabyne

shelf, and about 300m further on, two lookout points offer views over Piles Creek and a small waterfall. Next, cross a creek via a bridge and pass through some sheltered bush. The track crosses two more small creeks then rises up onto a drier ridge area for 500m before descending to Rat Creek. Wildflowers are excellent in this area in springtime. Cross Rat Creek and continue up and over a small ridge to a track junction near a creek.

Turn right (west) onto a section of the Great North Walk. After 150m the track crosses Piles Creek (bridge washed away). Once across the creek, turn left (west) and follow Piles Creek further downstream. The valley opens out and magnificent Deanes Gum and Turpentine can be seen. Near the junction of Piles Creek and Mooney Mooney Creek mangroves grow on the saline mudflats. Go as far as the grassy banks beside Mooney Mooney Creek, where you cross a vehicle track and stop for lunch.

Return 1.6km to the track junction near the Piles Creek crossing. Take the left (north) branch and stay on the western side of Piles Creek. The track climbs some stone steps and passes below some cliffs as it winds back up the Piles Creek valley. There is a final creek crossing near the picnic area below the car-park.

Grade: Easy, 130m asc.

Distance: 10km.

Best Seasons: Spring and Autumn.

Public Transport: Gosford-Old Sydney Town bus, Busways, (043)68-2277.

Map 24 and CMA Gosford, NRMA Central Coast Holiday Map.

Stephen Lord and Jeanette Blomfield

NATIONAL PARKS
and other NP&WS areas comprise less than
five per cent
of the area of N.S.W.

28. BRISBANE WATER N.P.: WONDABYNE - KARIONG BROOK - WONDABYNE TRIG

The ridges in Brisbane Water National Park rise to 250m above sea level and offer extensive views of the surrounding countryside. In contrast, the gullies that have resulted from creeks cutting their way through the Hawkesbury sandstone are sheltered and intimate. This walk takes you to both these extremes - Wondabyne Trig, with 360° views and Kariong Brook, a protected creek, lined with rainforest. In Spring, there are spectacular displays of wildflowers. Much of the walk is along the well-marked Great North Walk.

The walk starts from Wondabyne station. Alight from the rear door of the last carriage. View the sandstone sculptures 100m NE of the station, then return to the station and take the Great North Walk which heads south for a few metres. The track swings north past a dwelling, then climbs steeply to the top of a ridge where there are views over Mullet Creek.

Head north along the Wondabyne Track, past the Pindar Cave branch track on the left at 1.2km, to a track junction on the right (2.3km from the station). Take this track which descends steadily, then crosses fairly level country to pretty Myron Brook. Next head east up and over a ridge to Kariong Brook, where there is a deep round rock pool, a broad waterfall, a rock overhang, rainforest and ferns.

After a break continue up some steps to a fire trail (300m). Turn right, and walk along this trail for 1.3km, then take the track that branches off to the right. Follow this track for 400m to where it passes under a power-line and meets the service trail that is routed over the Wondabyne railway tunnel. Turn right along this trail a short distance then take the signposted track on the left that climbs gradually towards Wondabyne Trig. Near the summit, turn left onto the side-track which leads up to the trig. There are wonderful 360° views of the ridges and gullies of Brisbane Water National Park and the waterways and the ocean.

After admiring the views and a lunch break, return to Wondabyne station by the same route.

Grade: Medium, 500m asc.

Distance: 17km.

Best Season: Spring.

Public Transport: Train to Wondabyne.

Map 25 and CMA Gosford and Gunderman.

Val Lincoln

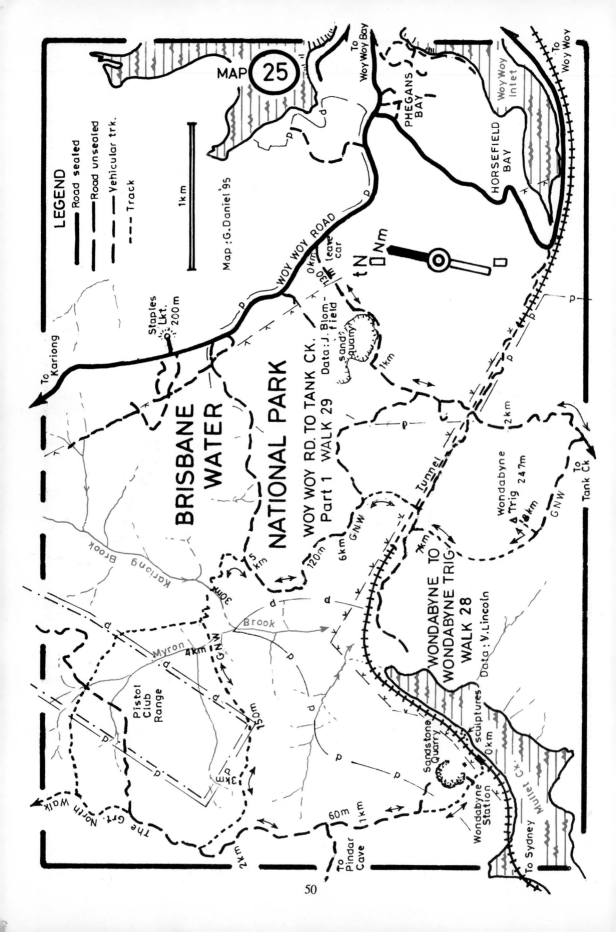

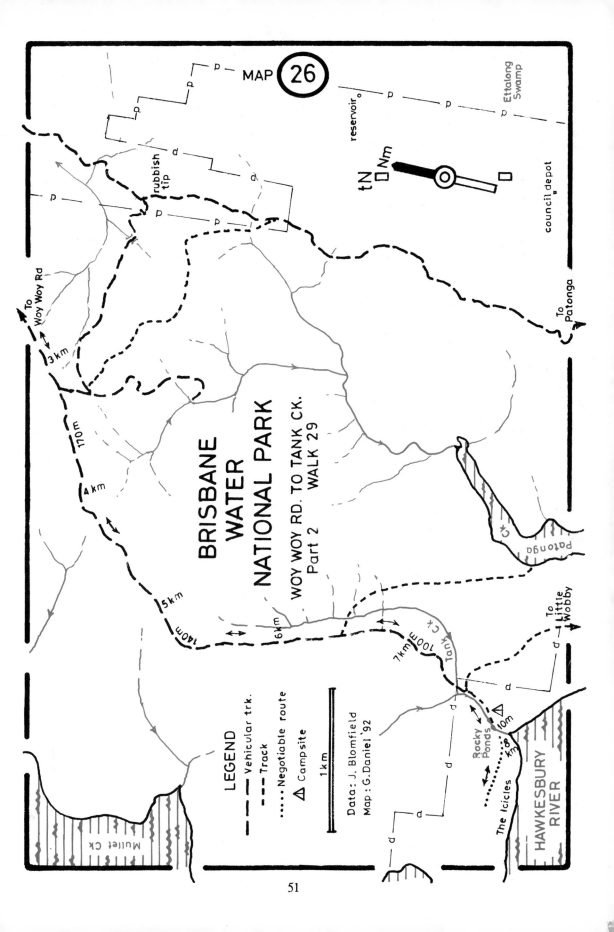

MAP 26

BRISBANE
WATER
NATIONAL PARK

WOY WOY RD. TO TANK CK.
Part 2   WALK 29

LEGEND
Vehicular trk.
Track
Negotiable route
△ Campsite

1 km

Data: J. Blomfield
Map: G. Daniel '92

To Woy Woy Rd

3 km

170 m

4 km

5 km

140 m

6 km

Mullet Ck

reservoir

Ettalong Swamp

council depot

To Patonga

rubbish tip

Tank Ck

7 km

100 m

10 m

8 km

Rocky Ponds

The Icicles

Patonga Ck

To Little Wobby

HAWKESBURY RIVER

tN   Nm

29. BRISBANE WATER N.P.: WOY WOY RD - WONDABYNE TRIG - ROCKY PONDS, TANK CREEK

Rocky Ponds is a series of appealing pools and waterfalls on Tank Creek in southern Brisbane Water National Park. From Rocky Ponds, and nearby hillsides, there are beautiful views of the Hawkesbury River and Dangar Island.

Leave the F3 Freeway at the Gosford/Woy Woy Exit. Turn right at Kariong towards Woy Woy. Stop at Staples Lookout, 5km past Kariong. The lookout has views of Brisbane Water and Barrenjoey Head. Drive south along the Woy Woy Road to the fourth fire trail on the right (1.3km), where there is an entrance gate to a sandy quarry. Park the car here.

Walk around the gate and along the trail for 2km, ignoring side tracks. Proceed under a power-line, past the sand quarry and under a second power-line to a locked gate which denotes the entrance to Brisbane Water National Park.

Continue for another 1km, then at a junction, take the right hand track up a minor fire trail which gently climbs towards Wondabyne Trig. Turn right along a narrow track through sandstone boulders to the summit and trig. This is an ideal place for morning tea with extensive views of the National Park and beyond.

From the trig, retrace your steps to the main fire trail via the track and minor fire trail. Turn right (SW) and walk for 600m to another track junction. Take the right (WSW) track (signposted Rocky Ponds and Patonga).

The next section (4km) is fairly level. Two tracks branch off to the left along the way. The destination, Rocky Ponds, is very scenic. Water from this creek used to be piped to small craft below. Climb to the top of the hillside above the Icicles for great views over the Hawkesbury.
After a break and lunch, return to Woy Woy Road by the same route.

Grade: 19km, 140m asc.
Distance: Medium.
Best from Autumn to Spring.
No Public Transport.
Maps 25, 26 and CMA Gosford, Broken Bay.
Jeanette Blomfield

30. BRISBANE WATER N.P.: UMINA - PATONGA

The forested ridges between Pearl Beach and Patonga offer brilliant wildflower displays and wonderful views over Broken Bay.

From the Umina Surf Club walk to the southern end of the beach. Take the old Pearl Beach road around the headland below the cliff face. Next walk along Pearl Beach. Near the southern end of the beach, look for Amethyst Street. Head west along this street and walk to its end, then take a track on the right which leads up to a lovely waterfall. There is a lookout to the NE (200m away) on a rocky ledge, and a rock swimming pool 250m further upstream.

Return the same way till you reach Diamond Street, turn right then right again into Crystal Avenue which will take you to a fire trail passing beneath a large rock overhang towards Warrah Trig. There is a short track off to the left to Warrah Lookout. The view out over Broken Bay is magnificent, a lovely spot to have a break. Continue on the track for 300m, and branch left down hill on the Patonga Trail towards Patonga. On reaching a point above Dark Corner, turn left at a junction and walk down to the rocks and a lovely little beach. Next, walk along Patonga Beach to the mouth of Patonga Creek. A optional extra is to follow the eastern bank of Patonga Beach for about 1.5km upstream. Return by the same route to Umina.

If a car shuttle can be arranged, there are spots worth exploring on the drive back to Umina. Firstly, note the tessellated pavement on the left side of the road. Then a little further on, on the right is a minor track to Elephant Rock, a vast expanse of sandstone, with views of the lower Hawkesbury River. The next stop is Waratah Patch, on the left, named for its abundance of Waratahs - in flower around October. Drive further on, past the Pearl Beach turn-off (200m) and turn right onto a side-road at a reservoir to Mt Ettalong for fantastic coastal views.

Grade: Medium, 230m asc.
Distance: 17km (rtn).
Transport: Train to Gosford; Bus to Umina, Busways (043)68-2277; Ferry, Brooklyn-Patonga (02)985-7566, Palm Beach-Patonga (02)918-2747.
Map 27 and CMA Broken Bay, NRMA Central Coast Holiday Map.   Val Lincoln

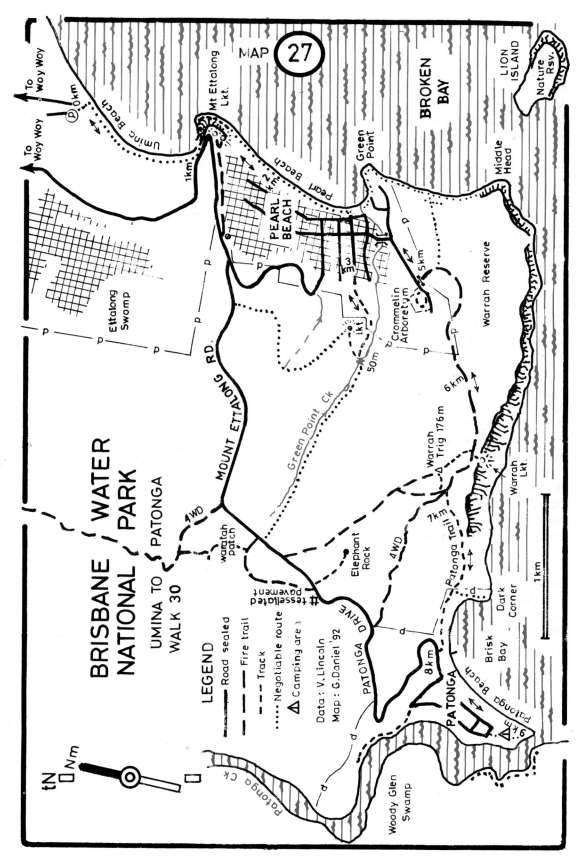

MAP 27

BROKEN BAY

BRISBANE WATER NATIONAL PARK

UMINA TO PATONGA
WALK 30

LEGEND

Road sealed
Fire trail
Track
Negotiable route
Camping area

Data : V. Lincoln
Map : G. Daniel '92

tN
Nm

To Woy Woy
To Woy Woy
To Woy Woy

Umina Beach

Mt Ettalong Lkt.

Pearl Beach

PEARL BEACH

Ettalong Swamp

MOUNT ETTALONG RD.

4WD

waratah patch

tessellated pavement

Elephant Rock

PATONGA DRIVE

PATONGA

Patonga Beach

Patonga Ck

Woody Glen Swamp

Green Point Ck

Green Point

Crommelin Arboretum

Warrah Reserve

Warrah Trig 176m

Warrah Lkt.

Middle Head

LION ISLAND

Nature Rsv.

Patonga Trail

4WD

Brisk Bay

Dark Corner

lkt

50m

1 km
2 km
3 km
5 km
6 km
7 km
8 km
9 km

1km

1 km

31. BOUDDI N.P.:
MAITLAND BAY CENTRE - MT BOUDDI - MAITLAND BAY CIRCUIT

Bouddi National Park protects a wonderful section of scenic coastline between the Hawkesbury River and McMasters Beach on the Central Coast. One of the jewels of the park is the secluded and unspoilt Maitland Bay. This walk takes you to this delightful spot, and in addition, there are extensive views of the coastline on both the inward and outward tracks.

To reach the walk starting point, drive from Woy Woy or Kincumber along Empire Bay Drive and turn into Wards Hill Road. Climb up two hairpin bends, then turn left into Maitland Bay Drive. Follow Maitland Bay Drive to The Scenic Road. The car-park at the Maitland Bay Centre (old Maitland Store) is opposite. Park the car here.

For a circuit walk to Maitland Bay, swing left behind the Maitland Bay Centre and follow a level fire trail which parallels The Scenic Road. After 2km you reach the narrow sealed Mt Bouddi Road. Turn right and follow the road to the Mt Bouddi picnic area and car-park. Find a walking trail behind the Dingledei shelter shed. A fairly level track leads to lookout rocks with views of Maitland Bay, Box Head and Barrenjoey Head. The track then drops steeply down the ridge to a "T" junction. Take the right hand track to Maitland Bay. Explore the headland of Bouddi Point, and the rocks below, which at low tide reveal the remains of the boiler of the paddle-steamer Maitland which was wrecked in a violent storm in 1898 with the loss of 27 lives.

Maitland Bay is a delightful spot to relax or swim. The track back to the Maitland Centre leaves the southern end of the beach, and climbs, via many steps, back to the top. A rock shelf near the top gives a delightful view of Maitland Bay.

Grade: Easy, 150m asc.   **Distance:** 7km.
Public Transport: Gosford-Wagstaff Buses, Busways (043)68-2277.
Suits all seasons.
Map 28 and CMA Broken Bay, NRMA Central Coast Holiday Map.

Jeanette Blomfield

32. BOUDDI N.P.:
MT BOUDDI - LITTLE BEACH CIRCUIT

This circuit walk takes you from high on the Bouddi Peninsula to the ocean then across the wonderful Bombi Moor to clifftop lookouts and pretty Little Beach. The final leg of the walk is via the Scenic Road.

To reach the walk starting point, drive from Woy Woy or Kincumber along Empire Bay Drive and turn into Wards Hill Road. Climb up two hairpin bends, then turn left into Maitland Bay Drive. Follow Maitland Bay Drive to The Scenic Road. Turn left and drive for 2km, then turn right into the Mt Bouddi Road picnic area and car-park.

Walk south along the trail to the rocky lookout over the Bouddi coastline, then descend the spur to a "T" junction (1.2km from Mt Bouddi). Turn left (east) along a narrow undulating walking track with glimpses of sandstone cliffs and shoreline. After 1.8km there is a fire trail junction. The trails in this section of the Park traverse Bombi Moor, which is a unique vegetation community growing on perched sand on a sandstone shelf high above the ocean. Casuarinas and Wallum Banksia form a dense low cover and in Spring every patch of heath sprouts masses of subtle and delicate flowers. Veer right and continue for 100m to a second junction. Turn right and walk out to Bombi Head for good coastal views. Return to the main trail, turn right (NE) and walk for 500m to another trail junction. Turn right again and walk to another lookout on the cliff edge at Third Point. Return to the main trail again and continue towards Little Beach. Turn right at the next "T" junction. Little Beach is a pleasant place for lunch with grassed picnic and camping areas (booking essential for camping), and a rocky beach.

Return up the main fire trail, or a more attractive walking track off to the right, to Grahame Drive past remnant rainforest and tall Blackbutts. Walk up Grahame Drive, turning left at The Scenic Road and back to Mt Bouddi car-park.

Grade: Easy, 160m asc.   **Distance:** 10km.
Public Transport: Gosford-Wagstaff Buses, Busways (043)68-2277.
Suits all seasons.
Map 28 CMA Broken Bay, NRMA Central Coast Holiday Map.

Jeanette Blomfield

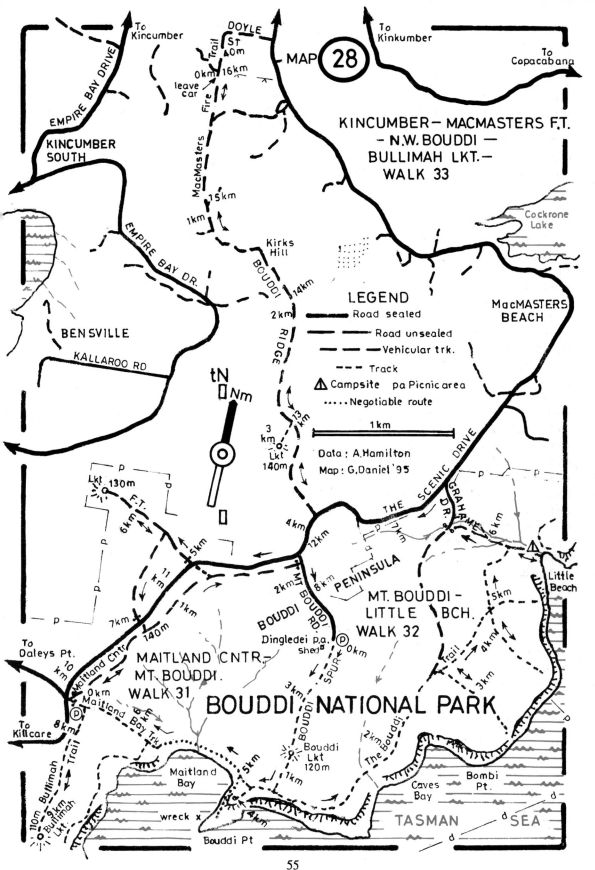

To Kincumber

DOYLE ST 40m

To Kinkumber

To Copacabana

MAP **28**

KINCUMBER — MACMASTERS F.T.
— N.W. BOUDDI —
BULLIMAH LKT. —
WALK 33

0km 16km
leave car

EMPIRE BAY DRIVE

KINCUMBER SOUTH

EMPIRE BAY DR.

MacMasters Fire Trail

15km

1km

Kirks Hill

14km

2km

BOUDDI RIDGE

Cockrone Lake

MacMASTERS BEACH

BENSVILLE

KALLAROO RD

tN Nm

13km

3 km

Lkt 140m

LEGEND

Road sealed
Road unsealed
Vehicular trk.
Track
⚠ Campsite   pa Picnic area
.... Negotiable route

1 km

Data : A. Hamilton
Map : G. Daniel '95

Lkt 130m

F.T.

6km

5km

4km

12km

THE SCENIC DRIVE

GRAHAME DR.

p

6km

2km MT BOUDDI

8km

PENINSULA

MT. BOUDDI —
LITTLE BCH.
WALK 32

5km

⚠ Little Beach

11 km

1km

BOUDDI RD.

7km 140m

MAITLAND CNTR. —
MT. BOUDDI.
WALK 31

Dingledei p.a. shed

0km

SPUR

Trail

4km

3km

To Daleys Pt.
10 km

Maitland Cntr

0km Maitland Bay Trk.

8km

To Kilcare

110m Bullimah Trail

9km Bullimah Lkt.

3km

BOUDDI NATIONAL PARK

Bouddi Lkt. 120m

2km The Bouddi

Maitland Bay

5km

1km

wreck x

4km

Bouddi Pt

Caves Bay

Bombi Pt.

TASMAN   **SEA**

55

33. BOUDDI N.P.: KINCUMBER SOUTH - N.W. BOUDDI - BULLIMAH LOOKOUT

North-west Bouddi is clothed in beautiful forest and offers great views over Brisbane Water.

From Kincumber, drive along the Scenic Road, and turn right into Doyle Street. Drive to the end of the bitumen and park the car. Walk up the fire trail ahead to a clearing with a 4-way track junction. Take the track on the right which heads down hill then up again along the top of the ridge. Just before the trail turns left and slightly downhill, note the huge rocky pinnacle (Mt Sugarloaf) on the right. Take the track that veers to the right to the top of some rocks for spectacular views of Copacabana, Brisbane Water and the ridges of Brisbane Water N.P. (5 mins climb). Return to the fire trail, turn right and follow the trail around the base of the pinnacle (past a branch track that leads left downhill), and walk up the steep hill to the Scenic Road.

Turn right and walk for 1.1km to where a service trail branches off to the right into the NW section of Bouddi National Park. Walk around the gate, and follow this trail for 300m and note a track on the left. Continue ahead for 500m to a lookout with sweeping views over Empire Bay, the Broadwater, Gosford and beyond. Return 500m to the track junction. Turn right and follow this track for 700m to the Scenic Road.

Cross the Scenic Road, go through a Service gate, and turn right onto a trail which leads to the rear of the Maitland Centre, and a car-park (700m). Take the track that heads downhill (SE) near the car-park for 100m to a track junction near a huge rock. Take the signposted Bullimah Trail on the right which heads SW to a lookout. Along the way there are extensive views of Maitland Bay, Barrenjoey Head, Pittwater and Broken Bay. The track passes by some ancient Grass Trees and the wildflowers are lovely in the Spring. At the lookout there are spectacular views of Patonga, Juno Head and West Head.

Return the same way except go via the fire trail that starts behind the Maitland Bay Centre and runs parallel to the Scenic Rd to Mt Bouddi Road. This saves 2km of road walking.

Grade: Easy/Medium, 140m asc.

Distance: 16km.

Suit all seasons. No public transport.

Map 28 and CMA Gosford and Broken Bay.

Ann Hamilton

34. BOUDDI N.P.: DALEYS POINT RIDGE - RILEYS BAY - HARDYS BAY

Bouddi N.P. currently protects only a narrow strip of coastal land. This walk is through proposed extensions to the park, which if added would assist the long-term viability of the area for nature conservation. Note that this walk must be done at low tide.

Drive along Empire Bay Drive from Woy Woy via The Rip Bridge. Turn up Wards Hill Rd, and after two hairpin bends, park at the top of the hill near a fire trail on the western side of the road opposite Maitland Bay Drive.

Start off along this fire trail. Walk past two left-hand fire trails, then after 1.6km at a Y-junction, take the right branch. This trail leads to a group of big boulders for a view over Cockle Bay N.R. - an important fish breeding and bird feeding refuge.

Return to the Y-junction and follow the left branch out on to a large area of flat rock with views over Brisbane Water. There are aboriginal carvings and axe grinding grooves near a small pool, whilst in caves under the main rocks there are more aboriginal carvings and a shell midden.

Continue on a track down the ridgeline almost to the Rip Bridge. There are views across to Booker Bay and Ettalong with Lion Island in the distance. Turn left, join Daley Ave and follow its recent extension around Fishermans Bay to Rileys Bay. Continue to the end of the road, then turn right and walk to the shoreline. Provided the tide is low, you can walk through the mangroves around to Hardys Bay. There are extensive shell middens on the banks. Have lunch in the parklands at Hardys Bay.

Return along Araluen Drive to Noble Road and follow it to its junction with Fraser Road. Turn left and walk up a concrete driveway, then turns right onto a track which leads up to the ridgetop. Once on top, at a T-junction with a fire trail, turn left and walk to a rock shelf for views over Hardys Bay and Bouddi N.P.

Return to the T-junction. Turn left and follow the 4WD track to Wards Hill Rd, then turn left back to the starting point.

Grade: Easy, 120m asc.   **Distance:** 9km.

Suits all seasons at low tide.

Public Trans: Busways (043)68-2277.

Map 29 and CMA Broken Bay.

Jeanette Blomfield

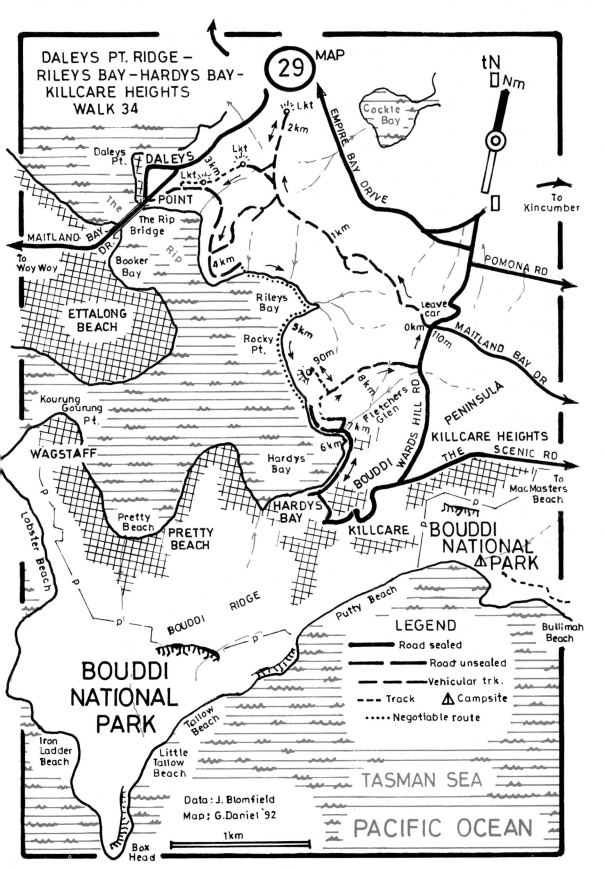

DALEYS PT. RIDGE –
RILEYS BAY – HARDYS BAY –
KILLCARE HEIGHTS
WALK 34

MAP 29

tN
Nm

Cockle Bay

To Kincumber

EMPIRE BAY DRIVE

Lkt
2km

Daleys Pt.

DALEYS

3km

Lkt

Lkt

POINT

The Rip Bridge

MAITLAND BAY DR

Booker Bay

To Woy Woy

1km

POMONA RD

The Rip

4km

Rileys Bay

leave car

Rocky Pt.

0km

110m

MAITLAND BAY DR

5km

90m

8km

PENINSULA

KILLCARE HEIGHTS

ETTALONG BEACH

Kourung Gourung Pt.

Fletchers Glen

7km

WARDS HILL RD

THE   SCENIC RD

6km

BOUDDI

To MacMasters Beach

WAGSTAFF

Hardys Bay

Pretty Beach

PRETTY BEACH

HARDYS BAY

KILLCARE

BOUDDI NATIONAL △ PARK

Lobster Beach

BOUDDI   RIDGE

Putty Beach

Bullimah Beach

LEGEND

Road sealed

Road unsealed

Vehicular trk.

Track   △ Campsite

Negotiable route

BOUDDI NATIONAL PARK

Tallow Beach

TASMAN SEA

Iron Ladder Beach

Little Tallow Beach

Data: J. Blomfield
Map: G. Daniel '92

1km

Box Head

PACIFIC OCEAN

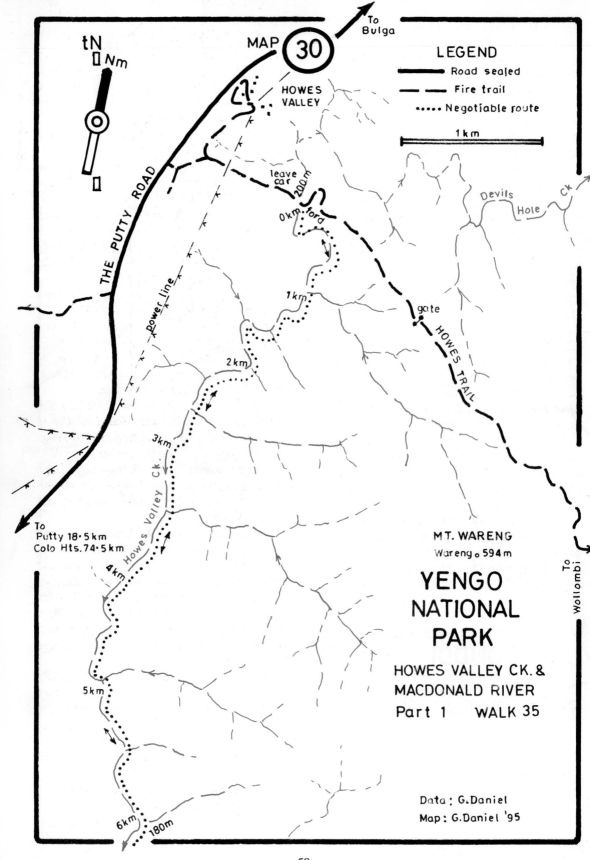

LEGEND
Road sealed
Fire trail
Negotiable route

1 km

MAP 30

To Bulga

HOWES VALLEY

THE PUTTY ROAD

leave car
200 m
0 km ford
1 km
Power line
2 km
3 km
Howes Valley Ck.
4 km
5 km
6 km   180m

To Putty 18·5 km
Colo Hts. 74·5 km

gate
HOWES TRAIL

Devils Hole Ck

To Wollombi

MT. WARENG
Wareng o 594 m

YENGO NATIONAL PARK

HOWES VALLEY CK. &
MACDONALD RIVER
Part 1   WALK 35

Data: G.Daniel
Map: G.Daniel '95

tN   Nm

NORTH WEST SECTOR

35. YENGO N.P.: HOWES VALLEY CREEK - MACDONALD RIVER

Imagine a two-day walk entirely along sandy, flat, wide and shady creek and river beds with only a couple of rocky boulders along the way. The beds of The MacDonald River and its tributaries offer such a walk - strange linear deserts within the maze of ridges that make up Yengo National Park.

Don't go on this walk if there has been heavy rain in the area, as there are no side tracks along the creek banks. Navigation is easy, just follow the creek and river beds. The creek beds are usually dry with just a trickle or no flow at all. At the MacDonald River it is not much different, although a small stream may flow at the camp-site.

Start off by driving north along the Putty Road. Cross the bridge over the MacDonald River (74.5km from Colo Heights). Then, 4.5km further on, there is an insignificant looking bush road on the right at Howes Valley - take it. Drive in for 800m and leave your car on the left hand side (200m before a ford across Howes Valley Creek).

Walk down to the ford, turn south, and enter the creek bed from the eastern side. You're on your way. You may encounter holes in the sand which have been dug by animals (kangaroos, wombats, dingoes etc.) seeking water.

After 11.7km you arrive at the MacDonald River - which should take about 4 hours. At this junction, turn left (south) and continue downstream for another 3.5km to a rock overhang on the right (west) side which would shelter about six people.

Camp here. Pitch tents on the dry sand on the rock bed beside the overhang. Good water should be available from the river at the camp-site. Boil it for the camp and the next day's walk out. Next day return via the same way.

Grade: Day 1 and Day 2; Easy, 80m asc, 15.5km walking along creek beds.
Total distance: 31km.
Suits all seasons. No Public Transport.
Maps 30,31 and CMA Howes Valley and Mount Yengo.

George Daniel

36. BLUE MOUNTAINS N.P.: GROSE VALE - CABBAGE TREE CREEK - BURRALOW CREEK - GROSE RIVER

The lower Grose River area of Blue Mountains N.P. offers opportunities for creek walking, rock hopping and plenty of swimming - great for the summer months.

At North Richmond, turn south into Terrace Road (which later becomes Grose Valley Road) and continue in a westerly direction before turning left into Cabbage Tree Road. This is a bitumen road for 2.7km but then becomes a dirt road, near a small horse yard on the left. Proceed along this dirt road through open gates and park your car in the second clearing on your right (before a "Y" intersection in the road). The distance from the gates is about 100m.

The first part of the walk is trackless and your objective is to reach Cabbage Tree Creek by proceeding NW for about 50m and then SW along the upper part of a ridge to the SW side of a gully. Descend to the creek in a NW direction and as you reach the bottom you will see a cleared paddock on the other side of the creek.

Walk along either side of the creek in a SW direction to its junction with Burralow Creek. Continue generally in a westerly direction up Burralow Creek mostly on the southern side. You can go as far as time will permit but a good lunch spot is found 1.5km from the Cabbage Tree Creek junction, where there are two small waterfalls and a large swimming hole.

Return along Burralow Creek, past the junction with Cabbage Tree Creek until you reach the Grose River. Cross to the southern side and proceed SE by the river. There are plenty of tempting areas for swimming. After 1.5km the river becomes quite shallow and there is a sand bank. At this point, cross over to the north side and climb the embankment to a disused four wheel drive trail.

Take this trail which ascends 170m before levelling out. Thereafter, continue along the trail for about 1km ignoring the two turn-offs to the left until you get to a definite "T" intersection. Turn right and walk a final 700m to the car.

Grade: Medium, 160m asc, rock-hopping and trackless sections. **Distance:** 8km.
Best in summer. No public transport.
Map 32 and CMA Kurrajong.

Rosemary MacDougal

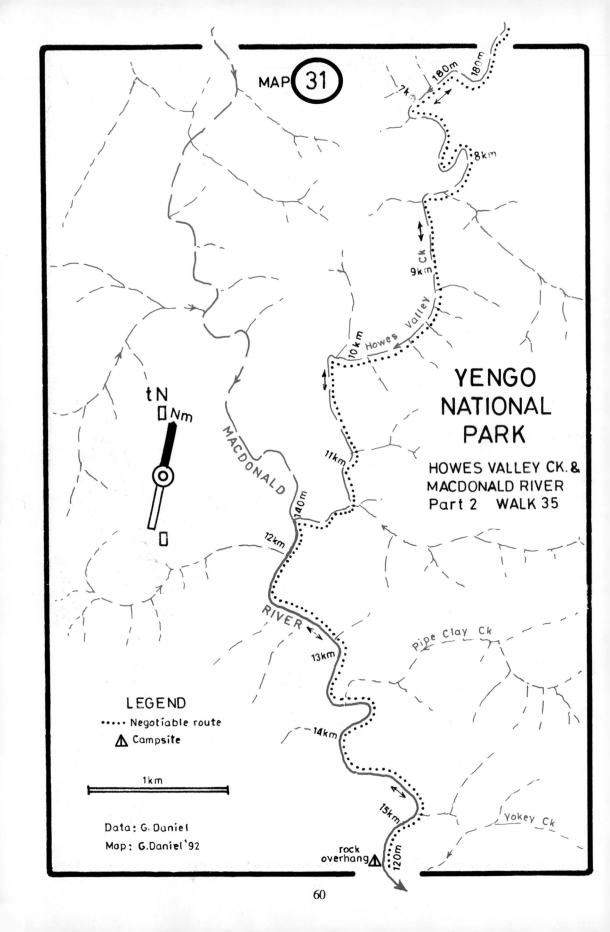

MAP ③①

180m 180m

7k

8km

Ck

9km

10km Howes Valley

YENGO
NATIONAL
PARK

HOWES VALLEY CK. &
MACDONALD RIVER
Part 2   WALK 35

11km

MACDONALD

140m

12km

RIVER

Pipe Clay Ck

13km

14km

15km

Yokey Ck

rock
overhang ⚠

120m

t N
☐ Nm

LEGEND
•••• Negotiable route
⚠ Campsite

|————— 1km —————|

Data: G. Daniel
Map: G. Daniel '92

60

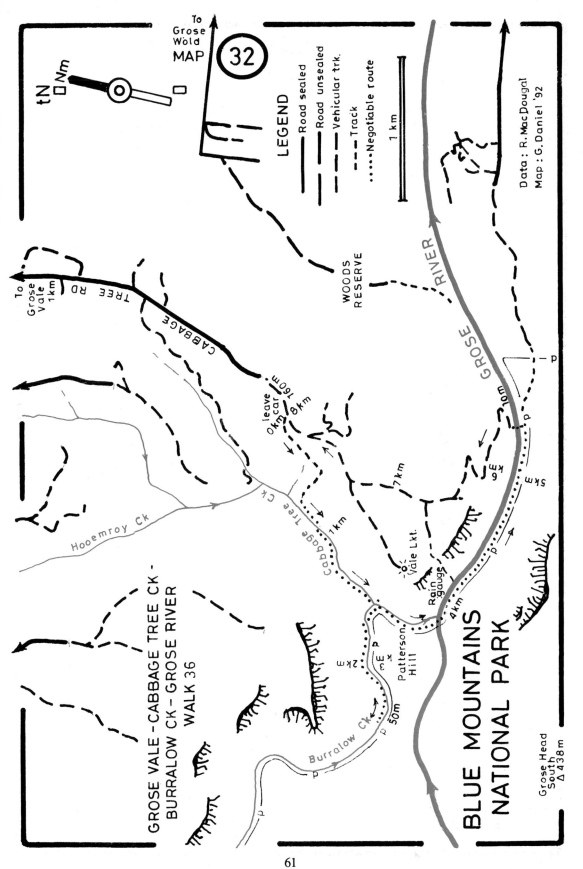

GROSE VALE - CABBAGE TREE CK -
BURRALOW CK - GROSE RIVER
WALK 36

BLUE MOUNTAINS
NATIONAL PARK

MAP 32

To Grose Wold

To Grose Vale 1km

CABBAGE TREE RD

WOODS RESERVE

GROSE RIVER

Hooemroy Ck

Cabbage Tree Ck

leave Oki car

160m

8km

7km

1km

9km

5km

10m

4km

Vale Lkt.

Rain gauge

P

P

P

Patterson Hill

2km

3m

50m

P

Burralow Ck

Grose Head South △438m

Data : R. MacDougal
Map : G. Daniel '92

LEGEND

Road sealed
Road unsealed
Vehicular trk.
Track
Negotiable route

1 km

tN □Nm
□

37. WOLLEMI N.P.: DEEP PASS

Deep Pass is an old farm site, hidden away in a corner of Newnes Plateau. Picture a large grassy clearing almost hemmed in by cliffs with a beautiful babbling brook, birds and other wildlife, and all sorts of interesting rock formations to explore. It's an easy walk in along an old road which is badly eroded on the final descent into Deep Pass. The only hard part of this trip is navigating through the maze of forest and fire roads on Newnes Plateau. The walk is not suitable after heavy rain as the roads become boggy.

To start the walk, drive up the Bells Line of Road from Windsor, and 6km past Bell turn right (left if coming from Lithgow) at the Zig Zag Railway. The road you want goes up the hill between the railway siding and a quarry, which is signposted to "The Glow Worm Tunnel".

Follow this road past a saw-mill entrance then through the sand mines to a "T" intersection (left to Lithgow and right to the Glow Worm Tunnel and Deep Pass). Turn right (watch for this intersection on your return) and follow the road as it runs through Newnes State Forest, in which there are pine plantations. At the end of the twelve mile pine plantation, turn right into Boundary East Forest Road. Drive through the first cross road, then at the next cross road turn left, then 500m further on, the road forks. Take the right fork (the left goes out to Mt Budgary and is very boggy).

After 2.5km a further turn-off to the right is taken. After half a kilometre or so, Dinner Gully is reached. Usually this is about the limit for two wheel drive vehicles, as often there is a large boggy patch that is very difficult to negotiate. However, if it is dry you can drive on to a car-park (with railway line barriers on two sides) above Deep Pass, another 2-2.5km further on.

From Dinner Gully, walk down the road past a branch road on the left. The trail is eroded and a bit steep, but is not very long, and then you're into the clearing that is Deep Pass. Cross the creek (Nayook Creek) to some superb camp-sites.

There are four short walks suggested for your stay at Deep Pass.

1. Follow Nayook Creek upstream (rough going in places) to a delightful pool and waterfall in a small canyon, great for that summer dip.

2. Follow the track on the southern side of Nayook Creek downstream about 250m through great cliffs. Cross the creek and at the western cliff-base look for a series of small caves, complete with glow worms. Head back on the northern side of the creek, along the cliff-base for about 150m to a miniature Standley chasm in the cliff-wall. The chasm ("T" shaped in plan view) has 25m and 50m long arms. Exit the same way you entered. Return to the camp-site by a track on the northern side of the creek.

3. From the clearing, walk toward the chasm, but follow a track north around the cliff-face to a ramp between two cliff-walls. Scramble up the ramp, then up onto the left hand bluff where there are eroded sandstone formations and views over the camp-site.

4. Walk south along the vehicle track which goes toward Bungleboori Creek for 1km to Deep Pass (the actual geographical feature after which the area is named). Turn right up an old eroded trail to a fire trail at the ridge-top for more views to the south of pagodas on the ridge-tops above a tributary of Bungleboori Creek.

How long you spend at Deep Pass will depend on how much food and time you have. After enjoying this special place, return the same way, taking care to carry all rubbish out with you to keep it special.

On your return, if time permits, visit the Glow Worm Tunnel overlooking the Wolgan Valley. Drive back to the main forest road, and where Boundary East Forest Road joins it, turn right and follow the signs. Do not turn right at the sign-posted Deanes siding. Drive past an information board, through a dry tunnel to a parking area. From here it is a 1km walk to the Glow Worm Tunnel which is 700m long, so you will need a torch. (For a more complete description of this area, look up Walk No. 30 in Bushwalks in the Sydney Region, Vol 1).

Grade: Easy, 150m asc.

Distance: 6km.

No Public Transport

Best in Spring or Summer.

Map 33 and CMA Rock Hill plus CMA Lithgow and Cullen Bullen for the access roads.

Phil Foster

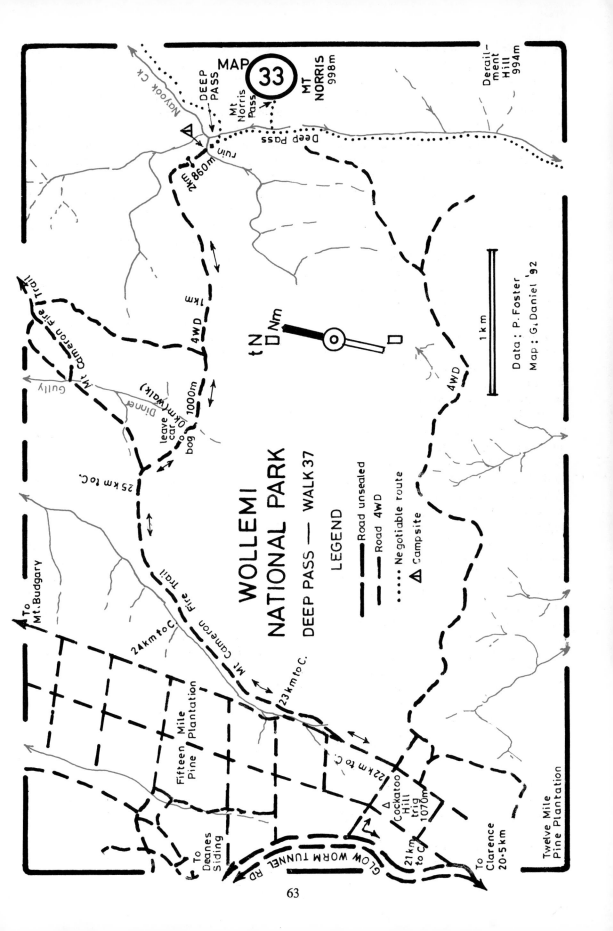

MAP (33)

WOLLEMI
NATIONAL PARK

DEEP PASS — WALK 37

LEGEND

Road unsealed
Road 4WD
Negotiable route
△ Campsite

Data : P. Foster
Map : G. Daniel '92

1 km

MT NORRIS 998m

Derail-
ment
Hill
994m

DEEP PASS

Mt Norris Pass

Deep Pass

Ngyook Ck

ruin

2 860 m

4WD

1 km

1000 m

Mt Cameron Fire Trail

Gully

Dinner (Qtmtwalk)

leave car

bog

25 km to C.

Mt Cameron Fire Trail

24 km to C.

23 km to C.

22 km to C.

Fifteen Mile Pine Plantation

To Mt. Budgary

To Deanes Siding

GLOW WORM TUNNEL RD

△ Cockatoo Hill trig 1070 m

21 km to C.

To Clarence 20·5 km

Twelve Mile Pine Plantation

63

WESTERN SECTOR

38. BLUE MOUNTAINS: HISTORIC RAILWAY WALK: LAPSTONE - GLENBROOK

The Blue Mountains presented a major challenge to the builders of the western railway line. Initially a zigzag line was opened in 1867 to enable trains to ascend and descend the Lapstone geosyncline. In 1913, a new line was completed which included a long tunnel which enabled trains to negotiate the steep climb on a continuous line.

This walk starts at Lapstone railway station. From the station walk south along Explorers Road and cross a gully via a concrete footbridge opposite the corner of Hume Road. Turn left after crossing the bridge and pass through the railway gate at the bottom of Grover Street. Walk to the railway line and turn right.

Walk beside the railway line until a cutting is reached and climb up the hill, keeping the cutting on the left, to a reserve at the rear of houses in Byrne Street where there are spectacular views of the Nepean River, Glenbrook Gorge and the railway line.

Proceed to the railway gates at the end of Governors Road where there is a sign "Bluff Lookout Unmade Track". Follow this track. There are various lookouts on the way and tracks which may be confusing but generally bear left towards the railway line.

After 1.7km there is a sign "Tramway Terminus". Early this century, a special railway track to sidings was constructed for delivering bricks for the lining of the Glenbrook Gorge Railway Tunnel. The bricks were transported by rail from the plains via the old single line 1892 tunnel to the old Glenbrook railway station and then via this construction line. The bricks were lowered to the tunnel site using a light funicular line. Glenbrook railway station was then situated at the site of present day Glenbrook Park. On May 11, 1913 a single line for trains climbing the mountains was put into service while those descending the hill continued to use the old tunnel. The double line was opened on September 25, 1913 and Glenbrook railway station was relocated to its present position.

Follow this "Tramway Route" track to the north via the Primary School, and cross over Explorers Road where there is a sign "Lapstone Tunnel". The path ends at a gully where the line once crossed by a wooden trestle bridge, long since burnt down in bush fires. Back track a short distance and then follow "Lapstone Tunnel" signs to the old 1892 Glenbrook Tunnel. Return to the "Tramway Terminus". Allow at least an hour for this side-trip along the Tramway Route.

Turn right and continue along above the railway line. After a short distance there is a sign "Windinghouse Base" and the remains of two concrete floors and bolts which were used to mount the engine house and winding gear for the funicular railway.

Walk down the wooden steps to a sign "Funicular Route". Follow this very steep path (which is now a water drain) a short distance down to the present railway line at a point not far from the eastern end of the Glenbrook Gorge Tunnel. Return to the main track and walk up to the picnic shelter/tables in Bluff Lookout Reserve.

During the construction of the railway, The Bluff became a tent town for the workers who had their own shops, hall and two-up school. The children attended Glenbrook School and School Of Arts.

Keep left and follow the path to the lookout which faces west. Walk down the track on the right hand side of the lookout to near the railway line just north of the bridge that leads to Blue Mountains National Park.

Turn right and walk up Bruce Road to Glenbrook railway station.

Grade: Easy, 80m asc.
Distance: 12km.
Public Transport: Train to Lapstone.
Map 35 and CMA Penrith.
Reference: Lapstone Zig Zag by William A. Bayley. Austrail Publications.

Ian Schleter

THE NATIONAL PARKS ASSOCIATION
is an independent non-profit community organisation dedicated to preserving our natural heritage.
Sydney Office, PO Box A96, Sydney South, N.S.W. 2000

39. BLUE MOUNTAINS N.P.: GLENBROOK - EUROKA CLEARING - NEPEAN RIVER

Euroka Clearing in the lower Blue Mountains N.P. is a large cleared area that was once used for farming. It contains a number of delightful spots for picnicking and camping.

Turn south off the Great Western Highway at Glenbrook into Ross Street, which is signposted "Blue Mountains N.P." Follow Ross St through Glenbrook shops, then turn left into Bruce Road which takes you into the National Park.

It is best to park in the NP&WS Visitors' Centre car-park at the park entrance and walk down (500m) to the Glenbrook Creek causeway.

Cross the causeway and head south up the road for 400m to a hairpin bend. Take the signposted "Euroka Walking Track" on the left - it is wide and well defined. It follows a gully, and generally takes an easy uphill slope through thick scrub. You pass over a small wooden footbridge and walk up some short steeper parts via wooden steps.

The track meets the intersection of Euroka and Mt Portal Roads. Cross Mt Portal Road and take the signposted track to Euroka Clearing. There are various tracks leading in different directions but walk down the short steep track into the clearing. At the northern end of the clearing cross over a bridge, pass the toilets and follow Euroka Creek to a sign "Nepean Walking Track".

Follow this track alongside the creek through a narrow gorge where there is lush vegetation and thick leaf litter. Look for Coachwood and Lillypilly trees, vines and mosses, and birds such as Scrub Wrens, Golden Whistlers, Yellow Thornbills, Bare Headed Friar Birds and orange and white Nankeen Kestrels.

As the track bends to the right and the Nepean River comes into view various tracks go to the left but they all lead to the same place so follow the wide well-worn track down a short steep section to the Nepean River. The track to the right just before the river leads to Bennett Ridge Road.

There are sandy spots by the river suitable for a picnic. Return to Euroka clearing and Glenbrook by the same route.

Grade: Easy, 300m asc. **Distance:** 8km.
Suits all seasons.
Public Transport: Train to Glenbrook, 1.5km walk to Park entrance.
Map 35 and CMA Penrith.   Ian Schleter

40. BLUE MOUNTAINS N.P.: GLENBROOK GORGE - TUNNEL VIEW LOOKOUT - PORTAL LOOKOUT - MT PORTAL ROAD

The Tunnel View and Portal Lookouts in the Glenbrook section of Blue Mountains N.P. offer wonderful views of Glenbrook Gorge and the Cumberland Plain around Penrith.

From Glenbrook railway station, walk to the NP&WS Visitors' Centre and look for a sign "Glenbrook Gorge" near the car-park. Walk along a sealed road which leads to an NP&WS maintenance area and at a locked gate take the track on the right signposted "walking track to Glenbrook Gorge". Follow this track down into the gorge to Glenbrook Creek. Coming in to the Gorge on the left is another gully across which on the NE side is the railway line.

Where a very small creek comes in on the left (NW), cross Glenbrook Creek and walk up a water course on the other side next to a large dead rotten tree which has fallen down the hill. The track up to the cliff top is very steep and slippery. The track then leads SE then east along the cliff tops to Tunnel View Lookout. Have morning tea and enjoy the views of Glenbrook Gorge, the railway line and tunnel.

Follow the cliff line, generally easterly, passing through the heads of two gullies until you reach Portal Lookout where there are splendid views of the Nepean River, Penrith and the surrounding plains.

Head back along the Mt Portal Road. Pass the turn-off to Tunnel View Lookout at 1.4km then continue for a further 1.1km to where Euroka Rd branches off to the left (south). At this point, take a well-defined track on the right. This track leads back to The Oaks fire trail at a hairpin bend just south of Glenbrook Creek. Walk down the road for 400m, cross Glenbrook Causeway, then follow the road back up to the Visitors' Centre.

Grade: Easy/Medium, 270m asc, some rough sections.
Distance: 10km.
Best in Autumn, Winter, Spring.
Public Transport: Train to and from Glenbrook.
Map 35 and CMA Penrith.

Ian Schleter

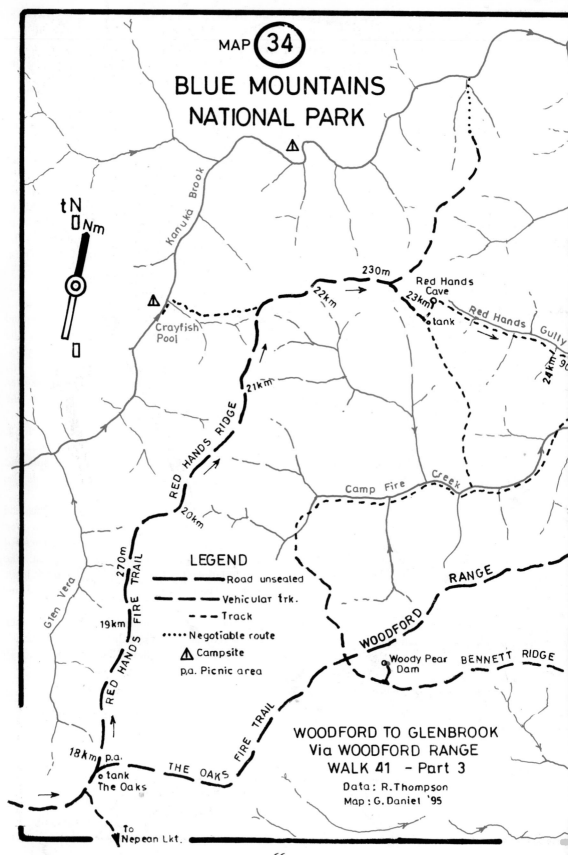

MAP (34)

BLUE MOUNTAINS NATIONAL PARK

tN
Nm

Kanuka Brook

Crayfish Pool

230m

Red Hands Cave

22km

23km

tank

Red Hands Gully

24km

90

RED HANDS RIDGE

21km

20km

Camp Fire Creek

270m

RED HANDS FIRE TRAIL

19km

Glen Vera

LEGEND

———— Road unsealed

– – – Vehicular trk.

- - - Track

••••• Negotiable route

⚠ Campsite

p.a. Picnic area

WOODFORD RANGE

Woody Pear Dam

BENNETT RIDGE

THE OAKS FIRE TRAIL

18km p.a.

tank
The Oaks

WOODFORD TO GLENBROOK
Via WOODFORD RANGE
WALK 41 – Part 3

Data: R.Thompson
Map: G.Daniel '95

To Nepean Lkt.

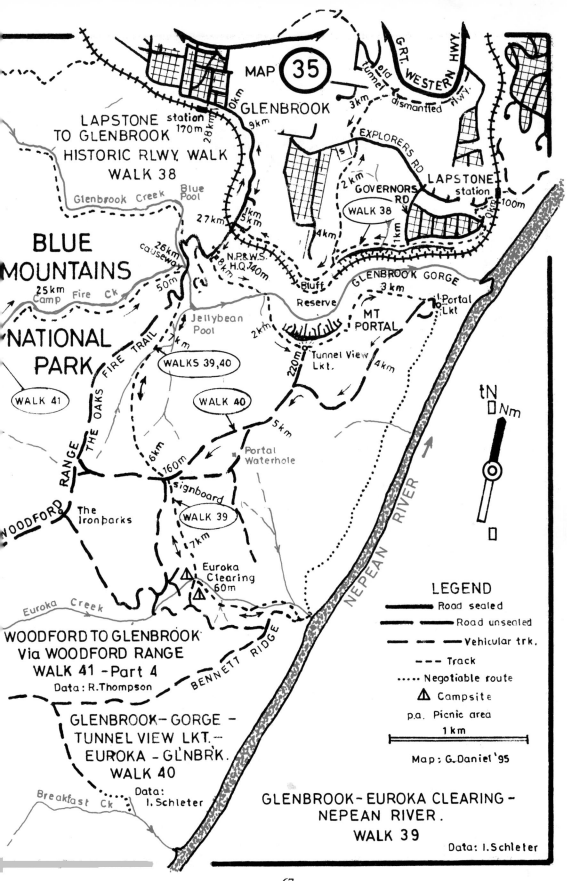

MAP 35 GLENBROOK

LAPSTONE TO GLENBROOK HISTORIC RLWY. WALK WALK 38

BLUE MOUNTAINS NATIONAL PARK

WALK 41

THE OAKS FIRE TRAIL

THE RANGE

WOODFORD

The Ironbarks

WOODFORD TO GLENBROOK Via WOODFORD RANGE WALK 41 -Part 4
Data: R.Thompson

GLENBROOK- GORGE - TUNNEL VIEW LKT.— EUROKA - GLNBRK. WALK 40
Data: I. Schleter

GLENBROOK-EUROKA CLEARING - NEPEAN RIVER. WALK 39
Data: I.Schleter

GRT. WESTERN HWY.

old tunnel dismantled

EXPLORERS RD

GOVERNORS RD
WALK 38

LAPSTONE station

NEPEAN RIVER

WALKS 39,40
WALK 40
WALK 39

Glenbrook Creek
Blue Pool

N.P.&W.S. H.Q.
Bluff Reserve

GLENBROOK GORGE
MT PORTAL
Portal Lkt.

Jellybean Pool
Tunnel View Lkt.

Camp Fire Ck

Portal Waterhole
signboard

Euroka Clearing 60m

Euroka Creek
BENNETT RIDGE

Breakfast Ck

tN
Nm

LEGEND

Road sealed
Road unsealed
Vehicular trk.
Track
Negotiable route
△ Campsite
p.a. Picnic area
1 km

Map: G. Daniel '95

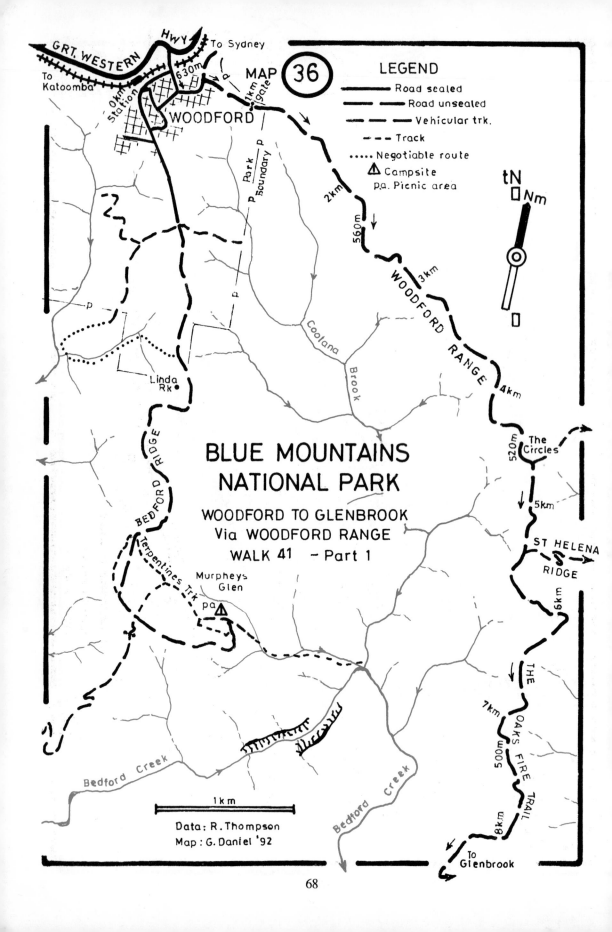

GRT. WESTERN HWY — To Sydney

To Katoomba

630m

0km Station

WOODFORD

MAP (36)

1km gate

Park Boundary

LEGEND

— — — Road sealed
– – – Road unsealed
— – — Vehicular trk.
- - - Track
······· Negotiable route
△ Campsite
p.a. Picnic area

tN □Nm

2km

560m

3km

WOODFORD RANGE

4km

520m The Circles

5km

ST HELENA RIDGE

6km

Coolana Brook

Linda Rk ●

BEDFORD RIDGE

BLUE MOUNTAINS NATIONAL PARK

WOODFORD TO GLENBROOK
Via WOODFORD RANGE
WALK 41 — Part 1

Terpentines Trk

Murpheys Glen

p.a. △

THE OAKS FIRE TRAIL

7km

500m

8km

To Glenbrook

Bedford Creek

Bedford Creek

1km

Data: R. Thompson
Map: G. Daniel '92

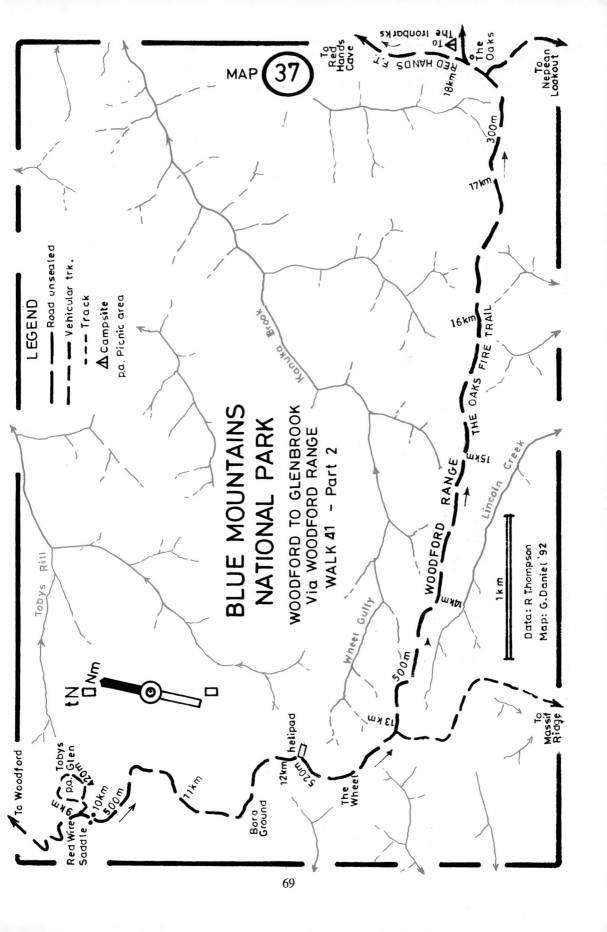

BLUE MOUNTAINS NATIONAL PARK

WOODFORD TO GLENBROOK
Via WOODFORD RANGE
WALK 41 – Part 2

MAP 37

LEGEND

— Road unsealed
▬ ▬ Vehicular trk.
--- Track
△ Campsite
p.a. Picnic area

Data: R T.Thompson
Map: G.Daniel '92

1 km

To Red Hands Cave
To The Ironbarks
RED HANDS F.T.
The Oaks
18km
To Nepean Lookout
300m
17km
16km
THE OAKS FIRE TRAIL
15km
Kanuka Brook
WOODFORD RANGE
Lincoln Creek
14km
500m
13km
Wheel Gully
The Wheel
12km helipad
520m
Bora Ground
11km
To Massif Ridge
10km
500m
9km
Red Wire Saddle
Tobys Glen p.a.
20m
To Woodford
Tobys Rill

69

41. BLUE MOUNTAINS N.P.: WOODFORD - GLENBROOK VIA THE WOODFORD FIRE TRAIL

The Woodford fire trails provides an opportunity for a very long (28km) day walk through the lower section of the Blue Mountains National Park. Although it is long there is plenty of steady downhill with no steep sections.

Start off from the south side of Woodford station. Walk east along Bedford Road, then south along the Appian Way, then east along Parker Street, then north along Taylor Road for 100m to the start of the Woodford Range Fire Trail.

Navigation is no problem - just follow the main fire trail. The first landmark, 5.4km after the start, is a branch road on the left. This road follows a long ridge towards St Helena (don't take it). Follow the main trail and after another 3km, the road descends sharply into Red Wire Saddle. A fire trail on left leads down into Tobys Glen, a volcanic neck full of thick vegetation including some massive Blue Gums. A small dam in Tobys Glen is a source of water (but not always) which should be boiled for use.

Continue on the main fire trail on a long section noting a small road on the left to a dam just beyond the now overgrown helicopter landing ground. About 1km further on a wheel in a tree on the right marks the area known as "The Wheel" and the start of a long gradual descent to the Oaks Picnic Area. At the road junction here, take the left branch to Red Hands Cave.

The trail to Red Hands Cave is level going. From the car-park at the trail terminus, walk down and admire the Aboriginal hand stencils in Red Hands Cave from a viewing platform. Next, take the track from the cave for 1km beside Red Hands Creek, then turn left at a junction and continue on for just over 1km along Camp Fire Creek to Glenbrook Causeway. Finally, walk up the sealed road past the Visitors' Centre and on to Glenbrook station via Bruce Street.

Grade: Hard, 220m asc.

Distance: 28km.

Public Transport: Train to Woodford and from Glenbrook stations.

Best in Autumn and Spring.

Maps 34-37 and CMA Katoomba, Springwood, Jamison, Penrith.

Richard Thompson

42. BLUE MOUNTAINS N.P.: WARRIMOO - FLORABELLA PASS - GLENBROOK CREEK - BLAXLAND

Florabella Pass is a very pleasant old track, which provides easy access to Glenbrook Creek.

To start the walk from Warrimoo station, cross the Great Western Highway on the crossing, turn right (west), along the highway, then left (south) into the Boulevarde and at Arthur St turn right, then a short distance along, left into Florabella St.

The track commences at the side of the last house in Florabella St, next to a large Angophora, and goes down some crude stairs. The track is eroded at first, but soon levels out and improves. Pulteneas (pea flowers), Eriostemons, (which have five petals and are mostly white) and many fine Boronias (which have four pink petals) - are a riot of colour in late Winter and Spring.

After crossing Florabella Creek a couple of times, the track crosses a side creek at a point where the creek waters drop through a plug hole.

Continue on the fairly level track for 700m to where a side-track leads up to a cave, which makes a good morning tea spot. Continue on the main track which contours around to another major track junction. Note the left branch which leads to Ross Crescent, the way out later on. Continue on the track ahead to sample the rainforest in Pippas Pass. Go as far as a creek crossing (600m) then return to the track junction. Locate a white arrow on the left near the ground which indicates the way down to Glenbrook Creek. Follow this steep track down to the creek, then walk downstream along a track to a sandy beach. Pass a side creek coming in from the east, then walk a further 25m to a large swimming hole - ideal for a lunch break.

After lunch, return to the track junction above Glenbrook Creek and take the track which leads uphill via well-made stone steps to the SE corner of Ross Crescent. Follow Ross Crescent around to Tarringha Street and onto the Great Western Highway. Head SE to Blaxland railway station.

Grade: Easy, 160m asc.   **Distance:** 6km.

Best in spring and summer.

Public Transport: Train to Warrimoo and from Blaxland.

Map 38 and CMA Springwood.

Phil Foster and Ian Schleter

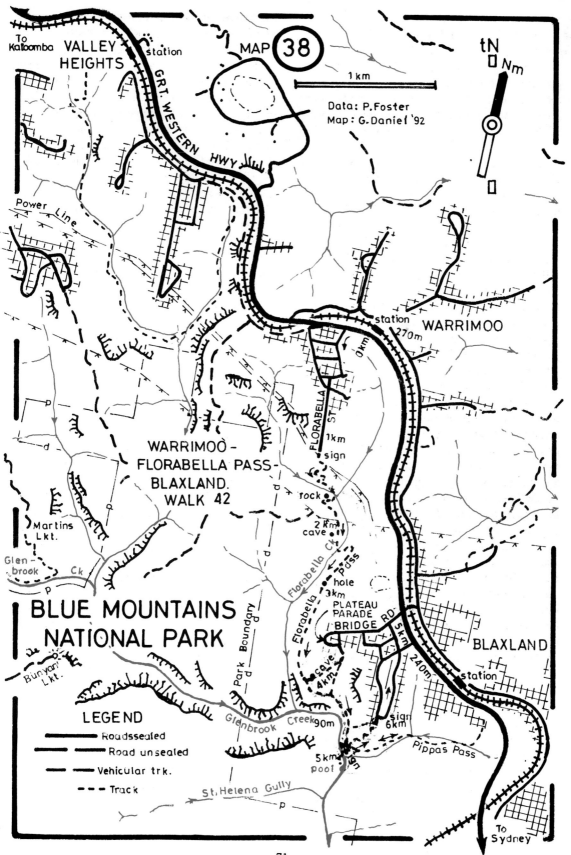

MAP 38

To Katoomba

VALLEY HEIGHTS

station

GRT. WESTERN HWY

1 km

Data: P.Foster
Map: G.Daniel '92

tN
Nm

Power Line

station
270m
WARRIMOO

0km

FLORABELLA ST

1km
sign

WARRIMOO -
FLORABELLA PASS -
BLAXLAND.
WALK 42

rock

2km
cave

Florabella Ck

Martins Lkt.

Glenbrook Ck

hole
3km

Pass

Florabella

PLATEAU PARADE BRIDGE

BLUE MOUNTAINS
NATIONAL PARK

5km
240m
BLAXLAND

station

Bunyan Lkt.

Park Boundary

cave
4km

LEGEND

Glenbrook Creek
90m

sign
6km

Pippas Pass

5km
pool

9m

St. Helena Gully

————	Road sealed
– – – –	Road unsealed
— — —	Vehicular trk.
- - - -	Track

To Sydney

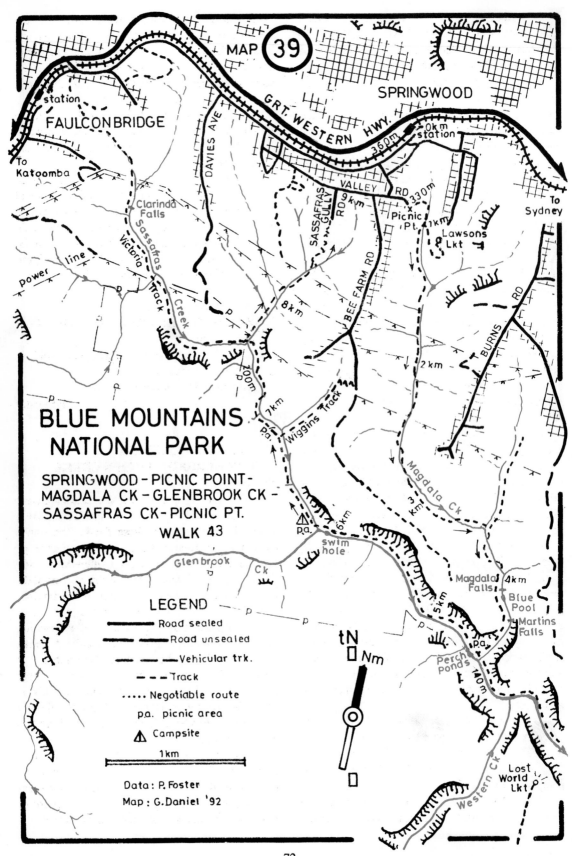

MAP **39**

SPRINGWOOD

FAULCONBRIDGE

station

To Katoomba

GRT. WESTERN HWY.

To Sydney

DAVIES AVE

VALLEY RD

SASSAFRAS GULLY RD

BEE FARM RD

BURNS RD

Clarinda Falls

Victoria Track

Sassafras Track

Sassafras Creek

power line

station 0km

360m

330m

9km

Picnic Pt. 41km

Lawsons Lkt

8km

2km

7km

p.a.

Wiggins Track

100m

Magdala Ck

3km

BLUE MOUNTAINS NATIONAL PARK

SPRINGWOOD – PICNIC POINT –
MAGDALA CK – GLENBROOK CK –
SASSAFRAS CK – PICNIC PT.

WALK 43

Glenbrook Ck

6km

swim hole

5km

Magdala Falls 4km

Blue Pool

Martins Falls

Perch Ponds

p.a.

140m

Lost World Lkt

Western Ck

LEGEND

———— Road sealed
– – – Road unsealed
— — — Vehicular trk.
- - - - Track
.... Negotiable route
p.a. picnic area
△ Campsite

|———| 1km

tN
□ Nm

Data: P. Foster
Map: G. Daniel '92

43. BLUE MOUNTAINS N.P.: SPRINGWOOD - MAGDALA CREEK - GLENBROOK CREEK - SASSAFRAS GULLY CREEK - SPRINGWOOD

This pleasant circuit walk along mountain creeks takes you to the most scenic spots in the Sassafras Gully area. The grades are fairly gentle, with no real knee trembling sections and no unpleasant road bashing. The area is great for wildflowers in Spring, and swimming in Summer.

If driving from Sydney, turn left off the Great Western Highway at the Springwood sign opposite the Shell Service station, into Macquarie Road. Follow Macquarie Road through Springwood shops, keeping the railway on the right. At the subway, keep left until Homedale Street. Turn left into Homedale St, then at the "T" intersection at the bottom of the hill, turn left again. Ignore the road on the right and continue on a short way to the picnic area at Picnic Point.

If coming by train, the newly reopened Fairy Dell Walk which starts from Springwood Ave, next to the Scout Hall and opposite the shoppers' car-park, leads into this walk.

Walk down the track at the edge of the car-park. It is a little eroded at first, but gradually levels out to a most pleasant walking track. In Spring you may spot Flying Duck Orchids (Caleana) growing close to the edge of the track. Waratahs may also be seen here in September and October. After 400m, ignore the track on the left that goes up the hill to Lawsons Lookout. The track crosses and re-crosses Magdala Creek and after 3.2km there is a prominent track junction. Turn right (south) here, as the left (north) fork is a dead end. After a short distance, you come to Magdala Falls, then a few hundred metres further on, Martins Falls. Notice the flora changing. You're now under a canopy of Coachwoods and Sassafras trees, with many mosses and fungi evident. After a short walk past the falls, the junction of Magdala Creek and Glenbrook Creek is reached. This spot, called Perch Ponds, is a great spot for that summer swim and lunch.

After lunch, follow the track on the north side of Glenbrook Creek upstream to its junction with Sassafras Creek. Here there is a large pool, great for a swim. Up a small rise there is quite a good camp-site, although it is a little over-used.

Cross Sassafras Creek on the rocks at the creek junction. At first the track hugs Sassafras Creek, and overhanging rocks add to the atmosphere of dimly lit rainforest. Then, as you wind up the valley, the vegetation opens out and hosts of wildflowers are seen here in Spring. After 800m, Wiggins Track branches off to the right. This track goes up to Bee Farm Road. After another 800m, another track branches right to Sassafrass Gully Road. This is the one you want. The other track goes on to Faulconbridge - the Victoria Track.

As the track tops the last rise you will notice the foundations of an old picnic shelter. A small track goes off to the left here to a lookout, which is worth a visit. Retrace your steps to the main track, then on to Sassafras Gully Road. Go up the road, turn right into Valley Road past Bee Farm Road to Picnic Point. Springwood station is a further 700m on.

Grade: Easy, 130m asc.
Distance: 8km from Picnic Point, 11km from Springwood station.
Public Transport: Train to Springwood station.
Best season: Summer.
Map 39 and CMA Springwood.

Phil Foster

44. BLUE MOUNTAINS N.P.: FAULCONBRIDGE - LINDEN CREEK TRIBUTARY

Just north of Faulconbridge is a short, pleasant walk with scenic views across the Lower Blue Mountains towards the Grose River. The upper catchment of Linden Creek has many rare or uncommon plant species, including the Faulconbridge Mallee, an attractive smooth-barked small tree, with a very limited distribution. The Mallee, along with other plants is only one of the reasons the Lower Mountains Conservation Society, with help from the National Parks Association and the Colong Committee, is pressing for this area to be added to Blue Mountains National Park. Although the walk is short, the track is indistinct in places and there a number of fallen trees across the path making this an easy/medium grade walk.

Turn right (north) off the Great Western Highway 100m west of the Faulconbridge shops into Grose Road. Turn left into Meeks Crescent and park the car just beyond the public school or in the bus bay outside the school on weekends.

Take the track which starts off as a steep scramble down a grassy bank 50m west of a pebbled drive and Sydney Water sign on Meeks Cresent.

As you wind your way down the slope, you will come to a few stone steps which date back 60 years or so. As the track levels out look for the Faulconbridge Mallee, (Eucalyptus burgessiana). It is a smooth barked tree of several stems. Its grey bark sheds in strips to reveal a tan colour. It has long thin leaves with a thickened margin.

The track descends to the creek from a rock crevice near where a small tributary enters from the left. Here there is a waterfall and a series of cascades with a large shallow pool. This is Peggy's Pool which was a popular swimming spot years ago, but has silted up. Enjoy a break here, and look for some aboriginal axe grinding grooves on the rocks just below the pool.

Head downstream for 25m on the right bank, cross over to the left bank for 100m, then cross back to the right bank. Keep a lookout for Waratahs in September/October. You will soon find yourself on a wide gully floor with the forest canopy high overhead. The very tall trees with the greenish/blue smooth bark are Deanes Gums. They only grow on deep soils in valleys, often reaching 60m.

The track switches back to the left bank after 600m. At a track junction 100m further on, where a very large tree has fallen, continue downstream on the left bank for 300m to the top of a second waterfall. The track then veers away from the creek to cross a small tributary. It then swings back and steeply descends to the main creekbed. Walk back upstream through thick ferns and rainforest to the base of this pretty waterfall. A large pool is at its base, although like Peggy's Pool it is partly silted up.

After a break at this delightful spot, return by the same route.

Grade: Easy/Medium, 110m asc.

Distance: 3km.

Public Transport: Train to and from Faulconbridge station - 1.3km to Grose Road.

Map 40 and CMA Springwood.

Book: Native Plants of the Lower Blue Mtns by Jill Dark.

Phil Foster

45. BLUE MOUNTAINS N.P.: FAULCONBRIDGE - GROSE RIVER - WENTWORTH CAVE

The middle Grose River features good swimming pools, undisturbed vegetation and an interesting cave. Access to the area is difficult, however, and this medium/hard 2 day walk involves 10km of rock hopping, which can be very slow going.

From the Great Western Highway at Faulconbridge, turn north into Grose Road and drive for approximately 4km. Hereabouts the road deteriorates so park the car and walk approximately 5.5km to the Grose River Track which is on the right. A parking area is opposite.

The Grose River Track is steep and descends 400m. Pay careful attention to the route as the 1993 bush fires have made the track difficult to locate in parts. Care should also be taken where the track traverses rocky sections, particularly in the wet. Good water can be obtained from a small creek that is crossed three times on the way down. The descent to the Grose takes about 45 minutes.

There are good swimming spots here, but keep in mind the river is polluted.

Next, walk upstream on the left bank for about 1km to a bend where the river is quite wide. The going along the Grose is very rough with a lot of rock scrambling. After another 2km you cross Linden Creek coming in from the south, where care should be taken on the wet slippery rocks.

Continue on for another 2km to Wentworth Creek, where twisted Watergums make it difficult to cross. Wentworth Cave is just up from the bank (NE of the crossing point). It makes a good camping cave in wet weather.

Water in Wentworth Creek, as well as the Grose, is polluted and should be boiled. The best water in the area is dripping down from the cliffs. The safest way is to bring water with you.

On day 2, explore the area, then return to Grose Road by the same route.

Grade: Day 1. Medium/Hard, 13km, 400m descent.

Day 2. Medium/Hard, 13km, 400m asc.

Total Distance: 26km, (33km from and to Faulconbridge station).

Best in Spring through Autumn.

Maps 40,41 and CMA Springwood, Kurrajong.

Dick Weston

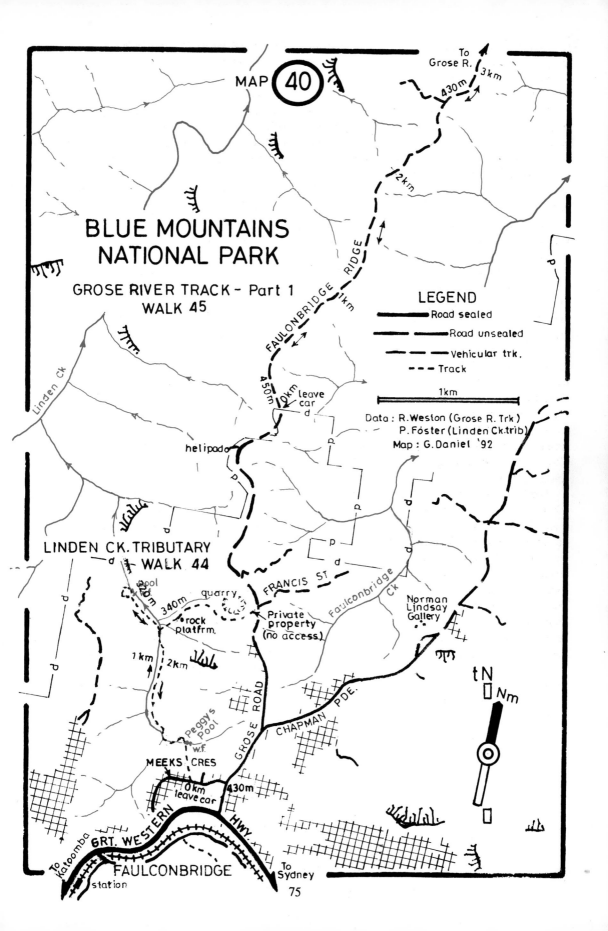

MAP **40**

BLUE MOUNTAINS NATIONAL PARK

GROSE RIVER TRACK – Part 1
WALK 45

To Grose R.
3km
430m

FAULCONBRIDGE RIDGE
2km
1km
450m   0km leave car
d

helipad

LEGEND

▬▬▬▬	Road sealed
▬ ▬ ▬	Road unsealed
━ ━ ━	Vehicular trk.
- - - -	Track

1km

Data : R. Weston (Grose R. Trk)
P. Foster (Linden Ck. trib)
Map : G. Daniel '92

LINDEN CK. TRIBUTARY
WALK 44

Linden Ck

Pool
d   340m
quarry
rock platfrm.
1km   2km

FRANCIS ST
Faulconbridge Ck

Norman Lindsay Gallery

Private property (no access)

Peggy's Pool
w.f.

GROSE ROAD

CHAPMAN PDE.

MEEKS CRES
0km leave car   430m

↑N
Nm

GRT. WESTERN HWY
To Katoomba
To Sydney
FAULCONBRIDGE station

75

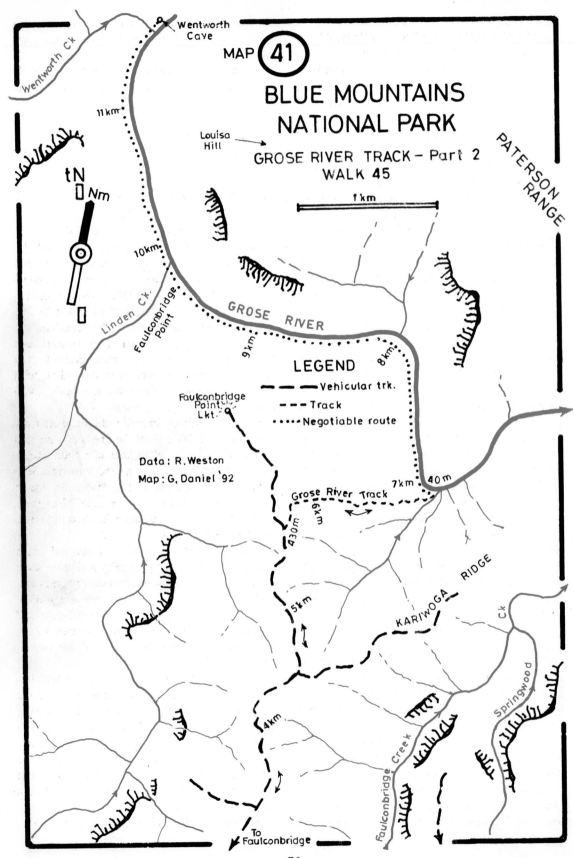

MAP **41**

BLUE MOUNTAINS
NATIONAL PARK

GROSE RIVER TRACK – Part 2
WALK 45

Wentworth Cave

11 km

Louisa Hill

PATERSON RANGE

tN
Nm

1 km

10 km

Linden Ck.

Faulconbridge Point

GROSE RIVER

9 km

8 km

LEGEND
— — — Vehicular trk.
- - - Track
······ Negotiable route

Faulconbridge Point Lkt.

Data: R. Weston
Map: G. Daniel '92

7 km 40 m

Grose River Track
6 km
430 m

5 km

KARIWOGA RIDGE

Springwood Ck

4 km

Faulconbridge Creek

To Faulconbridge

46. BLUE MOUNTAINS N.P.: LAWSON - DANTES GLEN - EMPIRE PASS - FREDERICA FALLS - LAWSON

The bushland north of Lawson in the mid Blue Mountains contains many delightful waterfalls, creeks and ferny glens. Please note that many of the signs mentioned in this text are attached to trees and can be easily missed.

On the north side of Lawson railway station turn left into Loftus Street, then right into Bernards Drive. Walk past the swimming pool and continue on through the picnic and camping area. Locate and take the signposted track "Dantes Glen", "Empire Pass" at the NE side of the picnic area. After 50m note the path on the right which leads to Fairy Falls - this track is used for the return trip. Continue straight ahead to some stairs with a handrail. Descend the stairs to Dantes Glen where there is a wooden bridge over a creek.

This area is very beautiful. There are some very tall trees which provide a sheltered canopy. At ground level, the logs and rocks are covered with moss. Walk by the creek for about 50m, then look for a sign on the other side of the creek. Cross over, turn right and proceed to Saint Michaels Falls.

After returning to the creek, continue on the Empire Pass route which follows the creek on the eastern side. After 500m a track leads to the right to Echo Point; don't take this path but walk straight on and after another 250m cross the creek. The track follows the western side of the creek for about 400m then re-crosses and dips down deep into a gorge. Where the track starts to rise take a smaller track to the left which goes down to the creek and ends in a small area with shady ferns enclosed with trees to form a canopy.

Go back to the main track and after 500m you reach Frederica Falls. Follow the track above the falls, don't cross the creek but walk to the right and follow the track for 1km to the intersection of several fire trails. Here you will see the remains of a shelter. Also high up in the trees are signs indicating the track which leads to Echo Point and Fairy Falls.

Take this track and after 400m, the track diverges (left to Fairy Falls). Continue ahead, past a rocky outcrop to the lookout at Echo Point.

Return to the track to Fairy Falls and follow it around the mountain where you will pass a rocky area with direction signs painted on the rocks.

The track crosses the creek at Fairy Falls and it is just a short distance back to the picnic area. Retrace steps to the railway station.

Grade: Easy, 180m asc.   **Distance:** 7km.
Public Transport: Train to and from Lawson station.
Suits all seasons.
Map 42 and CMA Katoomba.

Ian Schleter

47. BLUE MOUNTAINS N.P.: HAZELBROOK - ADELINA FALLS - TERRACE FALLS - HAZELBROOK

The Terrace Falls area is a naturalist's delight. It is not overcrowded with bushwalkers, which is often a problem in some of the more well known walks in the Blue Mountains. The vegetation ranges from dry open sclerophyll forest to fine examples of rainforest with Coachwoods, Sassafras, King Ferns, terrestrial orchids and colourful fungi. There are some marked trees along the track. The area is usually alive with birds. Watch out for the many Lyrebirds - you may be lucky enough to see one.

From Hazelbrook station, walk along Railway Parade (on the SW side of the line) and turn into Terrace Falls Rd for 100m, then take Baths Road. Follow Baths Road for 1km and turn right into Broad Street and walk for 800m to where Livingstone Street joins on the right. Here there are signs on the left indicating Adelina, Junction, and Federal Falls.

Follow a wide track which heads off south until you reach a rocky outcrop and then some stone steps. Further on there are hand rails and wooden steps before reaching an intersection. Turn right here, cross over a wooden bridge and shortly Adelina Falls is reached. Return to the intersection and follow the path down further into the gully.

The track crosses above Junction Falls, then descends into the gully. From here you see the two water falls and the creeks combine in a very beautiful sheltered area. A short distance further on, a track branches left to Cataract Falls but carry on another 150m to Federal Falls where there is a sandy spot and picnic table. Go back 150m and turn right up stone stairs to a lookout and then onto Cataract Falls.

Follow the fire trail which leads SE up to

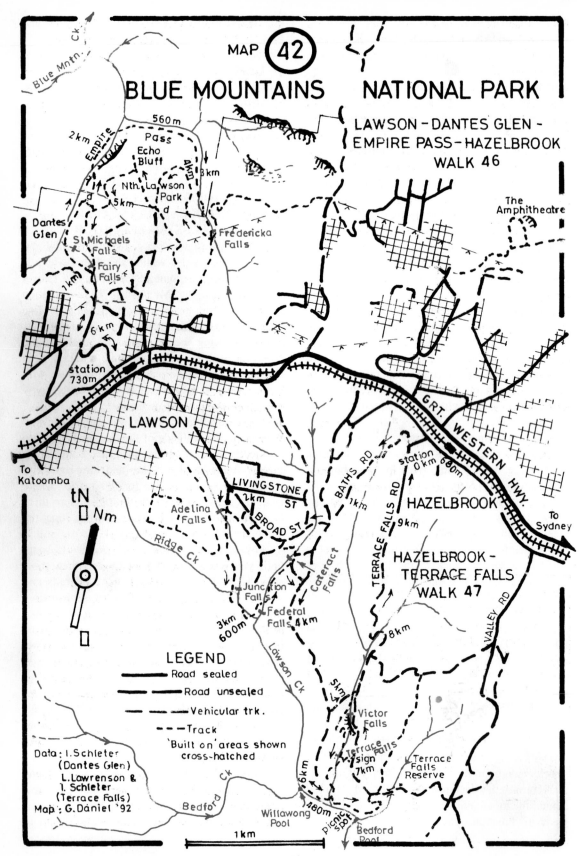

MAP **42**

BLUE MOUNTAINS   NATIONAL PARK

LAWSON - DANTES GLEN -
EMPIRE PASS - HAZELBROOK
WALK 46

The Amphitheatre

Blue Mtn. Ck.

Empire Pass

560m
2km
Echo Bluff
4km
3km
Nth. Lawson Park
5km
Dantes Glen
St. Michaels Falls
Fairy Falls
Fredericka Falls
1km
6km

station 730m

LAWSON

G.R.T. WESTERN HWY.

station 0km 680m
HAZELBROOK

To Katoomba

tN
Nm

LIVINGSTONE ST
2km
BROAD ST

Adelina Falls

Ridge Ck

Junction Falls

Cataract Falls

Federal Falls 4km
3km 600m

BATHS RD
1km

TERRACE FALLS RD
9km

To Sydney

HAZELBROOK -
TERRACE FALLS
WALK 47

8km

VALLEY RD

Lawson Ck

5km

Victor Falls

LEGEND
——— Road sealed
– – – Road unsealed
— - — Vehicular trk.
- - - - Track
'Built on' areas shown
cross-hatched

Data: I.Schleter
(Dantes Glen)
L.Lawrenson &
I. Schleter
(Terrace Falls)
Map: G.Daniel '92

Bedford Ck

6km
480m
picnic spot

Terrace Falls
Terrace sign
7km

Terrace Falls Reserve

Willawong Pool

Bedford Pool

1km

78

Baths Road. Turn right and walk for 1km to a junction. Turn left and walk for 200m to where a track leads off to the right (just before a ford and Terrace Falls Road).

Take this track which winds down to Victor Falls and then just a short distance further on to Terrace Falls. The track then crosses the creek and back again before Bedford Creek is reached. Before leaving Terrace Falls Creek, check out the remains of an old iron bridge across the creek. Cross Terrace Falls Creek and walk up Bedford Creek to the Lawson Creek junction and Willawong Pool - a good swimming hole.

From the Willawong Pool retrace your steps to Terrace Falls Creek and continue further downstream along Bedford Creek for 250m to a sandy beach at Bedford Pool. You can walk through the shallow water or follow the strategically placed stepping stones across the creek (probably put there by someone whose toes fell off when they waded across in winter). This is usually a lovely sunny spot for lunch.

Retrace steps to Terrace Falls, then up to Terrace Falls Road. Turn left and walk 2.5km to Railway Parade and Hazelbrook station.

Grade: Easy, 220m asc, with some rock hopping at creek crossings.
Distance: 10km.
Suits all seasons, but cool in winter. Some swimming spots for cooling off in summer.
Public Transport: Train to Hazelbrook station.
Map 42 and CMA Katoomba.

Les Lawrenson and Ian Schleter

RAIN JACKETS:
Jackets made from nylon material and pvc coated on the inside are good value - about $50. They are light (0.65kg for size OS), come with a hood and can double as a wind jacket. Their major disadvantage is that perspiration can build up. Choose a large size, (to cover bottom of shorts).
'Gore-Tex' jackets breathe better, but are heavier and quite costly. Waterproofed Japara (fine cotton) jackets are also good but need reproofing about every five years. They are dearer than nylon jackets.

---

48. BLUE MOUNTAINS N.P.: WIRRAWAY PLANE CRASH SITE AND INGAR AREA

On the 1st of August, 1940, one of two Wirraways on a training flight from Richmond air-base developed engine trouble in misty conditions over the Blue Mountains. The plane came down crashing into a ridge. The two occupants were killed in the crash and a bush fire ensued. The noise of the faulty engine and crash were heard by Hazelbrook resident M. Campbell who raised the alarm and directed police to the scene. This walk through the bush is pleasant and will appeal to those interested in aviation history.

To reach the starting point, turn SW off the Great Western Hwy at the top of Boddington Hill (at Wentworth Falls) into Tableland Road and drive 1.7km. Turn left and drive along Queen Elizabeth Drive for 400m to a minor road junction. Veer right here, to a car-park, 200m on. Take the signposted track to a lookout and an Aboriginal site - sharpening grooves. This diversion takes about half an hour.

Next, drive back to the minor road junction. Turn right and drive east on Murphys fire trail (which continues on from Queen Elizabeth Drive) for 3km to a gate on the left at the head of Wirraway Ridge fire trail. Leave your car here.

Walk along Wirraway Ridge fire trail (slightly) down hill for 3.4km and locate a large cairn about 1m to the left of the trail. Note the rocky ridge to the right of the trail here.

From the cairn walk (147 degrees true) for 75m on an indefinite track, which brings you to the ridge. Locate a small pile of rusty tubes etc. from the wreck. From here bear 114 degrees (true) for 35m over the ridge to the wreck.

All that is left after the ravages of time, souvenir hunters and bushfires is a jagged piece of the centre wing section adjacent to the main spar. It is about 2.7m long, 1m wide and 0.3m high. There are also other miscellaneous pieces. Do not remove any of it - leave it for others to visit. After contemplating the scene return via the same route to the car.

For the third part of the day's excursion, drive a further 7km along Murphys fire trail to Ingar Picnic/Camping Ground.

Have a swim in a man-made dam on Ingar Creek. After a break and lunch, take the track which starts at the eastern end of the camping area and follows the southern side of Ingar Creek

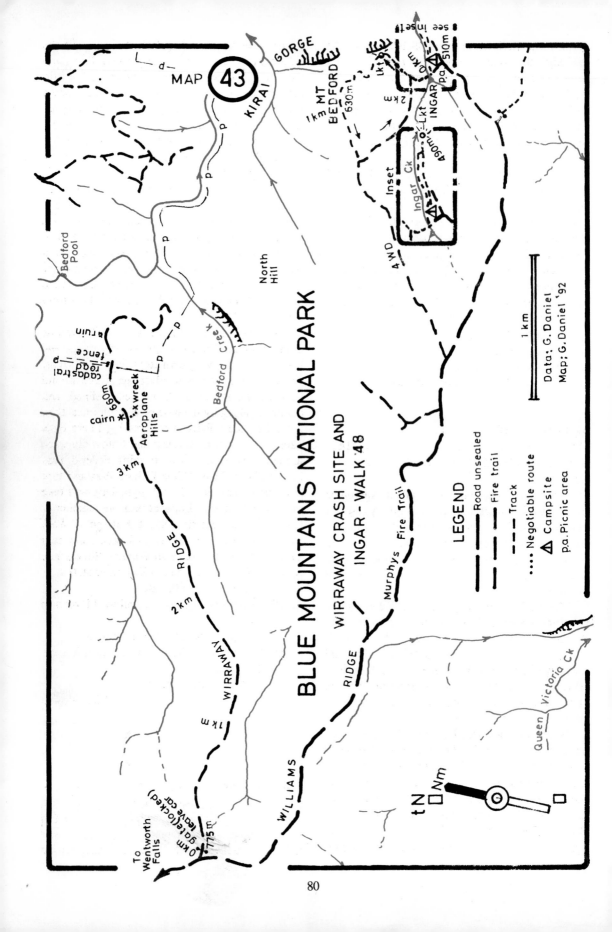

BLUE MOUNTAINS NATIONAL PARK

WIRRAWAY CRASH SITE AND INGAR - WALK 48

MAP 43

LEGEND

Road unsealed
Fire trail
Track
Negotiable route
△ Campsite
p.a. Picnic area

1 km

Data: G. Daniel
Map; G. Daniel '92

KIRAI GORGE

MT BEDFORD 630m

Bedford Pool

North Hill

Bedford Creek

cairn *xwreck 660m
Aeroplane Hills
a ruin
cadastral road
fence

3 km
RIDGE
2 km
1 km
WIRRAWAY

To Wentworth Falls
gate (locked) leave car 775m

WILLIAMS RIDGE

Murphys Fire Trail

Queen Victoria Ck

Inset
4WD
Ingar Ck
490m Lkt
INGAR p.a.
Lkt
2 km
510m
see inset

downstream. Follow the creek all the way to the cliff-edge, then find your way up on the right to a large flat rocky view point some 30m from the creek. From here, there are good views over Bedford Creek gorge. Look for the well defined track which returns you to the camping area. It comes out about 20m from the start of the creek-side track.

A second short circuit walk is the track up and over Mt Bedford. The track starts at the northern end of the dam. It is 450m to Bedford Creek lookout and 550m further to Mt Bedford. Continue on for 400m then turn left at a fire trail junction and return to the picnic area.

Grade: Easy/Medium. Mostly on fire trails.

Distance: Wirraway section: 7km, 120m asc. Ingar section: Gorge lookout, 1km, 20m asc; Mt Bedford circuit, 2km, 120m asc.

No Public Transport.

Suits all seasons.

Map 43 and CMA Jamison.

George Daniel and Helen Fastovsky

49. BLUE MOUNTAINS N.P.: WENTWORTH FALLS - KATOOMBA VIA ROBERTS, LINDEMAN AND FEDERAL PASSES

This route from Wentworth Falls to Katoomba follows tracks which date from the early days of bushwalking. From vantage points along the way there are inspirational views over the Jamison Valley. Certain sections of the tracks have become ill-defined, so allow at least six hours for the walk.

The walk starts at Wentworth Falls station. From the station walk south and turn right along the Great Western Highway for 300m to Falls Road. Walk south along Falls Road for 1.3km and turn right into Fletcher Street. At the end of Fletcher St bear left and walk to the Conservation Hut and tea-rooms at the end of Valley Road in Wentworth Falls.

Walk down towards Lodore Falls to a 4-way track junction. Turn right to Lillians Glen and walk for 300m to a track junction. Turn left, cross Lillians Bridge over Valley of the Waters Creek, then follow the track to a golf course. Walk around the 14th and 16th fairways and locate Roberts Pass track which heads off directly opposite from where the track emerges at the golf

course. Before descending Roberts Pass, take the side-track on the right to Inspiration Point and then the side-track on the left to Moya Point to take in the extensive views. The track down Roberts Pass then becomes steep and a metal ramp and steps have to be negotiated (the original steps were burnt out in bushfires). After a further 10-15 minutes you meet Lindeman Pass which is marked by the letter "L" on a tree.

Turn right and follow a fairly good track around the base of Inspiration Point. Cross a creek and follow the track as it ascends slightly to a beautiful overhang which has extensive views of the valley. This provides good shelter and would be a good place for morning tea. Continue for another 10-15 minutes to Gladstone Creek and the junction of the Gladstone Pass track (1.1km from Roberts Pass).

Continue along Lindeman Pass towards Sublime Point. The track here is very rough and hard to find in overgrown ferns and vines areas. The route is marked with silver tags. Once around Sublime Point the track is well defined and continues along by the base of Gordon Falls, then around to Leura Falls. After crossing Leura Falls Creek, cross a concrete strip and follow the track around a bend to where it joins Federal Pass below Linden Falls. Climb Federal Pass and turn left where there is a "kiosk" sign. This will take you up to Jamiesons Lookout near the junction of Cliff Drive and Merriwa Street, Katoomba. Walk west along Merriwa Street and turn right into Lurline Street, then left into Waratah Street, then right into Katoomba Street to Katoomba station.

Grade: Medium, 400m asc.

Distance: 13km station to station, 11km with car shuttle.

Best in Spring through to late Autumn.

Public Transport: Train to Wentworth Falls and from Katoomba.

Map 44 and CMA Katoomba.

Dick Weston

```
┌─────────────────────────────────┐
│          SPOT HEIGHTS           │
│     Spot heights on the maps    │
│   indicate metres above sea level │
└─────────────────────────────────┘
```

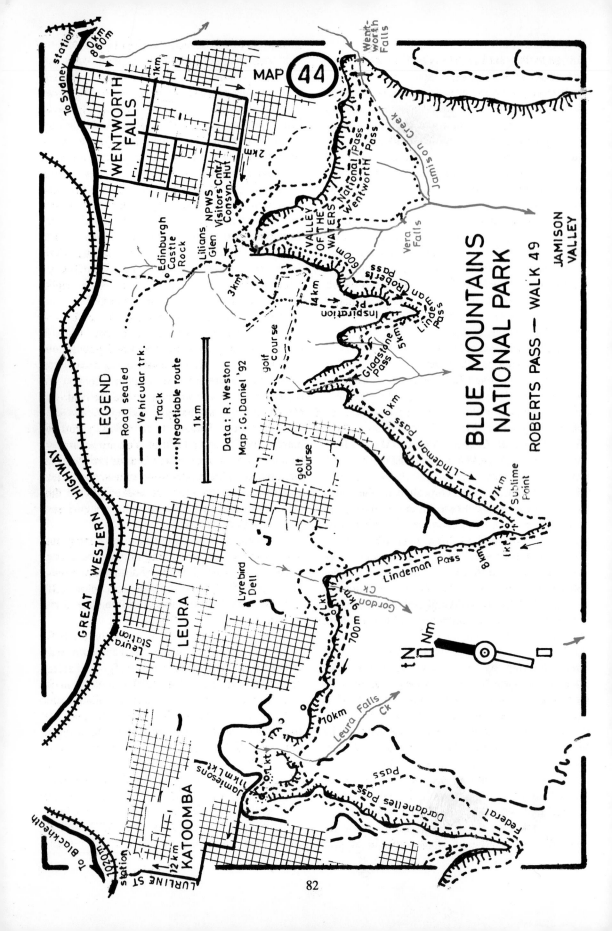

MAP 44

BLUE MOUNTAINS
NATIONAL PARK

ROBERTS PASS — WALK 49

LEGEND

Road sealed
Vehicular trk.
Track
Negotiable route

1km

Data: R. Weston
Map: G. Daniel '92

WENTWORTH FALLS

Wentworth Falls

Jamison Creek

JAMISON VALLEY

NATIONAL PASS
Wentworth Pass
VALLEY OF THE WATERS
NPWS Visitors Cntr.
Conservation Hut
Lilians Glen
Edinburgh Castle Rock

Vera Falls
Roberts Pass
Lindeman Pass
Inspiration
Gladstone Pass
600m

golf course
3km
4km
5km

golf course
6km
Lindeman Pass
7km
Sublime Point
Lkt.
8km
Lindeman Pass

Lyrebird Dell
LEURA
Leura Station

Gordon Ck
Lkt.
9km
700m
N↑ Nm

Leura Falls Ck
110km
10km

Lkt.
Jamisons
11km Lkt.

GREAT WESTERN HIGHWAY

To Sydney
0km 860m
1km
2km

To Blackheath
1020m
station
LURLINE ST
12km
KATOOMBA

Federal
Dardanelles Pass
Pass

82

50. BLUE MOUNTAINS N.P.: KATOOMBA TO WENTWORTH FALLS VIA MOUNT SOLITARY

This is one of the classic walks of the Blue Mountains. It is a real "wilderness" walk and covers all the major terrain and vegetation zones of the upper Blue Mountains from mountain heath through temperate rain and palm forest to dry and wet Eucalypt forest. Although the walk is on tracks for almost its full distance, it is a walk for parties led by experienced bush navigators only, because correct track identification in some parts is difficult. Day one requires 5 hours of walking and day two requires 7 plus hours of walking.

The suggested starting point for the walk is at the top of the Golden Stairs on Narrow Neck peninsula. From Katoomba station drive south down Katoomba St for 1.5km then turn right into Katoomba Falls Rd. Follow this road to Cliff Drive. Continue past the Scenic Railway car-park on the left. Approximately 300m past Landslide Lookout, Glenraphael Rd branches to the left along Narrow Neck. Follow this road for 2km to a car-park and sign at the top of the Golden Stairs. Alternatively, take a taxi from Katoomba station.

Walk down the Golden Stairs into the Jamison Valley. The track and stairs are well marked and there is one lookout 5 minutes walk from the top which will give a good perspective of the route along the valley and out onto Mount Solitary. The stairs descend to the base of the cliff-face, meeting the Federal Pass (Mt Solitary track). Turn due south on the track. The track from here to the base of Mount Solitary is well defined and signposted. It is best to commence the walk at first light to take advantage of the early morning sun as it filters through the mixed Eucalypt and fern forest canopy.

Near the branch track to the Ruined Castle there is a spring, but during dry periods it should not be relied upon. The track is clearly defined as far as the base of Koorawall Knife Edge. At this point the track becomes ill defined with branches to the north and south of the knife-edge. It is advisable to keep to the knife edge to avoid side tracks. The track becomes clearer as it rises out of the forest onto Mount Solitary. After you reach the plateau you pass through a Casuarina grove which is an excellent location for morning tea.

The track then trends down for 800m to a series of rock overhangs known as Chinamans

Caves. There maybe water in a nearby creek.

There are side tracks to lookouts at the north and south walls. At a three-way junction here, take the left (NNE) track which follows Chinamans Creek to the cliff-edge for good views over Kedumba Valley. Return to the three-way junction and take the right-hand (south) track behind the first overhang which goes up a rise. It then leads in a NE direction over uneven ground from near the southern wall to near the northern wall. It is important to keep to the high ground and avoid false trails trending off the ridge line. Approximately 1.2km further on, you reach the highest point of Mt Solitary, and a further 500m on the track approaches the northern cliff-edge. Camp overnight in the small valley on the right. Water is available from a spring-fed creek.

Next morning, continue along the track as it follows the northern wall of Mt Solitary. There is a confusion of competing tracks and you should keep to the north face to avoid being drawn into the interior. There are some white markers on the correct track. In a depression toward the centre of Mount Solitary is a hanging swamp. At the east face of Mount Solitary there are two descent points - the Col and a lookout. You are advised to take the lookout track. There is a visitors' book at the lookout and it is interesting to read the details of routes taken by previous walkers. From this point there are extensive views south and east over Lake Burragorang.

The descent from this point is very steep and follows the knife-edge of the ridge. It is a very beautiful area with glimpses of distant mountains. The track is fairly clear to the 600m contour (GR Jamison 537577) but at that point the track forks to follow two diverging ridge-lines.

Follow the track down along the main E-W spur line to an area where soil washed down from higher areas has formed a relatively flat natural terrace (the vicinity of the 500m contour line). Rich vegetation, Lyrebirds and rock wallabies can be found in this area totally unspoilt by man. At the terrace turn sharp left (north) on a faint track, then bear NE then east. One feature of this secluded terrace area is a huge perfectly formed Eucalypt tree (probably a White Ash). The track down beyond this point is steep. A good flat camp-site suitable for a large group is located at a knoll on the track (GR Jamison 544578). Water can be obtained from a watercourse 400m WNW

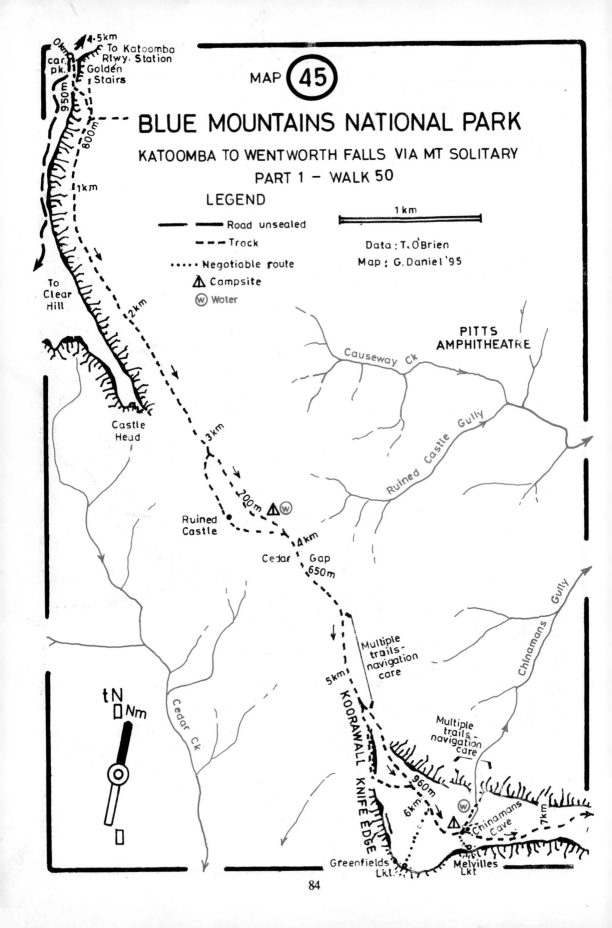

MAP 45

BLUE MOUNTAINS NATIONAL PARK
KATOOMBA TO WENTWORTH FALLS VIA MT SOLITARY
PART 1 – WALK 50

LEGEND

———— Road unsealed

- - - Track

····· Negotiable route

⚠ Campsite

Ⓦ Water

1 km

Data : T. O'Brien
Map : G. Daniel '95

4·5km
To Katoomba
Rlwy. Station
Golden Stairs
0 km
car. pk.
950 m
800 m
1 km

To Clear Hill

2 km

Castle Head

PITTS AMPHITHEATRE

Causeway Ck

Ruined Castle Gully

3 km

700 m

⚠ Ⓦ

Ruined Castle

4 km

Cedar Gap
650 m

5 km

Multiple trails - navigation care

Multiple trails - navigation care

Chinamans Gully

KOORAWALL KNIFE EDGE

960 m

Ⓦ

6 km

7 km

Chinamans Cave

⚠

Cedar Ck

↑N
☐ Nm

Greenfields Lkt.

Melvilles Lkt.

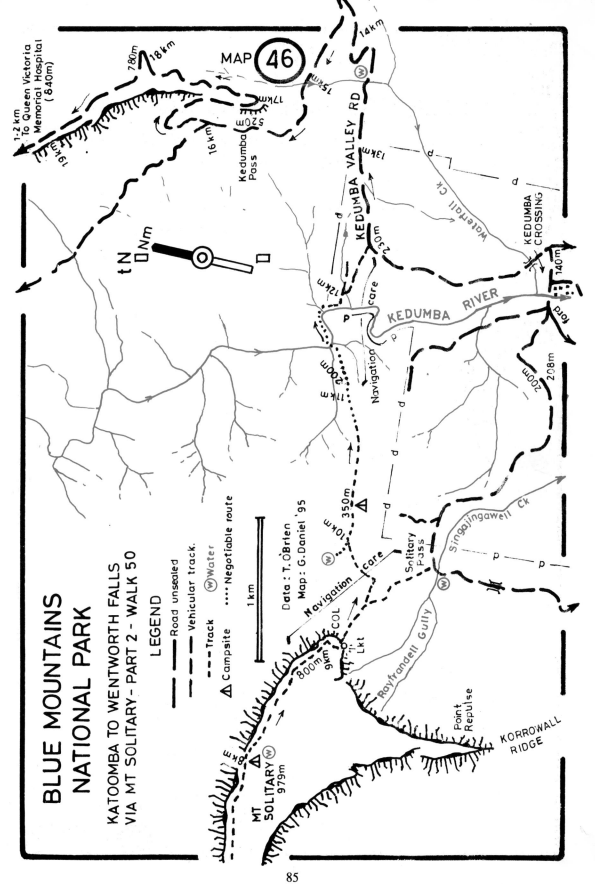

BLUE MOUNTAINS
NATIONAL PARK

KATOOMBA TO WENTWORTH FALLS
VIA MT SOLITARY - PART 2 - WALK 50

LEGEND

——— Road unsealed
▬▬▬ Vehicular track.
- - - Track
Ⓦ Water
△ Campsite
.... Negotiable route

1 km

Data : T.O'Brien
Map: G.Daniel '95

MAP ⦿46

↑Nm ↑tN

KEDUMBA VALLEY RD

KEDUMBA RIVER

Waterfall Ck

KEDUMBA CROSSING

Singajingawell Ck

Rayfandell Gully

Point Repulse

KORROWALL RIDGE

MT SOLITARY
979m

Solitary Pass

Navigation care

Navigation care

Kedumba Pass

To Queen Victoria
Memorial Hospital
(840m)
1·2 km

18 km
780m

19 km

16 km

17 km
520m

14 km

15 km

13 km
230m

12 km

11 km
300m

10 km
350m

9 km
800m

8 km

COL

Lkt

140m

208m
200m

85

of the camp-site (GR Jamison 540579).

Next, follow the track from the knoll as it leads east along the ridge-line then down to a tributary of the Kedumba River (1.1km). The track becomes vague after 500m, but keep on a bearing 85° to a creek, then follow it to the Kedumba River. Have a lunch break here.

The river is easily crossed except during or after heavy rain periods. In these circumstances some walkers have been forced to retrace their steps back across Mt Solitary. Note Kedumba River has a very high bacteria count and should not be drunk without appropriate treatment.

Once across the river, follow it downstream for 250m to where a creek enters from the north. Walk up this creek a few metres, then bear sharply south to climb above the steep river bank. Continue south above the river, then descend via an old overgrown vehicle track to a gully and take a 4WD track. Follow it west for 50m to a junction. Take the right branch and after 400m the trail meets the Kedumba Valley Road (a fire trail).

Turn left and follow Kedumba Valley Road to the Kedumba Pass intersection. Keep right and proceed up the Pass to the Queen Victoria Hospital on Kings Tableland Road. The road is well graded and passes through a number of mature wet and dry Eucalypt groves. The Kedumba Pass intersection is a pleasant place for lunch and a rest before the steep ascent. It takes four hours to walk from Kedumba River to Queen Victoria Hospital. There may be water where Waterfall Creek crosses the road.

Grade: Day 1 - Medium/Hard. 8km mostly on tracks, about 310m ascent.
Day 2: Medium/Hard. 12km mostly on tracks/road, about 610m ascent.
Distance: 20km (Golden Stairs - Queen Victoria Hospital); 32km (Katoomba station - Wentworth Falls station).
Public Transport: Train to Katoomba station and taxi to the Golden Stairs (4.5km). On return, walk to Wentworth Falls station (6.2km) or call for a taxi from the hospital. Those travelling by car may park at Queen Victoria Hospital (advise reception) and call a taxi for the trip to Golden Stairs.
Maps 45,46 and CMA Katoomba, Jamison.

Terry O'Brien

51. BLUE MOUNTAINS N.P.: PIERCES PASS - GROSE RIVER - BLUE GUM FOREST

The beautiful Blue Gum Forest in the Grose Gorge is one of the most majestic features of the Blue Mountains. This walk to the Blue Gum from Pierces Pass is graded medium because it entails a 470m descent and ascent and 9km of riverside walking. It is suggested you start off by 8.30am.

To reach the starting point, drive along the Bells Line of Road towards Lithgow. At 1.6km beyond the turn-off to Mount Banks, take the signposted road to Pierces Pass on the left. Drive in 1km and park at the picnic area.

Take the very well defined Hungerfords track. Initially, it leads through dry open forest then down into Hungerfords Ravine where there is rainforest with Coachwood and Sassafras trees. Have a short break here to look at Fairy Grotto - a shady fern lined gully. Beyond the ravine the track passes along a shale terrace where there are views of Blackheath Walls and the landslide scar on Burramoko Head. The track then zigzags through open forest down to the Grose River.

Once at the Grose River there are great spots for morning tea on large rocks on the river bank. Cross the river, turn left at a track junction and take the track that follows the river downstream. In about an hour and a half you should reach the Blue Gum Forest - 4.5 km from the river crossing.

There are many ideal spots by the river to have lunch and appreciate the beauty of the Blue Gum Forest. There are magnificent views of the cliff bluffs including Banks Wall. At the Perrys Lookdown track junction there is an information board which gives details about how the magnificent Blue Gums were saved by early conservationists. [Note camping and fire lighting are prohibited in the Blue Gum Forest but allowed 600m up Govett Creek at Acacia Flat.]

After lunch return the way you came along the Grose River. Be careful to cross over at the correct point and have a rest in preparation for the hard climb out (allow one and a half hours).

Once back, if time and energy permit, take the track that heads south for 500m to Rigby Hill lookout for panoramic views of the Grose Gorge.

Grade: Medium, 470m asc. **Distance:** 11km.
Best in Autumn, Winter, Spring.
No public transport.
Map 48 and CMA Mt Wilson.   Ian Schleter

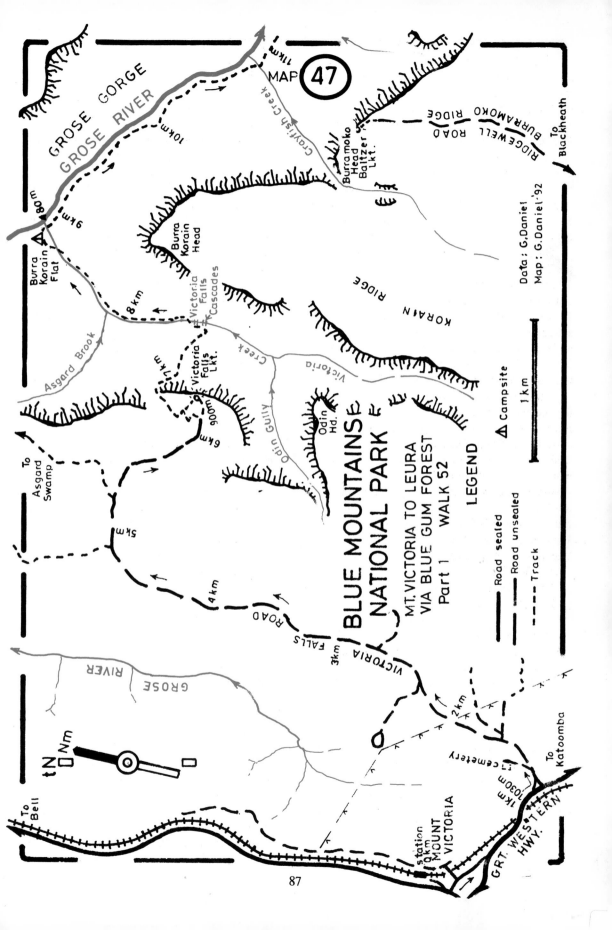

MAP 47

GROSE GORGE
GROSE RIVER
Crayfish Creek
10km
1km

To Blackheath
RIDGEWELL ROAD
BURRAMOKO RIDGE

Burramoko Head
Baltzer Lkt.

Burra Korain Head

80m
9km
Burra Korain Flat
△

Asgard Brook
8km

Victoria Falls
Cascades

KORAIN RIDGE

Victoria Falls Lkt.
7km
600m
6km

Victoria Creek

Odin Gully Creek

Odin Hd.

To Asgard Swamp

5km

4km

VICTORIA FALLS ROAD
3km

2km

Cemetery
1km

Data: G.Daniel
Map: G.Daniel '92

△ Campsite

1km

BLUE MOUNTAINS NATIONAL PARK

MT.VICTORIA TO LEURA
VIA BLUE GUM FOREST
Part 1   WALK 52

LEGEND

Road sealed
Road unsealed
Track

GROSE RIVER

tN Nm

To Bell

GRT. WESTERN HWY.

To Katoomba
1030m
1km

Station
1km
MOUNT VICTORIA

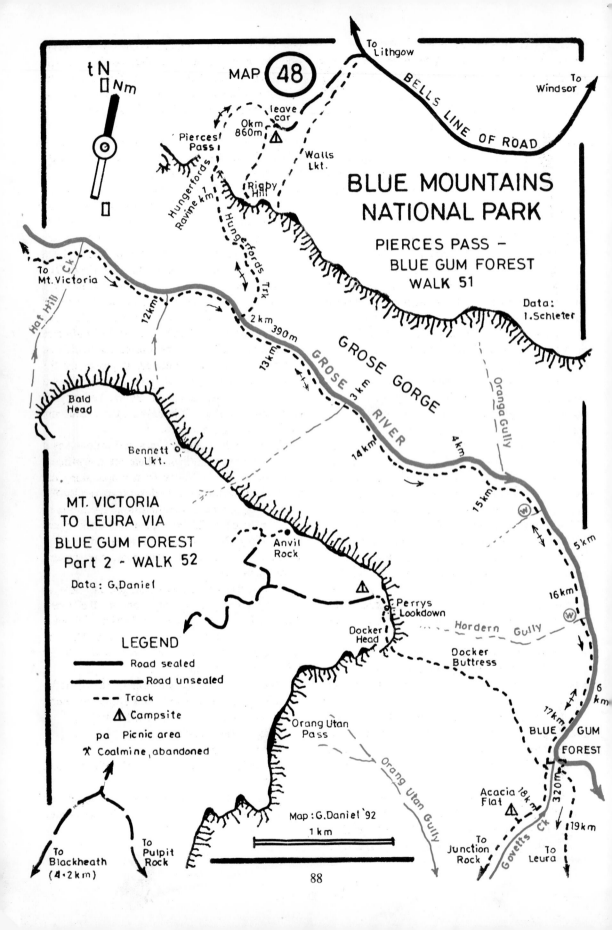

MAP 48

To Lithgow

To Windsor

BELLS LINE OF ROAD

tN
Nm

Pierces Pass

leave car

0km 860m △

Walls Lkt.

Hungerfords Ravine km

Rigby Hill

Hungerfords Trk

To Mt. Victoria

Hat Hill Ck

12km

2km 390m

13km

GROSE GORGE

GROSE 3km RIVER

Oranga Gully

BLUE MOUNTAINS NATIONAL PARK

PIERCES PASS – BLUE GUM FOREST WALK 51

Data: I. Schleter

Bald Head

Bennett Lkt.

14km

4km

15km

Ⓦ

5km

16km

Ⓦ

MT. VICTORIA TO LEURA VIA BLUE GUM FOREST
Part 2 – WALK 52

Data: G. Daniel

Anvil Rock

△

Perrys Lookdown

Docker Head

Hordern Gully

Docker Buttress

6km

17km

BLUE GUM FOREST

LEGEND

⎯⎯⎯ Road sealed
⎯ ⎯ Road unsealed
- - - Track
△ Campsite
pa Picnic area
⚒ Coalmine, abandoned

Orang Utan Pass

Orang Utan Gully

Acacia Flat △

18km

320m

19km

To Junction Rock

Govetts Ck

To Leura

Map: G. Daniel '92

1 km

To Blackheath (4.2km)

To Pulpit Rock

52. BLUE MOUNTAINS N.P.:
MT VICTORIA - BLUE GUM FOREST - DU FAUR BUTTRESS - LOCKLEY PYLON - LEURA

The walk from Mt Victoria to Leura via the Grose Gorge has many fine features including the majestic cascades on Victoria Creek, Victoria Falls, the Blue Gum Forest, the great camp-site at Acacia Flat, the challenging climb up Du Faur Buttress, the panoramas from the top of and near Lockley Pylon and the Pinnacles.

Try to be away from Mt Victoria station by 8.30 am. Walk 200m uphill (south) and turn into the first street on the left which will take you to the Great Western Highway after 300m. Take the Highway SE past the historic Toll House at the railway overpass for 600m to signposted Victoria Falls Road. Turn left into it, avoid minor branches of the road to arrive at the picnic area at the end of the road and then Victoria Falls Lookout - 6.3km from the station.

From the lookout take the track which descends to The Cascades on Victoria Creek (1km). A further 200m on, have morning tea whilst admiring Victoria Falls. Below the Falls, cross Victoria Creek to a sign-board. The track runs along the eastern side of the creek and basically follows it past Asgard Brook junction on the left at 8.1km (good water). The track crosses Victoria Creek then arrives at Burra Korain Flat which is at the junction of Victoria Creek and the Grose River. Cross back over Victoria Creek just before the junction and take the track which follows the Grose River downstream on the SW side.

Crayfish Gully Creek enters the Grose from the SW at 10.9km out. This is the suggested lunch spot. Continue on, cross Hat Hill Gully Creek at 11.4km (good water). Once across Hat Hill Gully Creek avoid the track going up the ridge and return close by the Grose River and continue downstream.

The Pierces Pass track coming in from the left over the Grose River at 12.6km is the next position fix. A gully at about 15.4km may have good water as well as Hordern Gully at about 16.2km. Collect enough water for the camp and the next day's walk. The track stays on the south side all the way to the Blue Gum Forest (4.8km from the Pierces Pass junction). At the Blue Gum Forest there is a track junction with a large sign-board. The right branch leads up to Perrys Lookdown whilst the track ahead leads to Acacia Flat. Press on for 500m to Acacia Flat, a large flat and grassy camp-site. There is little firewood around, so use it sparingly or take a stove.

Next day return 500m to the big sign-board. [Pullout option via Perrys Lookdown 1.5km + 7.8km via Hat Head Road to Blackheath station]. Go past the sign-board for 25m and take a faint track on the right. Cross Govetts Creek near its junction with the Grose River. At the base of the buttress there is a yellow marker on a tree indicating the way along a track to the right which leads up around and onto the spur. Ascend Du Faur Buttress via a track to Du Faur Head. The ascent is about 450m and takes approximately 1 hour 20 minutes. Once on the plateau take a break for morning tea then wind your way via a rocky track further up the Head near the SW cliff-face and cross a small dry water course. The track now becomes more clearly defined. It passes by the base of Lockley Pylon. A cairn marks the point where you side-track up the Pylon. Leave your pack and go on up - it is only a 30m ascent and worth a photo from the top.

Return to the Lockley Track and follow it as it swings from south to east. There are magnificent views of the Grose Valley from points along the track here. The track settles down to generally SE. Later, you pass the eroded sandstone formation of The Pinnacles at 23.5km, then the track meets Mount Hay Road at 23.9km where there is a concrete water tank (possibly containing water). Have lunch here.

Follow the Mount Hay Road, generally SW as it undulates along a ridge-top to the Great Western Highway at Leura at 33.5km - about 2 hours walk. Turn west for 500m to the intersection of the Mall. Turn south and walk for 150m to Leura station.

Grade: Day 1; Easy/medium, 18km, 650m descent on fire trail and track. Day 2; Medium, 16km, 590m asc on track and fire trail.

Total Distance: 34km.

Best in Spring and Autumn.

Public Transport: Train to Mt Victoria and from Leura.

Maps 47-50 and CMA Mount Wilson and Katoomba.   George Daniel

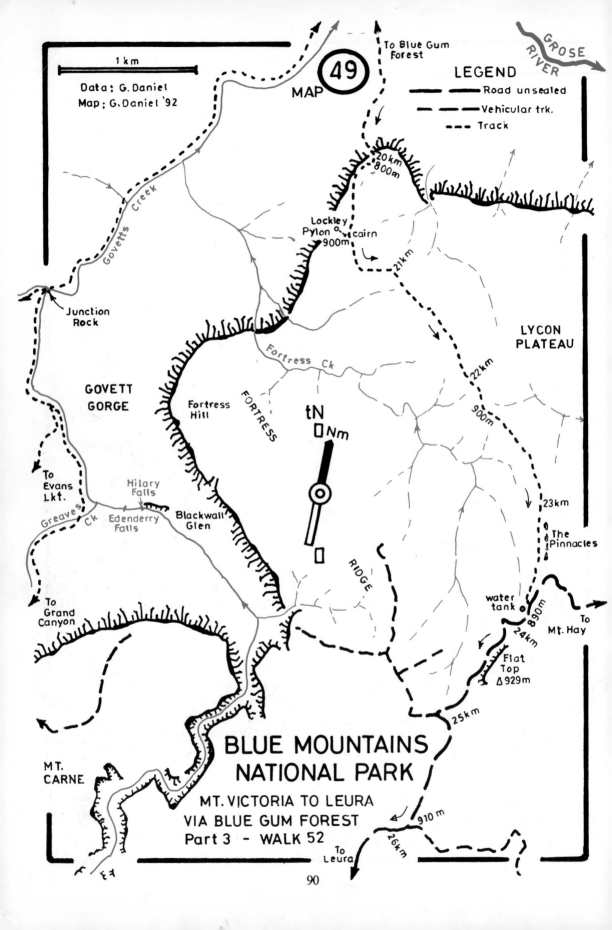

BLUE MOUNTAINS
NATIONAL PARK
MT. VICTORIA TO LEURA
VIA BLUE GUM FOREST
Part 3 - WALK 52

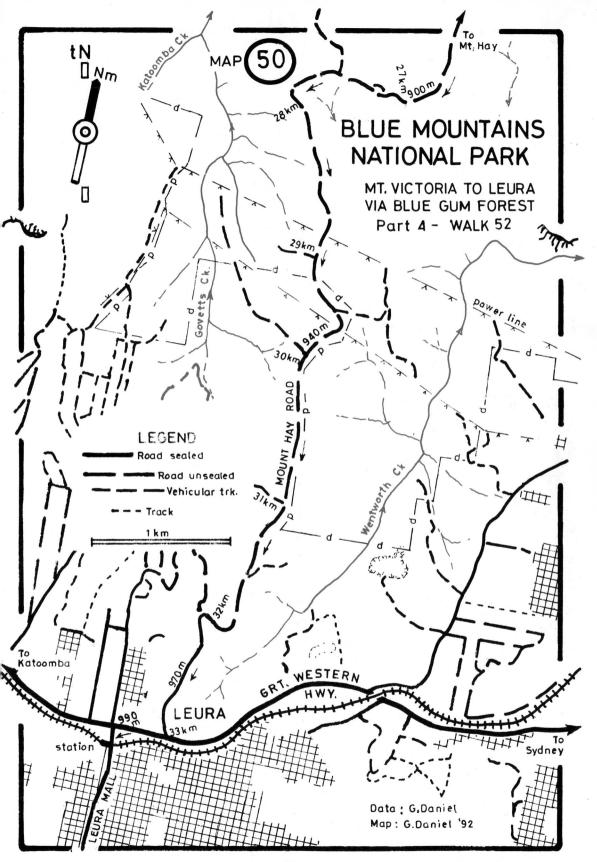

MAP 50

BLUE MOUNTAINS
NATIONAL PARK

MT. VICTORIA TO LEURA
VIA BLUE GUM FOREST
Part 4 – WALK 52

LEGEND
Road sealed
Road unsealed
Vehicular trk.
Track

1 km

To Katoomba

LEURA

station

LEURA MALL

GRT. WESTERN HWY.

To Sydney

power line

MOUNT HAY ROAD

Katoomba Ck

Govetts Ck.

Wentworth Ck.

To Mt. Hay

27km 900m

28km

29km

940m

30km

31km

32km

970m

990m

33km

Data : G.Daniel
Map : G.Daniel '92

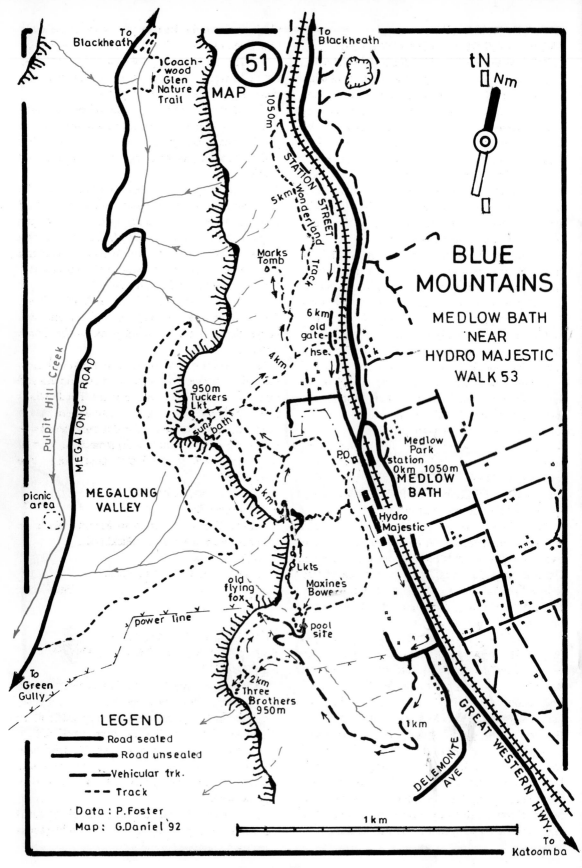

MAP 51

To Blackheath

Coach-wood Glen Nature Trail

To Blackheath

tN Nm

BLUE MOUNTAINS

MEDLOW BATH NEAR HYDRO MAJESTIC WALK 53

1050m

STATION STREET

5km wonderland Track

Marks Tomb

6km old gate-hse.

4km

950m Tuckers Lkt

sun bath

MEGALONG ROAD

Pulpit Hill Creek

picnic area

MEGALONG VALLEY

3km

PO

Medlow Park station 0km 1050m
MEDLOW BATH

Hydro Majestic

Lkts

old flying fox

Maxine's Bower

power line

pool site

To Green Gully

2km Three Brothers 950m

1km

DELEMONTE AVE

GREAT WESTERN HWY.

1km

To Katoomba

LEGEND

———— Road sealed
— — — Road unsealed
– – – Vehicular trk.
- - - - Track

Data: P. Foster
Map: G. Daniel '92

53. BLUE MOUNTAINS:
HYDRO MAJESTIC, MEDLOW BATH - THREE BROTHERS - TUCKER LOOKOUT

If you've ever been across the Blue Mountains by road or rail, you will have noticed the Hydro Majestic Hotel opposite Medlow Bath station. It is visible from as far away as Kanangra Walls. Between the Hotel and the escarpment, there is a network of walking tracks developed by the Hotel years ago. This walk takes you to a number of the most interesting features in the area. Take time out after the walk to sit and sip a coffee or tea in the Coffee Shop at the Hydro. There is no better view in this part of the Mountains.

To start the walk, either park your car in front of the Hydro, or walk across from the station. Walk south towards Katoomba for 500m then turn right into Bellevue Crescent. A few metres down the crescent past Delemonte Ave, find the fire trail turning left as Bellevue Crescent turns right. Walk down the fire trail until it passes under a power-line, and 100m past this, a track turns off to the left back under the power-line. Walk on down the track, and after a short distance, a further track turns left down the hill to the rock formation known as the Three Brothers.

Return to the main track which now loops back to the fire trail. Follow the power-line for a few metres to look at the old flying fox site. This was used to haul produce up from the Megalong Valley to the Hydro in years gone by.

Next, follow the fire trail down the hill to the old swimming pool site. A dam here used to hold back a pool some 2m deep and up to 200m long. Unfortunately, due to increased erosion caused by removal of the tree cover, the pool is now silted up. The dam wall is not apparent until you lean over and look down the creek.

A track leads off up the hill to the right (north). This goes back to the Hydro. Instead, take the track on the southern side of the pool site down the creek. It is a little eroded in places, but easy enough to follow. After a few hundred metres you will pass a large cave. This is Maxines Bower which is worth a few minutes appreciation.

Continuing along the track, watch for a small track off to the left (south) going to a small lookout. After crossing the creek, (a bridge once stood here), go up the slope, then turn left (south) to a platform overlooking the valley. Take time to enjoy the view and speculate on how and why the platform was built. Retrace your steps to the creek (don't recross) and find the track going up the gully. This track is overgrown and a bit of a bash, but don't worry, there is a good track that circles this gully, so head up until you meet it.

Walk north on this good track. There are many vantage points until the track enters a mixed forest of Banksias, Eucalypts and Casuarinas. After 250m, turn left (NW) to reach the Wonderland Track.

At another junction (200m on) turn left to the Sun Bath. Originally the Sun Bath was enclosed with a high fence, and men and women (separately) took the sun long before we worried about UV radiation and ozone depletion. This is a good spot for lunch, as through the bushes is a fine view over the Megalong Valley.

Take the Wonderland Track to Marks Tomb. The track is in good condition and a metal sign points the way off the main track to the Tomb (800m).

After resting and admiring this curious rock formation, retrace your steps to the main path and turn left (north). The Wonderland Track winds along without any great undulations, and eventually comes out on the dirt road alongside the railway. Turn right (south) from here: it is an easy stroll back to the Hotel. Don't forget the Coffee Shop.

Grade: Easy, 110m asc.

Distance: 7km.

Public Transport: Train to Medlow Bath, or bus from Katoomba or Blackheath.

Suits all seasons.

Map 51 and CMA Katoomba.

Phil Foster

54. BLUE MOUNTAINS N.P.:
EVANS LOOKOUT - GRAND CANYON - NEATES GLEN

Some of the most outstanding scenic features of the Blue Mountains are the deep canyons, although most are remote and very difficult to negotiate. The Grand Canyon, near Blackheath, is one of the few that is easily accessible with only medium grades. The track through the canyon is clearly defined and signposted and is a very popular walk.

At Blackheath, take the Evans Lookout Road for 2.9km to a parking area on the right (about

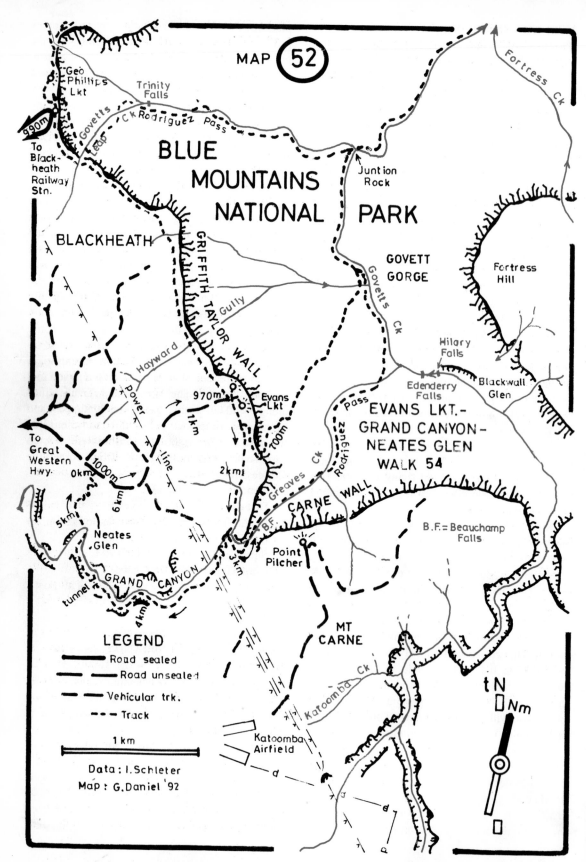

MAP 52

BLUE
MOUNTAINS
NATIONAL PARK

Geo Phillips Lkt
Trinity Falls
Rodriguez Pass
Govetts Leap Ck
990m
To Blackheath Railway Stn.

BLACKHEATH

Junaction Rock
Fortress Ck

GOVETT GORGE
Fortress Hill

GRIFFITH TAYLOR WALL
Gully
Hayward
Power line
0km 1000m 6km 5km
970m
Evans Lkt
1km
2kmi
700m
Govetts Ck
Hilary Falls
Edenderry Falls
Blackwall Glen

EVANS LKT.-
GRAND CANYON-
NEATES GLEN
WALK 54

To Great Western Hwy.

Neates Glen
GRAND CANYON
tunnel
4km
3km
B.F.
Greaves Ck
Rodriguez Pass
CARNE WALL
B.F.=Beauchamp Falls

Point Pilcher

MT CARNE

Katoomba Ck
Katoomba Airfield

LEGEND
——— Road sealed
– – – Road unsealed
— — Vehicular trk.
- - - Track

|———— 1 km ————|

Data : I. Schleter
Map : G. Daniel '92

tN
Nm

94

1.3km short of Evans Lookout). There are signs "Neates Glen" and "Grand Canyon" at the trackhead here. Leave the car here.

Walk along the road to Evans Lookout where there are spectacular views of the Govett Gorge. At the lookout there is a picnic area and shelter shed. Walk to the right hand side of the lookout and follow the track as it steeply descends. After 200m there is a track junction. Take the right branch which leads down to Greaves Creek and the Rodriguez Pass walking track - a descent of 270m from Evans Lookout. On the way down, as you pass through a lush rainforest with a canopy of Coachwoods, look for grey barked Sassafras, Lillypilly, giant ferns, thick mosses and tangled masses of vines and creepers.

At Greaves Creek there is a sign "Beauchamp Falls" pointing to the left, the right hand track leads to the Grand Canyon.

Take the very pleasant short walk to the falls where you can sit atop huge boulders, have morning tea and enjoy the waterfall and surroundings.

Return to the track junction and continue toward the Grand Canyon where you can see Greaves Creek flowing far below. In places the creek has cut a narrow chasm 30m deep and only a couple of metres wide right beside the track.

You will see ferns, small waterfalls and moss covered overhangs. Floods have piled up logs and other debris in the creek.

Along the way you will pass through a short tunnel and into an open area where there are Cedar Wattles.

Cross Greaves Creek in Neates Glen and climb the steep track through Banksias, Tea Trees, Sydney Golden Wattle and Casuarinas to the parking area on Evans Lookout Road.

Grade: Medium, 300m asc, steep and slippery in parts.

Distance: 7km.

Best in Autumn or Spring.

Public Transport: Train to Blackheath. 4.7km from Blackheath station to car-park on Evans Lookout Road.

Map 52 and CMA Katoomba.

Ian Schleter

55. BLUE MOUNTAINS N.P.: KATOOMBA - MEGALONG VALLEY - DEVILS HOLE - KATOOMBA

This interesting one-day walk takes you on a section of "The Six Foot Track" and returns via a cleft in the cliff line known as Devils Hole.

Start at Katoomba by leaving your car near the corner of the Great Western Highway and Valley Road (which runs into Narrow Neck Road and Cliff Drive). A convenient parking spot is near a water tower about 150m along Valley Road.

Walk along the highway for about 1.6km to Explorers' Tree (Eucalyptus concretus), then turn left into Pulpit Hill Road. About 250m in, the road forks. Take the left branch - The Six Foot Track. It soon drops steeply past the old quarry and into Nellies Glen - care is required on the large, rough steps down into the valley. On the way down the track passes close to Bonnie Doon Falls.

About 2km from Explorers' Tree the track merges into a trail - The Nellies Glen Road. Further on, about 2km, there is a road branching to the left - the Devils Hole route which goes to Dixons Ladder. Before taking this turn, cross the bridge over Diamond Creek and continue straight on past a road branching to the right (which crosses Megalong Creek) for 150m to view a miners' village site. Some horse stables stand on the clearing.

Return to the road branching off across Megalong Creek and have lunch by the creek "on the rocks".

After lunch cross the bridge and take that right hand road towards Dixons Ladder. About 750m along (say 10 minutes) look for a small track off the road heading NE (it may be marked with a small cairn or marker).

Follow it across a couple of small branches of Devils Hole Creek. The track bears more easterly as it climbs up the lower slopes toward the cliff face. Markers (50mm aluminium squares) denote the track up to the vicinity of the cliff-face where you should bear right till you locate the cleft which is the way up.

The striking feature here is the ominous rock wedged overhead in the cleft. You tend to hurry when you're directly beneath it - although it is difficult because it is steep and rough. Near the top the track divides. The left track involves a "jump up" of about 1.5m, whilst the right track

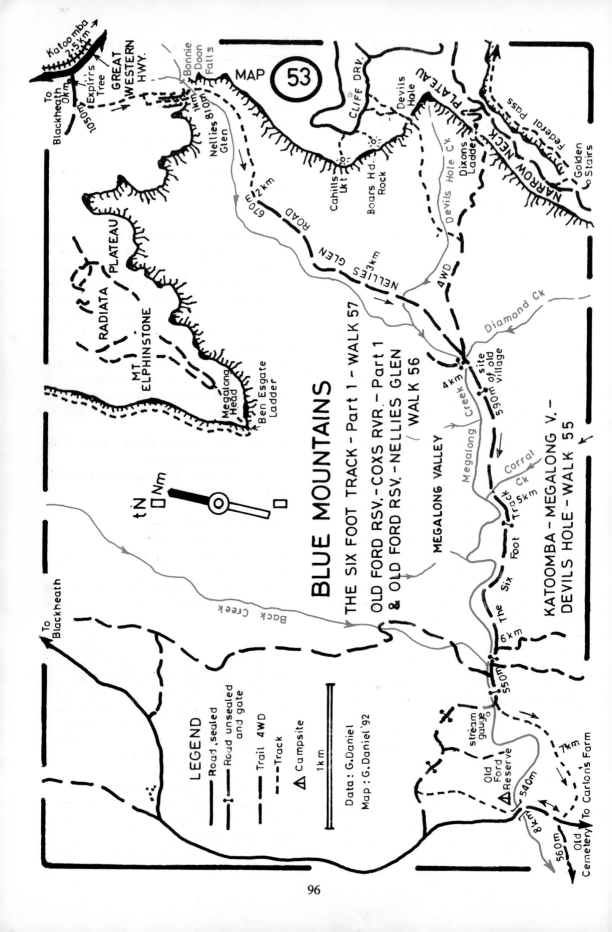

BLUE MOUNTAINS

THE SIX FOOT TRACK - Part 1 - WALK 57
OLD FORD RSV.-COXS RVR.- Part 1 & OLD FORD RSV.-NELLIES GLEN / WALK 56
KATOOMBA - MEGALONG V. - DEVILS HOLE - WALK 55

MAP 53

LEGEND

Road, sealed
Road, unsealed and gate
Trail 4WD
Track
△ Campsite

1km

Data : G. Daniel
Map : G. Daniel '92

follows a more gentle grade. Both tracks emerge at Cliff Drive where there are great views over the valley.

At Cliff Drive turn right then left into Narrow Neck Road from where it is about 1.6km to the car at the water tower.

Of course you can go by train and walk from and to Katoomba station - this adds a total of 2.5km to your walk.

Grade: Medium, 460m descent and ascent on track, rough and steep in places.

Distance: 10km.

Public Transport: Train to Katoomba.

Map 53 and CMA Katoomba.

George Daniel

56. BLUE MOUNTAINS:
OLD FORD RESERVE - COXS RIVER AND - NELLIES GLEN.

This car-based camping trip is ideal for beginners. The two one-day walks are sections of the historic Six Foot Track whilst the base camp is located in a very scenic spot on Megalong Creek. This way you can enjoy parts of the Six Foot Track without undertaking the whole walk. The walks are along fairly level tracks in the picturesque Megalong Valley.

Old Ford Reserve is 14km from Blackheath. At Blackheath, turn west via the railway level crossing and turn left immediately (south) along Station Street for 350m, then turn right into Shipley Road. Follow Shipley Road for 800m to a four-way intersection and turn left into Megalong Road (well signposted). Follow Megalong Road for 13km (no major junctions) to Old Ford Reserve, which is on your left where a concrete bridge crosses Megalong Creek.

Day 1. From Old Ford Reserve, drive south for 400m to where the Six Foot Track crosses Megalong Road (signposted). There is ample parking space. Of interest is the old cemetery on the left of the track just at the start of the walk.

Follow the 4WD trail westward as it undulates through farmland. Not far past where the track comes close to Megalong Creek there is a track fork. Take the left branch through a gate. There are some extensive vistas here.

The scenery changes at a point where you first see glimpses of the Coxs River, from open farmland to granite country. Fine views of the

Coxs River extend to the swing bridge over the Coxs River. Cross the bridge and walk for 1.1km to a camp-site where some grassy flats provide a good lunch spot.

Return the same way to Old Ford Reserve and camp for the night.

Day 2. After you have packed up your tent drive to the same starting point as for day 1.

Head east along the well-marked track which undulates through farmlands almost parallel to Megalong Creek. At 3.5km along you come to an old village site. There is not much evidence of the miner's dwellings that were one here - only a couple of horse sheds stand on the site now. It is near a ford across Megalong Creek. Continue on, cross the bridge over Diamond Creek to a road junction. Take the left hand branch (the right goes to Devils Hole) and follow it for 3km through Nellies Glen to below Bonnie Doon Falls. Some imagination is required to visualise how the Glen looked at the turn of the century. The track then zigzagged down from the top with ferny dells in the gullies - if you look carefully, traces of these may be seen.

Return the same way.

Grade: Day 1, Easy/Medium, 15km, 300m ascent on track and fire trail.

Day 2, Easy, 14km, 250m asc on track and fire trail.

Distance: 29km.

Best in Autumn and Spring.

No public transport.

Map 53,54 and CMA Katoomba, Hampton.

Pamphlet: Dept of Lands.

Book: From Katoomba to Jenolan Caves, The Six Foot Track by Jim Smith.

George Daniel

WATER BOTTLES AND CARRIERS:
Thin plastic bottles are OK. Three with 500ml capacity are the required minimum. Bottles which are oval in section, have a screw cap and a small cup can be obtained from supermarkets for less than a dollar.

For your 4 litre wine cask liner, make an nylon envelope-shaped container with two strap handles. This comes in handy at camp, saving trips to a water supply. It can also double as a wash basin.

57. KATOOMBA TO JENOLAN CAVES VIA THE SIX FOOT TRACK

Up until about 1880, access to Jenolan caves was via a lengthy route from Tarana railway station. The trip from Sydney by train and then horse and buggy took 24 hours. In 1884, a survey was undertaken to find a more direct route for a bridle track from Katoomba to Jenolan Caves. The track was to be six feet wide. By 1894, this 42km track was very popular as the travel time from Katoomba to the caves was only eight hours. However, maintenance ceased in the early 1900s and the track became little used by 1940. In 1985 the track was re-marked and re-opened by the Orange CaLM Office.

This three-day experience is "required walking" for enthusiasts. The actual walking time is about two days, with two half-days for transport. The track is well marked.

Start off from Katoomba by 9am, but first, book a coach seat for the return trip - Aussie Tours, 283 Main St, Katoomba (047) 82-1866. Walk from Katoomba along the Great Western Highway for 2.5km to the Explorers' Tree (blazed on Blaxland, Wentworth and Lawsons' exploratory expedition). Turn west off the Highway and follow the gravel road for 250m. At a road fork take the left branch and descend steeply to Nellies Glen. Care is required on the large steps. Notice the gravel spoil bulldozed into the gully in a failed attempt to make a fire trail down to the valley floor from the plateau.

It is about 2km to the bottom where the track meets a fire trail (Nellies Glen Road). Take a break here. Follow this road which undulates, and crosses Diamond Creek near its junction with Megalong Ck. Nearby is the site of an old mining village. Go 250m to a gate, pass through, and proceed 1km to the next gate ("Warri Warri"). Two more gates ("Crystal Brook" & "Oakburn") are negotiated before you reach Megalong Valley Road.

The suggested lunch spot is 500m north along Megalong Valley Road at Old Ford Reserve which is well worth a look. After lunch, return to the track, and explore the old cemetery on the southern side of the track.

Follow the 4WD trail westward as it undulates through farmland. Not far past where the track comes close to Megalong Creek there is a track fork. Take the left branch through a gate. The track is well marked with walking track logos in this section.

The scenery changes, at a point where you first glimpse the Coxs River, from open farmlands to granite country. Fine views of the Coxs River extend to the swing bridge which crosses it. Cross the bridge and walk for about 600m and collect water for the camp and next day's walk from a creek that crosses the track. Continue a further 600m along the track to a spacious camp-site with grassy flats. An alternative water supply is from Murdering Creek - just past the camp-site. The last resort is to use water from the Coxs River. So far you have walked 17.5km from the station.

Next day, follow the power-line service road up alongside Murdering Ck to a junction 2.6km on, near some stockyards. Bear left and go up to Mini Mini Saddle 450m above the river. There are grand views on a clear day. You can see the Hydro Majestic at Medlow Bath etc. Descend to beautiful Alum Ck. The track then passes through delightful country to the Little River crossing which is normally shin deep. About 400m beyond Little River, on a sharp bend in the road before a gate, pause and listen for Bellbirds. If you are in luck you may see and hear these secretive pretty birds at close range - a special treat.

Next, climb steeply up to Black Range. Half way up the road branches - keep left and near the top, on your left note the rain-gauge and road junction. Keep right and look for the next suitable clearing for lunch. From Little River the ascent is 440m.

Along Black Range the fire trail undulates through dry sclerophyll bush for 9km to Jenolan Caves Road. With an 8am start, you should be there about 3pm. You've walked 18.5km. Spacious camp-sites with water on tap are available here, one is just across the road opposite where the track emerges amongst some pines, the other is about 100m north along the Jenolan Caves Road. If you can't decide which is the better, spend half the night at each.

Next day it is a relatively easy walk down Jenolan Caves Road to Binda Flats (4km), then take the signposted track into the bush and down a steep scenic route to Jenolan Caves House (4.8km). If you arrive well before coach departure time you could go on one of the cave tours.

The coach departs at 3.30pm (check) and takes about 1.5 hours to reach Katoomba station. Trains

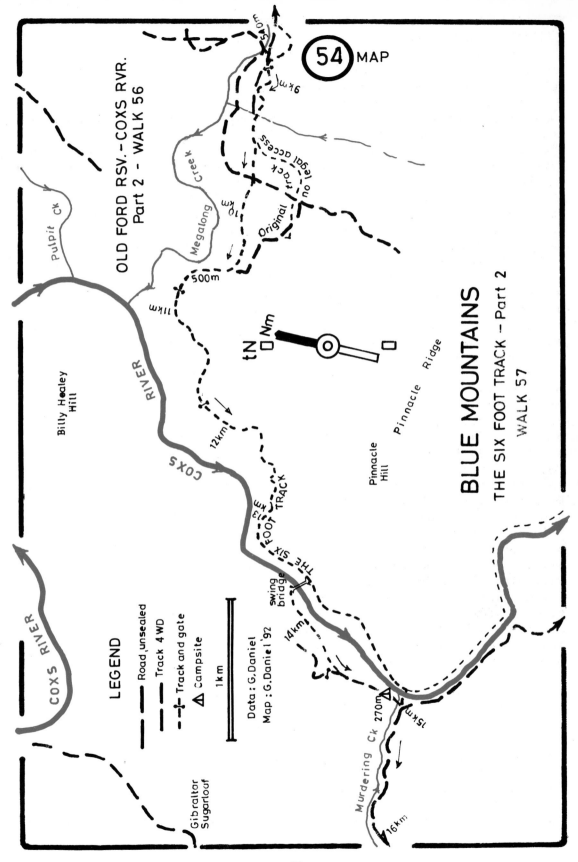

MAP 54

OLD FORD RSV.–COXS RVR.
Part 2 – WALK 56

BLUE MOUNTAINS
THE SIX FOOT TRACK – Part 2
WALK 57

LEGEND

Road, unsealed
Track 4WD
Track and gate
Campsite

1km

Data: G.Daniel
Map: G.Daniel '92

Pulpit Ck
Megalong Creek
no legal access
Original track access
Billy Healey Hill
COXS RIVER
COXS RIVER
THE SIX FOOT TRACK
swing bridge
Pinnacle Hill
Pinnacle Ridge
Murdering Ck 270m
Gibraltar Sugarloaf

tN
Nm

9km
10km
500m
11km
12km
13km
14km
15km
16km

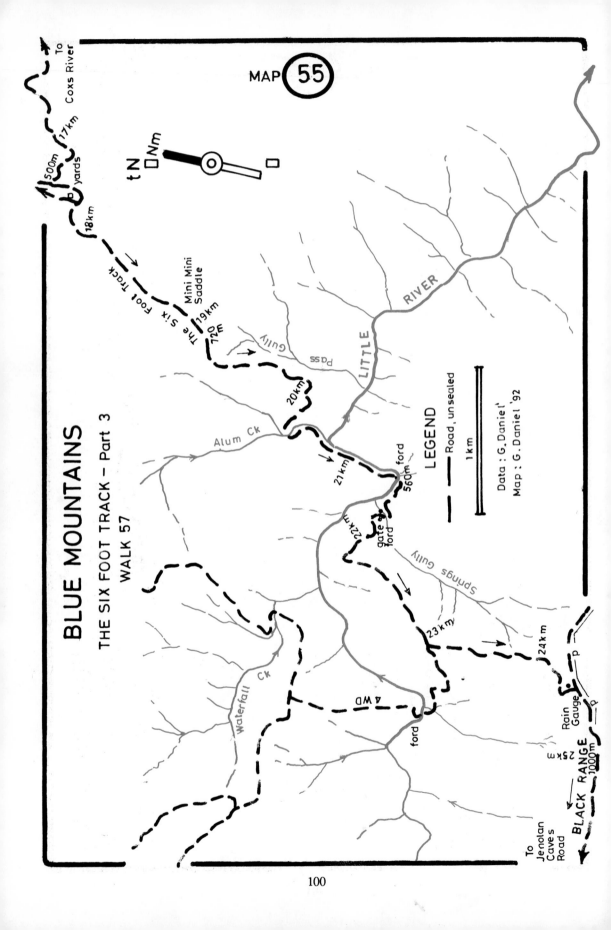

BLUE MOUNTAINS

THE SIX FOOT TRACK – Part 3
WALK 57

MAP **55**

To Coxs River

17km

500m
yards
18km

The Six Foot Track

Mini Mini Saddle
19km
720m

Gully
Pass

20km

LITTLE RIVER

Alum Ck

21km

560m
ford

LEGEND

Road, unsealed

1km

Data : G. Daniel
Map : G. Daniel '92

22km
gate
ford

Springs Gully

23km

24km

Waterfall Ck

4WD

ford

Rain Gauge

BLACK RANGE

25km
1000m

To Jenolan Caves Road

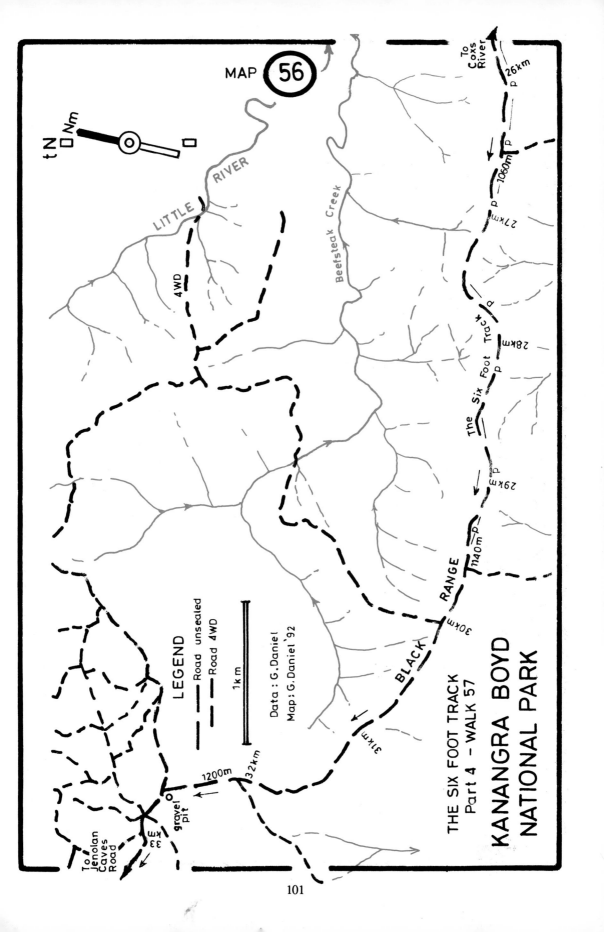

MAP 56

THE SIX FOOT TRACK
Part 4 – WALK 57

KANANGRA BOYD
NATIONAL PARK

LEGEND

Road unsealed
Road 4WD

1 km

Data : G. Daniel
Map : G. Daniel '92

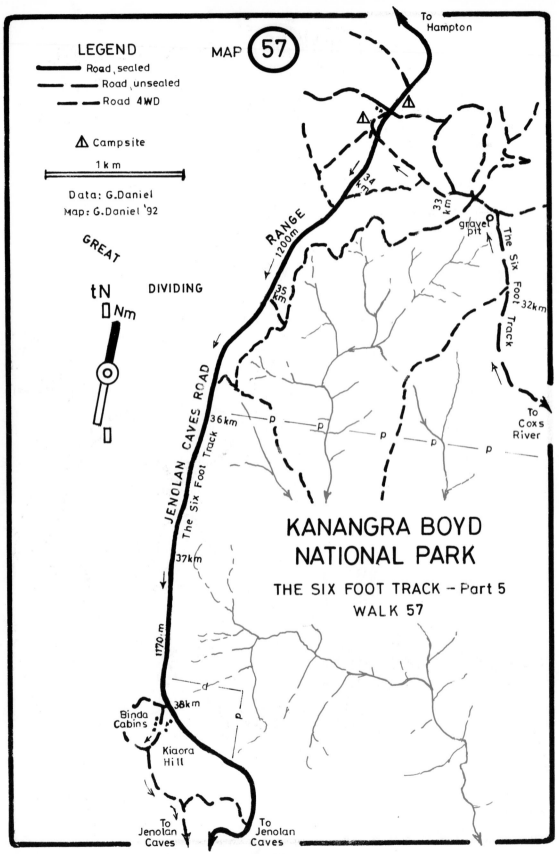

LEGEND
—— Road, sealed
— — Road, unsealed
– – – Road 4WD

⚠ Campsite

1 km

Data: G.Daniel
Map: G.Daniel '92

GREAT

tN
☐ Nm

DIVIDING

MAP 57

To Hampton

RANGE
1200m

34 km

33 km

gravel pit

The Six Foot Track

32km

To Coxs River

35 km

JENOLAN CAVES ROAD

The Six Foot Track

36km   p   p   p   p   p

37km

1170 m

KANANGRA BOYD NATIONAL PARK

THE SIX FOOT TRACK – Part 5

WALK 57

d
p

38km

Binda Cabins

Kiaora Hill

To Jenolan Caves

To Jenolan Caves

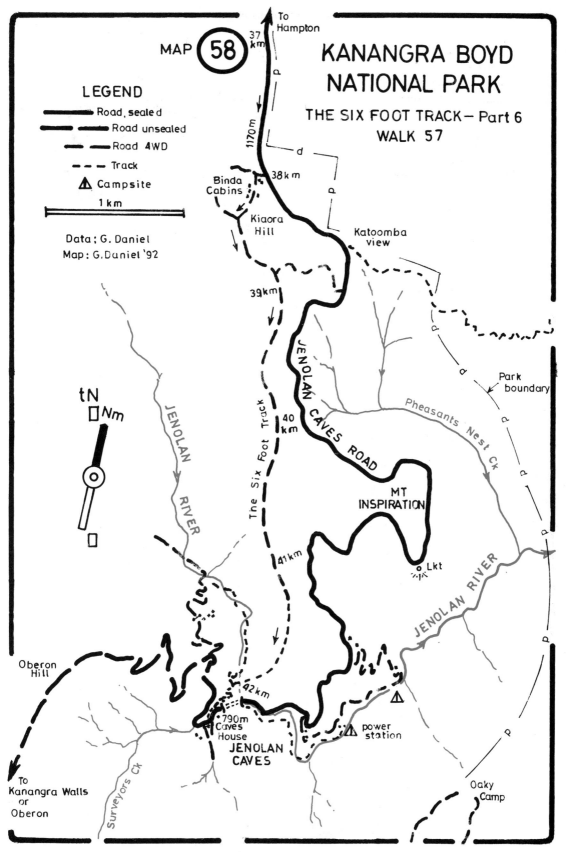

MAP 58

LEGEND

Road, sealed
Road unsealed
Road 4WD
Track
▲ Campsite

1 km

Data: G. Daniel
Map: G. Daniel '92

KANANGRA BOYD
NATIONAL PARK

THE SIX FOOT TRACK — Part 6
WALK 57

To Hampton

37 km

1170 m

38 km

Binda
Cabins

Kiaora
Hill

Katoomba
view

Park
boundary

39 km

tN
Nm

JENOLAN RIVER

The Six Foot Track

JENOLAN CAVES ROAD

Pheasants Nest Ck

40 km

MT
INSPIRATION

41 km

Lkt

JENOLAN RIVER

Oberon
Hill

42 km

790 m
Caves
House

JENOLAN
CAVES

power
station

Surveyors Ck

To
Kanangra Walls
or
Oberon

Oaky
Camp

from Katoomba to Sydney are usually hourly.

Remember that a lot of this track is through private property, and access is provisional only, so obey the signs. Camping is allowed only where shown on the map. Carry water for each day's walk and carry all rubbish out.

Grade: Day 1. Easy/medium. 17.5km, 780m descent on road, track and fire trail.

Day 2. Medium/hard. 18.5km, 955m asc on track and fire trail.

Day 3. Easy. 8.8km, 330m descent on road and track.

Total Distance: 44.5km (includes 2.5km from Katoomba station to Explorers' Tree).

Best in Autumn or Spring.

Public Transport: Train to and from Katoomba and Coach from Jenolan Caves to Katoomba.

Maps 53-58 and CMA Katoomba, Hampton and Jenolan.

Pamphlet from CaLM Offices.

Book: From Katoomba to Jenolan Caves, The Six Foot Track by Jim Smith.

George Daniel

FOOTWEAR

One-day walks: Joggers (weight 0.65kg for size 8) are good for most day walks. They have shock absorbing soles, are light and are soft on the heel - a factor that reduces the risk of blisters. They also drain better and dry more quickly than boots if 'in water' walking is encountered. Their main disadvantage is that they provide little ankle support.

Two-day and longer walks: With the heavier loads and longer durations involved, soft boots are better for the soles of the feet and ankles, particularly if the terrain is rocky. They are heavier, however, (1.6kg for size 8) and more likely to cause blisters.

For river crossings: To keep your other footwear dry, take an extra pair of joggers.

---

58. BLUE MOUNTAINS N.P.: CARLON'S FARM - MEDLOW GAP - KELPIE POINT - COXS RIVER - BUNGGALOOLOO RIDGE - WONGA MOUNTAIN - KOWMUNG RIVER

The Wild Dog Mountains and Kowmung River areas offer some of the best walking country in the Blue Mountains. Great views from mountain tops, giant Turpentine forests complete with Lyrebirds, and the last unpolluted major river in the Blue Mountains are but some of the features of this wilderness walk.

You must obtain a permit from Sydney Water before undertaking this walk as a section is through their prohibited zone, i.e. within 3km of the stored water of Lake Burragorang. Phone the Sydney Water Catchment Services Division on (02) 681-0313. Permission entitles you to pass through, but not to camp.

The starting place is Carlon's Farm in the Megalong Valley, about two and a quarter hours drive from Sydney. From Blackheath, follow the Megalong Valley Road past Old Ford Reserve (14km), then for a further 4.5km on a gravel road to a gate. Continue on for 2.5 km to the car-park at the end of the road. Carlon's Farm is shown on the Jenolan topographic map as "Green Gully".

Start off early (by 7am). After paying a parking fee at Carlon's shop, walk south up to the crest of a hill (about 400m) where three 4WD trails meet. Take the east branch for about 200m up a slight rise around a bend then look for a rough track up a hill by a fence. Follow this track for about 1km to the Bellbird Ridge track junction and take the left branch. After about 600m you arrive at a service road (the old Black Dog Track) opposite Carlon Head. Turn right.

There is a flat camp-site beside a creek 3.5km along this road which provides a refreshing spot for a break. An undulating walk of about 2km from the creek brings you to Medlow Gap (where there are Sydney Water signs, gates, a helipad and a water-hole (sometimes dry).

At Medlow Gap, take the road heading west. Walk down the road skirting Mt Mouin. After 2km find a lesser used trail than the one you are on, veering off right (south) along a ridgetop. Follow this until it ends, shortly before the end of the ridge (you can go down the left hand road to Kelpie Point, but it is longer and not as easy).

Throw off the load right at the end of this road and contemplate the magnificent vista. See if you

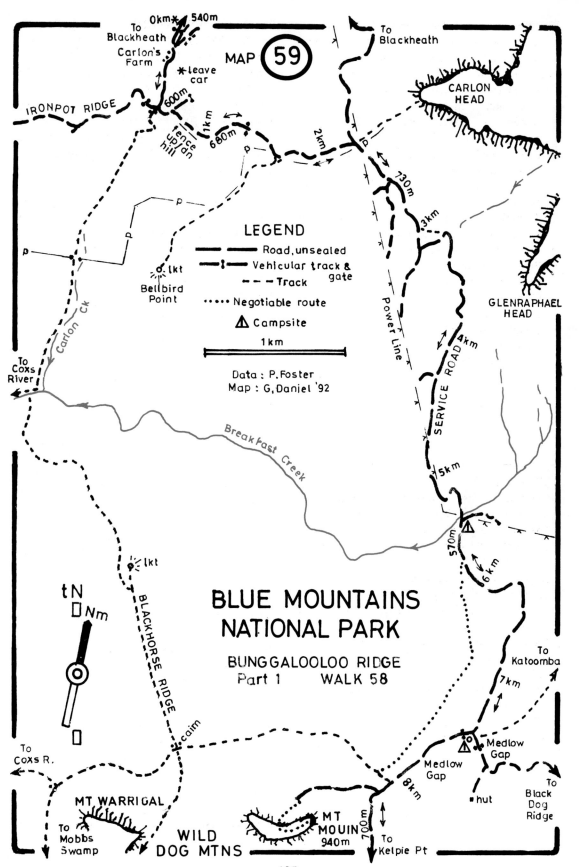

MAP 59

LEGEND

—— Road, unsealed
—□— Vehicular track & gate
— — — Track
...... Negotiable route
△ Campsite

|—— 1km ——|

Data : P. Foster
Map : G. Daniel '92

BLUE MOUNTAINS
NATIONAL PARK

BUNGGALOOLOO RIDGE
Part 1   WALK 58

IRONPOT RIDGE

To Blackheath
Carlon's Farm

0km 540m
*leave car

600m
Fence Up/dn hill

1km
680m

2km

Carlon Ck

To Coxs River

Bellbird Point

Carlon Ck

Breakfast Creek

To Blackheath

CARLON HEAD

730m

3km

Power Line

GLENRAPHAEL HEAD

SERVICE ROAD

4km

5km

570m

6km

tN
Nm

BLACKHORSE RIDGE

lkt

cairn

To Coxs R.

MT WARRIGAL

To Mobbs Swamp

WILD DOG MTNS

MT MOUIN
940m

700m

To Kelpie Pt

Medlow Gap

Medlow Gap

7km

To Katoomba

8km

hut

To Black Dog Ridge

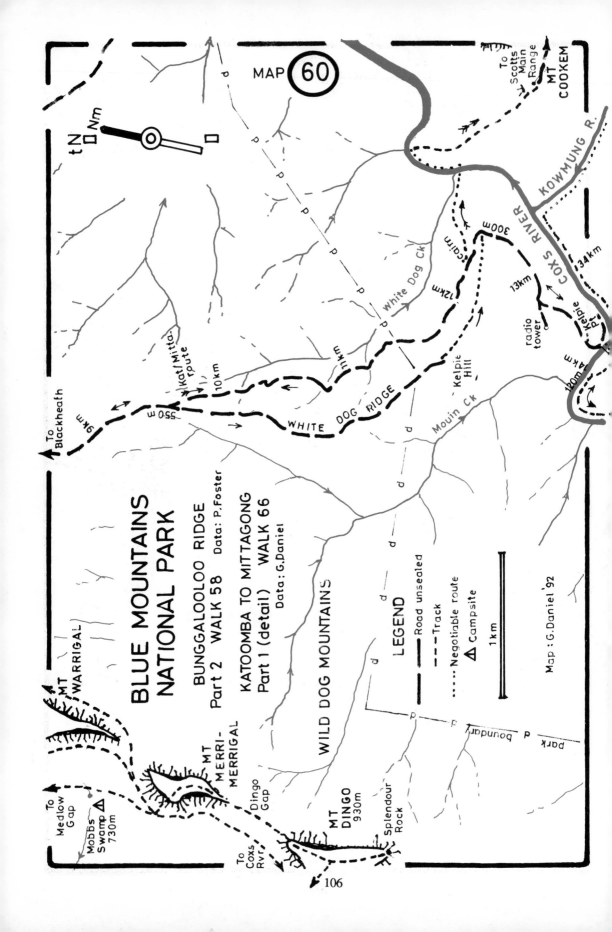

MAP 60

MT COOKEM
To Scotts Main Range

KOWMUNG R.

COXS RIVER

34km

White Dog Ck

13km

radio tower

12km

cairn

300m

Kelpie Pt

120m

4km

To Blackheath

Kat/Mitta-route

10km

550m

11km

9km

WHITE DOG RIDGE

Kelpie Hill

Mouin Ck

BLUE MOUNTAINS
NATIONAL PARK

BUNGGALOOLOO RIDGE
Part 2 WALK 58   Data: P.Foster

KATOOMBA TO MITTAGONG
Part 1 (detail)   WALK 66
Data: G.Daniel

WILD DOG MOUNTAINS

LEGEND

Road unsealed
Track
Negotiable route
△ Campsite

1km

Map: G.Daniel '92

park boundary

MT WARRIGAL

To Medlow Gap

Mobbs Swamp 730m

MT MERRI-MERRIGAL

Dingo Gap

MT DINGO 930m

Splendour Rock

To Coxs Rvr

106

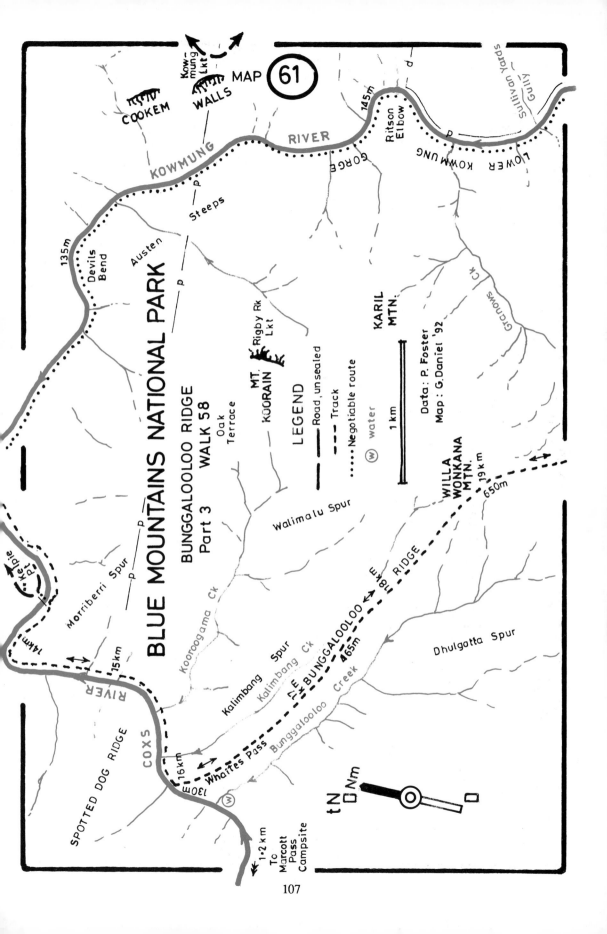

BLUE MOUNTAINS NATIONAL PARK

BUNGGALOOLOO RIDGE
WALK 58
Part 3

MAP 61

LEGEND

——————— Road, unsealed

— — — — Track

· · · · · · Negotiable route

Ⓦ water

|———————| 1 km

Data: P. Foster
Map: G. Daniel '92

COOKEM WALLS

Kowmung Lkt

KOWMUNG RIVER GORGE

Steeps

Devils Bend

135m

Austen

Oak Terrace

MT. KOORAIN

Rigby Rk Lkt

145m

Ritson Elbow

LOWER KOWMUNG

Sullivan Gully

Sullivan Yards

Gromows Ck

KARIL MTN.

Walimalu Spur

WILLA WONKANA MTN.

650m

19 km

18 km

BUNGGALOOLOO RIDGE

465m

Dhulgatta Spur

Kelpie Pt

14 km

Morriberri Spur

Kooroogama Ck

15 km

Kalimbang Spur

Kalimbang Ck

Bunggalooloo Creek

Whaites Pass

16 km

130m Ⓦ

COXS RIVER

SPOTTED DOG RIDGE

1·2 km
To Marcott Pass Campsite

N

107

can spot the ridge you will take from the Coxs River over to the Kowmung. It rises evenly without any bumps or humps. On then to the Coxs. Stay on the spine of the ridge; there is a faint track, but it fades on the way down to the Kelpie Point service road. Turn right along this for 1.3km to Kelpie Point on the Coxs River.

Cross the Coxs, near the flying fox at an old ford. Remember that the Coxs River is a fast and powerful stream, so take care after rain. Do not cross if the water is more than a metre deep. After crossing, have lunch by the river.

After a break begin walking upstream: it may be easier to walk in the river than along the side in this section - take additional Volleys or joggers for this. After passing two medium sized gullies (usually dry), find a cairn and a large dead Casuarina marking the start of Whaites Pass up Bunggalooloo Ridge (2.5km from Kelpie Point).

The first part of the ascent is steep, but it levels off a little after a kilometre or so. On the lower part of the ridge the track is faint, but more definite as you go on. Look for blazes on some trees (probably done from horseback). As you reach the top of the ridge it levels out and here huge Turpentines compete with Grey Gums and Forest Oaks whilst in the undergrowth you may spot a Lyrebird, especially in late winter or spring.

Keep to the trail as it veers SW (now marked with the occasional aluminium marker in this area where several ridges meet) across Willa Wonkana Mountain. It picks up Wonga Ridge across to Wonga Mountain. Notice that as the track turns along Wonga Ridge the vegetation changes: Turpentines give way to Ironbarks, and Native Holly, the scourge of bushwalkers, makes an appearance. Now the track turns down the hill on the left (east) side of the spur and zigzags a little until with trembling knees you reach the Kowmung.

Look for a camp-site 100m up river past Ti Willa Creek (which is usually dry and stony). Here there is a camp-site to satisfy even the most discerning camper. There are still traces of the Old Cedar Road in this area.

Next morning rise early for the return trip. In winter you will need to head off by 8am to arrive back at Carlon's Farm about 5pm.

Grade: Day 1. Medium/Hard, 23km, 530m asc. Day 2. Hard. 23km, 1060m asc.

Total Distance: 46km.

No public transport.

Map 59-62 and CMA Katoomba, Jamison, Bimlow, Kanangra, Jenolan.   Phil Foster

---

A BUSHWALKING CODE

Bushwalkers should have the spirit (or ethic) of respect for the bush. Go with idea of "minimal impact bushwalking" - enjoying the natural environment without disturbing it. Some points to consider:-

* Rubbish - Pack out what you pack in including foil, cans, plastic, glass and food scraps. Leave the bush as good as or better than you found it.

* Use marked or formed tracks where they exist, and avoid making new parallel tracks. Where tracks zigzag on steep slopes, keep to the track and don't take short cuts as steep direct tracks accelerate erosion.

* Trees, shrubs, rock formations, archaeological sites, and signs should not be damaged in any way.

* Use fuel stoves where possible and especially where wood is scarce (for instance at popular camping areas). For campfires, use only fallen branches and then only sparingly. Fallen timber is a limited resource and is a part of the ecosystem. Some National Parks have "stove only" rules already. Scatter or bury ashes (when cold) out of site. If camping in wilderness areas, leave no sign of the campfire.

* Bury, not merely cover, human waste well away from watercourses, camp-sites and tracks (depth 15cm). Burn or pack out used toilet paper (as animals can dig up and scatter it).

* Wash dishes, clothes and body away from watercourses with soap (not synthetic detergents).

* Try not to introduce weeds or plant diseases into the bush. Make sure your boots, joggers and car are clean before setting out.

* Have consideration for other walkers, leave radios at home or use with discretion.

* Of course, don't disturb native animals or take domestic pets, firearms or weapons into National Parks.

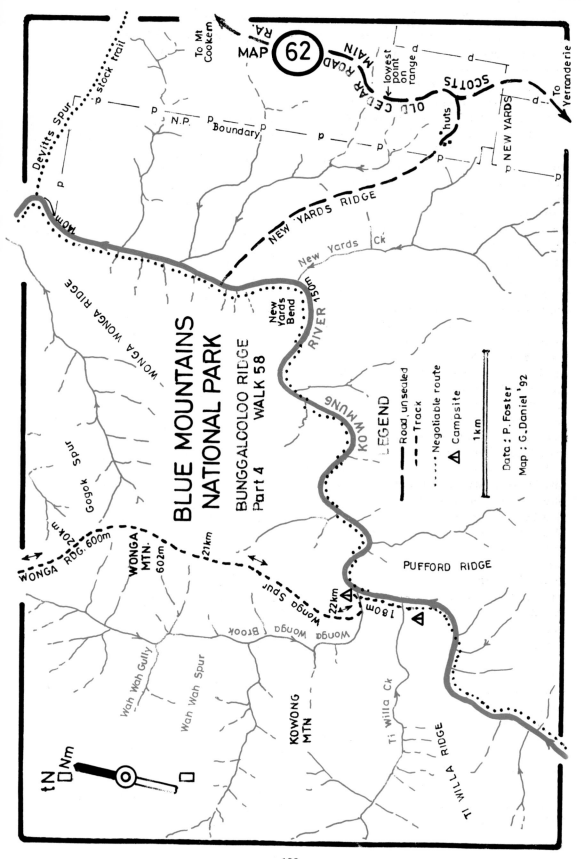

BLUE MOUNTAINS
NATIONAL PARK

BUNGGALCOLOO RIDGE
Part 4
WALK 58

MAP 62

LEGEND

Road, unsealed
Track
Negotiable route
Campsite

1km

Data : P. Foster
Map : G.Daniel '92

New Yards Ck

NEW YARDS RIDGE

New Yards Bend

RIVER 150m

KOWMUNG

PUFFORD RIDGE

WONGA WONGA RIDGE

Gogok Spur

WONGA RDG. 600m

20km

WONGA

WONGA MTN.
602m

21km

Wonga Spur

22km

180m

Wonga Wonga Brook

Wah Wah Gully

Wah Wah Spur

KOWONG MTN

Ti Willa Ck

TI WILLA RIDGE

Devitts Spur

stock trail

N.P. Boundary

To Mt Cookem

OLD CEDAR ROAD MAIN RA.

lowest point on range

SCOTTS

huts

NEW YARDS

To Verranderie

40m

Nm

59. KANANGRA BOYD N.P.: KANANGRA WALLS - MT CLOUDMAKER - DEX CREEK

The wilderness walk from Kanangra Walls to Mt Cloudmaker offers a panorama extending from Katoomba to Mittagong. Whilst this walk does not have some of the steep climbs found in other walks in the area, the country it traverses is rugged and prone to extremes of weather. For this walk you need to be well equipped and have some experience of the area and full pack bushwalking. The minimum size party should be four.

Kanangra Walls, the starting point for this walk, is 190km from Sydney via Jenolan Caves. From Jenolan Caves drive up Oberon Hill then on to a "T" junction (5km). Turn left and travel for 30km to Kanangra Walls car-park.

From the parking area follow the asphalt path to a sign indicating the way to the "plateau walk". Follow this path which crosses Blacks Pass (a small saddle) onto the Kanangra Walls plateau. The track then follows the top edge of the walls with spectacular views over Kanangra Creek. The plateau narrows 1.5km from the car-park where a relatively shallow valley comes in from the right (south). On the cliff-edge near here, there is a good vantage point above Kanangra Gorge. Just beyond this valley there is a track junction located on an exposed rock platform. Continue NE on the track closest to the cliff-edge to Brennan Tops.

About 1km from the track junction look for a cairn which marks the top of Smiths Pass. Here one can see Kilpatrick Causeway leading to Crafts Wall and the Mt Cloudmaker massif in the distance. The track down to Kilpatrick Causeway is via a steep rocky cleft (Smiths Pass). The track leaves a rock shelf on the plateau at the cairn, and drops into a small thickly wooded gully. It then descends the narrow cleft via a very steep rock scramble. The track then emerges below the cliffline. Walk left below the cliffline then veer north to the ridge top. The track along the causeway is occasionally indistinct but in general follows the ridge top. It rises to the base of the rock face of Crafts Wall. Follow the left track around the NW side of Crafts Wall. At the far end of Crafts Wall there is a track junction. Take the left branch which crosses a saddle, then climbs slightly to Mt Berry. A deep saddle - much loved by bushwalkers - called Gabes Gap follows. Navigation should be no problem as the track follows the most gradual descent.

At the bottom of Gabes Gap, the harder work begins. Firstly, climb steeply up the ridge to Mt High and Mighty, where there are great views. Next, follow the ridge around Mt Stormbreaker. The final section involves the climbs up Rip, Rack, Roar and Rumble (good views to the east) before reaching Mt Cloudmaker (no views at all). Mt Cloudmaker is marked by a cairn and a visitors book.

The best spot to camp is beside Dex Creek 1.7km NNE. The track commences at the NE corner of the mountain top. It heads NE for about 500m and then swings north along the ridge to upper Dex Creek. At the end of the ridge the track drops off the western slide to the camp-site areas in a small clearing at the junction of Dex Creek and a small creek coming in from the west. Both creek beds can be dry at that point, however there is always a small pool of good water a short distance upstream on the western creek where it drains from a swamp. The camping spot is marked on the Gangerang sketch map but not on the CMA topographic map. It is located in the upper catchment of the creek near a sharp bend just below Karrung Top.

Dex Creek is the only source of water on the walk and so water should be collected for the return trip.

The return walk follows the same route back to Kanangra Walls, with pauses to view the spectacular Thurat Spires in the light of a clear afternoon.

Grade: Day 1. Medium, 12km, 400m asc.
Day 2. Medium, 12km, 310m asc.
Total Distance: 24km.
Best in Autumn and Spring.
No Public Transport.
Maps 63,64 and CMA Kanangra and Gangerang (Sketch).

Richard Thompson

MAGNETIC VARIATION:
"Sydney Region" 1995 is 12.2° E
Annual change is +2 minutes of arc
i.e. approx 0.03 of a degree.

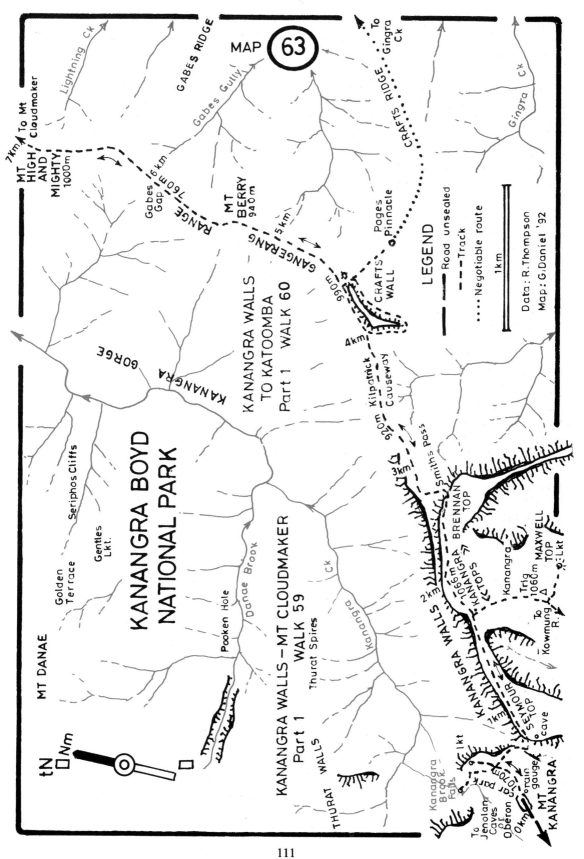

MAP 63

LEGEND

Road unsealed
Track
Negotiable route

1km

Data: R.Thompson
Map: G.Daniel '92

KANANGRA BOYD
NATIONAL PARK

MT DANAE

Golden
Terrace
Seriphos Cliffs
Gentles Lkt.
Pooken Hole

KANANGRA GORGE

Danae Brook

KANANGRA WALLS
TO KATOOMBA
Part 1   WALK 60

KANANGRA WALLS—MT CLOUDMAKER
WALK 59
Part 1

THURAT WALLS

Thurat Spires

Kanangra Ck

Lightning Ck

GABES RIDGE

Gabes Gully

MT HIGH
AND
MIGHTY 1000m

7km To Mt Cloudmaker

Gabes Gap
16km

RANGE 760m

MT BERRY 940m

GANGERANG

5km

CRAFTS RIDGE

To Gingra Ck

Gingra Ck

Pages Pinnacle

960m

CRAFTS WALL

4km

Kilpatrick Causeway

920m

Smiths Pass

3km

2km

BRENNAN TOP

1066m KANANGRA TOPS

Kanangra Trig
1060m MAXWELL TOP
Lkt

To Kowmung R.

KANANGRA WALLS

SEYMOUR TOP

1km

Cave

Lkt

Kanangra Brook Falls

car park
Drain gauge
1070m

To Jenolan Caves or Oberon

Okm

MT KANANGRA

tN
Nm

111

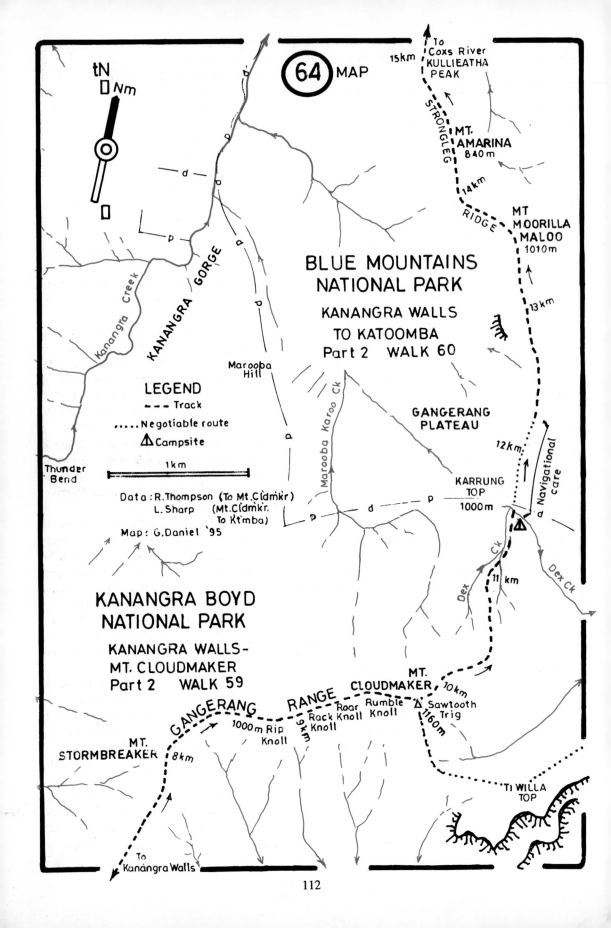

tN

Nm

(64) MAP

To Coxs River
KULLIEATHA
PEAK
15km

STRONGLEG
RIDGE

MT.
AMARINA
840m

14km

MT
MOORILLA
MALOO
1010m

13km

BLUE MOUNTAINS
NATIONAL PARK

KANANGRA WALLS
TO KATOOMBA
Part 2   WALK 60

GANGERANG
PLATEAU

12km
a Navigational
care

KANANGRA CREEK

KANANGRA GORGE

Marooba
Hill

Marooba Karoo Ck

LEGEND

- - -   Track

..... Negotiable route

△ Campsite

1km

Thunder
Bend

Data: R.Thompson (To Mt.Cldmkr)
L. Sharp (Mt.Cldmkr.
To Kt'mba)

Map: G.Daniel '95

KARRUNG
TOP
1000m

△

Dex Ck

Dex Ck

11 km

KANANGRA BOYD
NATIONAL PARK

KANANGRA WALLS-
MT. CLOUDMAKER
Part 2   WALK 59

MT.
CLOUDMAKER
10km

△ Sawtooth
Trig
1160m

GANGERANG   RANGE

Roar   Rumble
Rack Knoll   Knoll
9km   Knoll

1000m Rip
Knoll

MT.
STORMBREAKER   8km

To
Kanangra Walls

Ti WILLA
TOP

60. KANANGRA BOYD AND BLUE MOUNTAINS N.Ps.: KANANGRA WALLS TO KATOOMBA

This is one of the classic walks in Australia. It is a challenging three-day walk across the Kanangra wilderness, featuring Kanangra Walls, spectacular mountains, mountain passes, a river crossing, great camp-sites and a variety of vegetation types. There are magnificent views along the way. As this walk includes a crossing of the Coxs River, monitor the rainfall in the area in the week before the walk. Transport must be arranged to the starting point (Kanangra Walls). This description carries on from walk 59 (Kanangra Walls - Mt Cloudmaker). **Note this is a long wilderness walk and navigation skills are essential.**

On day 2, get an early start from the camp at Dex Creek. Initially scramble a short distance up the rocky point on the northern side of the small valley with the water supply. The track is not definite here and you will need to find the easiest way through the scrub while heading in a NNE direction to the top of the ridge where the scrub thins out. Continue to head NNE until the ground starts to drop steeply to the north. Turn NNW at this point for a short distance until you are on the ridge and among the taller trees. Head north along the ridge and the track should soon become obvious. The track passes west of Mt Moorilla Maloo 2km from Dex Creek, then crosses Mt Amarina 1km further on. It then undulates to Mt Strongleg (1.5km). The descent to the Coxs River is very steep. It branches into a multitude of tracks at the end of the ridge and it is a matter of picking the easiest one. Try to keep your party together here, otherwise they can become scattered along the banks of either Kanangra Creek or the Coxs River.

You will need at least one litre of water and possibly two in the warmer weather for the climb up Yellow Pup Ridge from the Coxs River. There is no water at the top. Fill your containers from Kanangra Creek, preferably upstream from the horse riding camp at Konangaroo clearing. Do not use the water from the Coxs River as it is polluted with the sewage from Lithgow.

The Coxs River is broad and deep in the vicinity of Kanangra Creek. Head downstream to your right until the Coxs is seen to narrow and starts to flow through Casuarinas. It is broad but only knee deep. This is the crossing point during normal river flows. The rocks on the river bed are slippery with algae. Walk slowly and carefully to the other side. A stout stick will help to keep your balance. Do not attempt to cross if the river is in flood (more than 1m deep) as it is extremely dangerous. Walk back to Kanangra Walls or make camp and wait for the river level to go down.

Once across, walk downstream until the cliffs on the ridge on your left disappear. The track up Yellow Pup Ridge then commences on the nose of the ridge. It is a steep climb (610m ascent in 3km) and it can take between one and two hours to reach the top of Mount Yellow Dog.

Before reaching the top, at a point where small rocky cliffs can be seen ahead, the track divides. Take the track to the left. It is easier as it contours along the side of the ridge instead of going straight over the top.

The track heads NE from Mount Yellow Dog to the top of the Brindle Dog Range where it then heads east to the base of Mount Dingo. The side-track up to Mount Dingo and Splendour Rock branches right near a cairn beside the main track.

The track to Mobbs Soak undulates along the base of the Wild Dog Mountains generally in a NE direction. Water can sometimes be found in pools down off the western side of the track from small streams. It takes approximately 30 to 45 minutes to walk from the base of Mount Dingo to Mobbs Soak (1.7km).

Mobbs Soak appears as a clearing at the end of a gentle slope on the track which has now become broader and rutted. The clearing is distinguished by an isolated group of three or four small gum trees near the track and a small group of boulders to the left of it with obvious signs of a fireplace.

You can camp here or further to the west among the Casuarina trees above the gully. Water can be found to the north a short distance along the main track from a small stream.

The best water is to be found upstream. However it is wise to boil all water in the area.

On day three, follow the main track which is well defined, ignoring side-tracks to the left and right for 3.5km to a service road. Turn left and walk a short distance to Medlow Gap. From the road junction at Medlow Gap, take the track heading uphill in an ENE direction. The distance to Taros Ladder is 2.3km via a well defined track. It will probably take you about an hour to reach the top. Climb the ladder (a series of rungs and

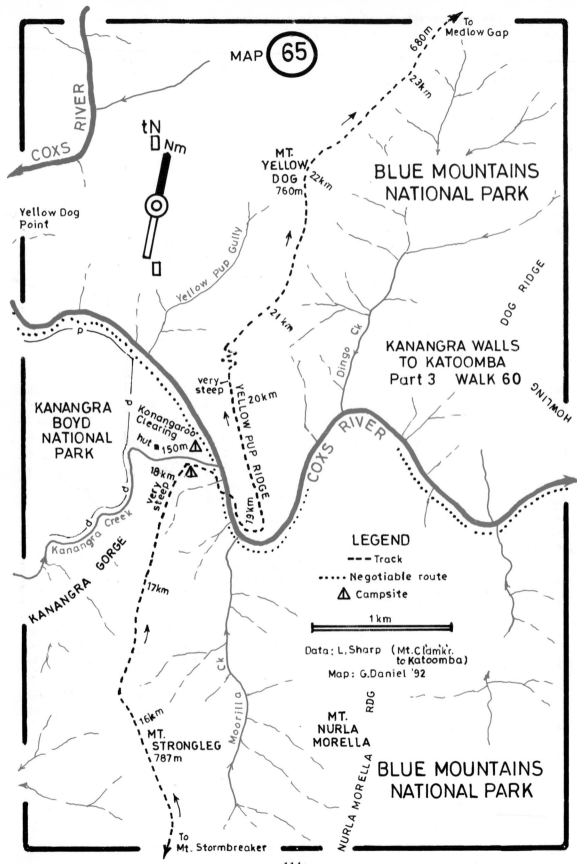

MAP 65

COXS RIVER

Yellow Dog Point

tN Nm

To Medlow Gap
680m
12.3km

BLUE MOUNTAINS
NATIONAL PARK

MT. YELLOW DOG
760m
22km

Yellow Pup Gully

21km

KANANGRA WALLS
TO KATOOMBA
Part 3   WALK 60

Dingo Ck

DOG RIDGE

HOWLING

KANANGRA BOYD NATIONAL PARK

Konangaroo Clearing

hut 150m

very steep

20km

YELLOW PUP RIDGE

18km
very steep

COXS RIVER

Kanangra Creek

KANANGRA GORGE

19km

LEGEND
— — Track
· · · Negotiable route
△ Campsite

1km

17km

16km

MT. STRONGLEG
787m

Moorilla Ck

MT. NURLA MORELLA

NURLA MORELLA RDG

Data: L. Sharp (Mt. Cloudmk'r. to Katoomba)
Map: G. Daniel '92

BLUE MOUNTAINS
NATIONAL PARK

To Mt. Stormbreaker

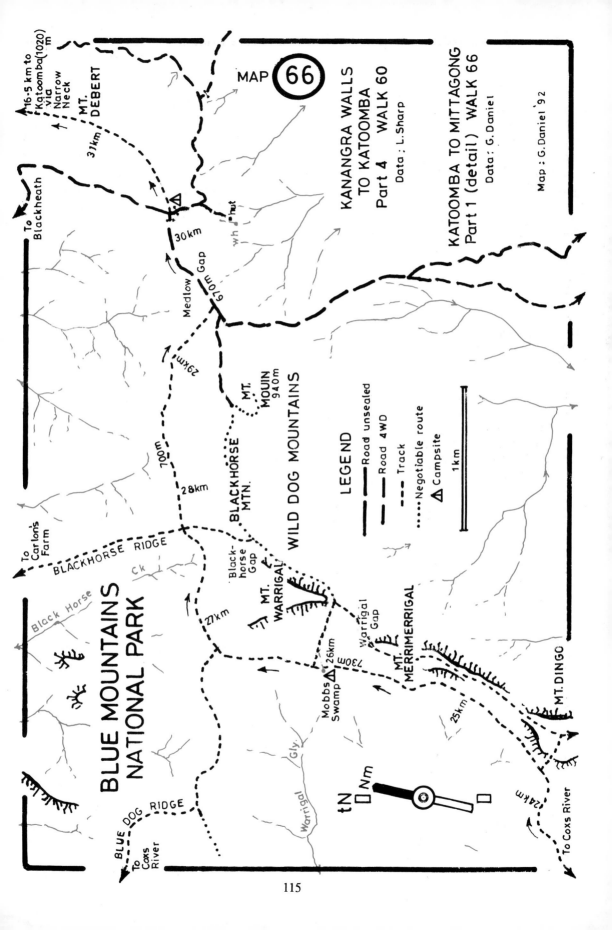

MAP 66

KANANGRA WALLS
TO KATOOMBA
Part 4   WALK 60

Data : L. Sharp

KATOOMBA TO MITTAGONG
Part 1 (detail) WALK 66

Map : G. Daniel '92   Data : G. Daniel

16·5 km to Katoomba (1020 m) via Narrow Neck

MT. DEBERT

31km

To Blackheath

30km

wh hut

Medlow Gap   610 m

29km

MT. MOUIN 940 m

BLACKHORSE MTN.

700 m

28km

WILD DOG MOUNTAINS

LEGEND
Road unsealed
Road 4WD
Track
Negotiable route
△ Campsite

1km

To Carlon's Farm

BLACKHORSE RIDGE

Ck

Blackhorse Gap

MT. WARRIGAL

27km

Black Horse

BLUE MOUNTAINS NATIONAL PARK

Warrigal Gap

Mobbs Swamp △ 730 M   26km

MT. MERRIMERRIGAL

25km

MT. DINGO

Gly.

Warrigal

N↑   Nm

BLUE DOG RIDGE

To Coxs River

24km

To Coxs River

115

spikes that extend for about 7m up the cliff wall) and walk further on around to the west and up a gully to Clear Hill (a few hundred metres) on Narrow Neck Road. You will be greeted with excellent views over Lake Burragorang, the Wild Dog Mountains, and the Kanangra area.

The total ascent from Medlow Gap to Clear Hill is about 370m. You will notice a plaque dedicated to Taro on the wall of a rock cleft between the ladder and Clear Hill.

Walk along the fire trail on the Narrow Neck peninsula to the car-park at the top of the Golden Stairs then continue on via Cliff Drive, Oak Street, Violet Street, Katoomba Falls Road and Katoomba Street to Katoomba station.

Grade: Day 1. Medium, 12km, 400m asc.
Day 2. Medium/Hard, 15km, 680m asc.
Day 3. Medium/Hard, 22km, 500m asc.
Total Distance: 49km.
Transport: Cales Car and Truck Hire, 163 Bathurst Road, Katoomba have 12-seater minibuses (which includes the driver) for hire. A class 1a license is required. The cost is $120/day or $60/half day plus fuel. The minibuses have adequate room for packs. Phone (047)82-2917. Cales can let you know how to arrange a driver. The cost is $50 for a half day or $15/hour - the return trip to Kanangra Walls takes four hours.
Best in Autumn and Spring.
Maps 63-66, 75 and CMA Kanangra, Jenolan, Jamison and Katoomba.

Richard Thompson and Len Sharp

BUSHLAND WEEDS
The following garden plants are some of the many that have the potential to become bushland weeds: Pampas Grass, Small-leaved Privet, Large-leaved Privet, Wandering Jew, Fishbone Fern, Asparagus Fern, Ochna, Cotoneaster and Lantana. The seeds and spores of these plants can be spread by birds, the wind and water. You can do your local bushland area a favour by removing such species from your garden and replacing them with endemic (local) species.

---

61. KANANGRA BOYD N.P.: BOSS PEAK - KOWMUNG RIVER - DINGO DELL - TUGLOW CAVES - KOWMUNG RIVER - BOSS PEAK - GILLESPIES LOOKOUT - BOX CREEK FALLS

The Boyd plateau area in Kanangra Boyd National Park contains the rugged Tuglow Caves limestone system, the magnificent Box Creek Falls and great camp-sites beside the upper Kowmung River. Note that whilst this walk takes you to Tuglow Caves, the cave entrances are barred by locked grilles. A permit, key, speleological experience and equipment are required for access. Include a light day pack for this walk.

To get to the walk starting point, take the Kanangra Walls Road at a "T" junction 5km past Jenolan Caves. At 18km from this intersection look for the signposted Kowmung River Fire Trail on the right. (If you miss it and arrive at the Boyd River camping area, you have come 5.5km too far).

The trail is negotiable for two-wheel drive vehicles as far as Boss Peak. At the start of the Kowmung Fire Trail set your trip meter to "O". After 4.5km, note but don't take the trail off to the right. A further 1km along, at a trail fork, take the right branch. Another 2km on, a rough road branches off to the right - Gillespies Lookout Road. Keep it in mind for the next day's part of the outing. A further 1.5km brings you to a sharp bend. A sign states "4WD from here on" as the trail drops steeply from here. There is ample parking space.

Walk down the fire trail for 1.5km and cross the Kowmung River at a ford to a camping area. Head on up the fire trail for 600m to a NP&WS sign-board where an old vehicle track branches off to the right to Tuglow Caves.

Leave your pack (and with a day-pack) continue SW along the fire trail for 1.9km past a private property access road on the right to Tuglow Hole Creek. Cross over to Dingo Dell - a large pleasant clearing/camping area. After exploring the area and a break return to the Tuglow Caves track junction at the sign-board and regain your pack.

Follow the old vehicle track which heads NNW over a small crest for 700m to Tuglow Caves. A track leads to a cave entrance a few metres to the north. Have lunch in the pleasant

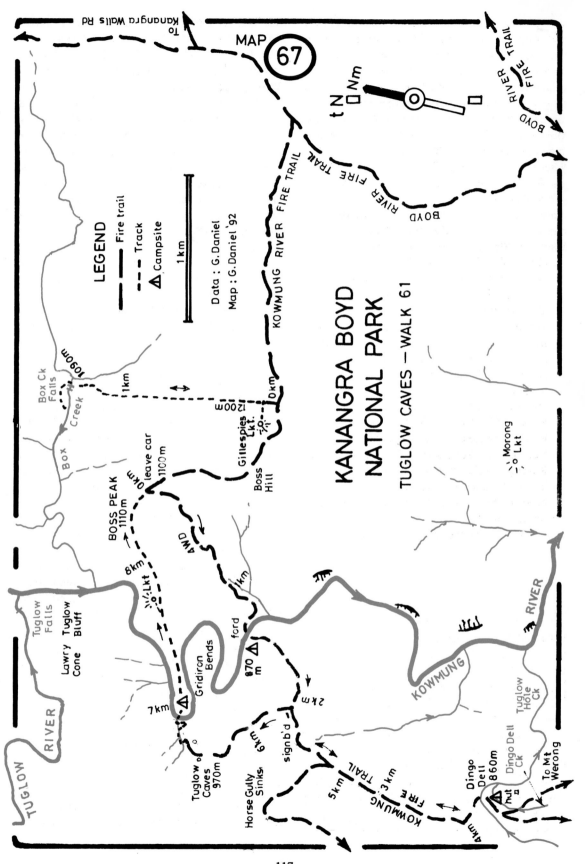

KANANGRA BOYD
NATIONAL PARK

TUGLOW CAVES — WALK 61

MAP 67

LEGEND
———— Fire trail
- - - - Track
△ Campsite

Data : G. Daniel
Map : G. Daniel '92

1 km

To Kanangra Walls Rd

BOYD RIVER FIRE TRAIL

KOWMUNG RIVER FIRE TRAIL

Box Ck Falls
Box Creek
1090m

1km

0km
Gillespies Lkt.
200m
Boss Hill

Morong Lkt

BOSS PEAK
1110m
leave car 1100m
0km
4WD
1km
8km
.'.'Lkt.
ford
870 m
2km
Gridiron Bends

Tuglow Falls
Lawry Tuglow
Cone Bluff

7km

Tuglow Caves 970m
Horse Gully Sinks
6km
sign'b'd
5km

KOWMUNG RIVER

KOWMUNG FIRE TRAIL
3km

Tuglow Hole Ck
Dingo Dell Ck
Dingo Dell 860m
Hut
To Mt Werong
4km

TUGLOW RIVER

117

surroundings here. After a good look around, take the track past the cave entrance down into the gully to the Kowmung River. The track is rough for the final descent to the river and can be very slippery.

Once at the river, the track runs beside it upstream for about 15m to a gravelly crossing place. Cross and head SE for about 50m to a good camp-site at the foot of the ridge from Boss Peak. Use Kowmung water (boiled) for the camp and next day's supply.

Next morning, head up the ridge towards Boss Peak via a well defined track. About halfway up there is a side-track which leads to a rock outcrop affording great views up the Kowmung toward the Box Creek/Kowmung junction and Tuglow Bluff. Return to the main track and climb steeply up to Boss Peak, which is only 200m from car.

Drive back 1.5km to Gillespies Lookout turn-off (mentioned earlier) and drive in approximately 20m to the trail end and park the car. A narrow track leads west for 50m to Gillespies Lookout. Take in the views from the rock outcrop and treat yourself to "high lunch".

After lunch return to the car, then take the faint track which heads north for 1.1km to the east of more rock outcrops, then bear NNE for 400m to Box Creek Falls. Cross the creek at a flat rocky area and scramble down below the falls for more spectacular views of the falls and the gully downstream. The pools below the falls are good for a dip.

Spend time exploring the falls area, before walking back along the track to the car.

Grade: Day 1. Easy/Medium, 7km, 200m ascent on fire trail and track (very rough in parts).

Day 2. Easy/Medium, 5km, 330m ascent on and off track (very rough in parts).

Total distance: 12km.

Best in Autumn and Spring. Watch for fire bans in Summer (Central Tablelands District) as the area may be closed. In Winter melted snow from Mount Werong and Shooters Hill may cause the Kowmung to flood.

No public transport.

Map 67 and CMA Shooters Hill plus Blue Mountains (Tourist) for road access.

George Daniel and Helen Fastovsky

62. KANANGRA BOYD N.P.: KANANGRA WALLS - BULLHEAD RIDGE MOUNTAIN - CAMBAGE SPIRE - KOWMUNG RIVER

On the 26th November, 1802, Ensign F. Barrallier's exploratory party camped at the junction of Kowmung River and Christys Ck. He was attempting to go as far west as possible and had come from Camden via Yerranderie, Byrnes Gap, Church Ck and the Kowmung River. Why did he turn up Christys Ck? Perhaps, because this was the first westward access from the Kowmung Valley he encountered, as he headed down river. Two days later, the party was forced to turn back at Johnston Falls on Wheengee Whungee Ck. This two-day walk takes you to the camp-site on the Kowmung in the rugged Kanangra wilderness.

This relatively short but physically demanding walk to the Kowmung River is recommended for experienced walkers only. Start by 9am and take water for the walk in. For directions to Kanangra Walls car-park, **see Walk 59.**

From the car-park, follow a path east to near Echo Head where there is a sign-board and track junction. Take the right track for the plateau walk down some steps then into Blacks Pass. At a track junction in the pass, take the left branch and climb up rough steps on to the Kanangra plateau. Follow the track along the top edge of the Walls. At several points there are fine views of Kanangra Gorge and Thurat Spires.

The plateau narrows 1.5km from the car-park where a relatively shallow valley comes in from the right (south). Just beyond this valley, as the track begins to ascend to Brennan Tops, there is a track junction which is partly obscured by heath.

Take the right branch which leads off through an area of bare rock and past a cairn in a SE direction. The track passes west of Maxwell Top. Just beyond, beware of a track on the left leading off to a lookout. The main track is well defined and crosses a narrow saddle, then ascends Murrarang Head where there are views south toward Mt Colong. Beyond Murrarang Top the track forks. Take the left fork which leads to a short rock scramble descent. Below the cliff and 50m E is the Coal Seam Cave. In the Coal Seam Cave there is a container usually filled with fresh water, which seeps from cracks in the cave roof.

Continue on the track as it descends SE for 200m to a track junction. The junction is difficult to see but is marked by a cairn. Take the right

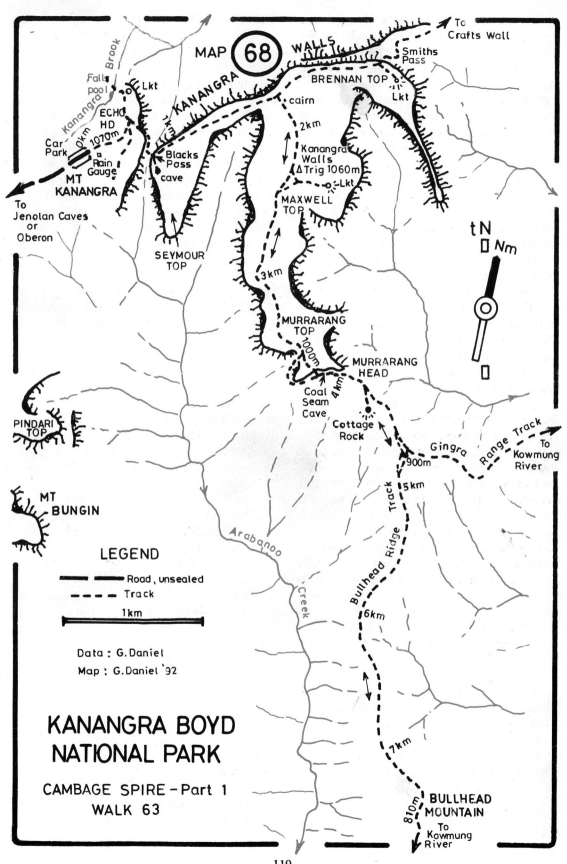

MAP **68**

To Crafts Wall

KANANGRA WALLS

Smiths Pass

BRENNAN TOP

Lkt

Falls pool
Lkt

Kanangra Brook

Falls Brook

ECHO HD 1070m

Car Park

0km

Rain Gauge

MT KANANGRA

To Jenolan Caves or Oberon

cairn

2km

Blacks Pass cave

Kanangra Walls △Trig 1060m

Lkt

SEYMOUR TOP

MAXWELL TOP

†N

☐ Nm

3km

MURRARANG TOP

1000m

MURRARANG HEAD

Coal Seam Cave

4km

Cottage Rock

900m

Gingra Range Track

To Kowmung River

PINDARI TOP

5km

Bullhead Ridge Track

6km

MT BUNGIN

Arabanoo Creek

LEGEND

──── Road, unsealed

- - - - Track

├───────┤ 1km

Data : G. Daniel

Map : G. Daniel '92

7km

KANANGRA BOYD NATIONAL PARK

CAMBAGE SPIRE – Part 1
WALK 63

810m

BULLHEAD MOUNTAIN

To Kowmung River

hand branch to Cottage Rock up a slight ridge. The track leads to the base of this rocky outcrop 5 mins away. A rock scramble then takes you to the top. The top of the rock is flat and offers superb views over the Kanangra area. From here, the path of the Kowmung River can be traced from Gingra Creek, up through Bulga Denis Canyon to the Christys Creek area. Scotts Main Range, Byrnes Gap and Yerranderie Peak can also be seen.

Return to the Gingra Track and about 400m on, locate a cairn and a track to the right which is Bullhead Junction. Follow the right-hand track which veers up a slight ridge to its high point which signifies the Bullhead Ridge start. The trees at this spot were felled to make an emergency helicopter landing pad.

Two tracks drop away from this cleared knoll, one from the middle (heading south) and one from the western end (also heading south). Both meet at about 100m along the ridge. Take either, continue along the sharp ridge on a fairly well defined track - it descends to a saddle which has a denser tree growth about 2km from Bullhead Junction. Care is required here as the track is poorly defined. If you lose it, keep bearing slightly west and stay on the high ground, till the ridge and track are again located. It climbs up to Bullhead Mountain. Near the summit, follow the track around the west side of the mountain to a grand lookout - just right for lunch. The outlook is to the south. The western face of Cambage Spire appears as a low conical hill in the foreground.

Now for the steep rocky bits. Follow the ridge track to the top of Cambage Spire and carefully descend. At a point where there is doubt about the route down, bear slightly east of south (till signs of previous walkers are found). Then at a point well down you come to the side of a sloping rock face with a narrow, steep, rough and rocky gully on each side. The nearer is safer (saves you having to go across the rock face by a rudimentary foot ledge). A tree trunk has conveniently become lodged in this nearer crevice which aids the descent. As a further aid lower backpacks with a rope (say 25mm circumference and 5m long).

Once down the worst bit, the going becomes only very steep and rough. The descent to the Kowmung from here follows a series of "steps" over about 1.5km with the route fairly obvious.

At the Kowmung "jelly legs", sore toes and knees may be evident. You should come out right at the Christys Creek junction. Cross Christys Ck (shin deep perhaps) and head south along the Kowmung for 50m to arrive at a fairly good camp-site. You should be there around 2.30pm. If you have time and energy you may wish to explore a little way up Christys Ck or along the Kowmung and reflect on Barrallier's effort.

You may also like to search for an old mine shaft. It is on the south side of Pippins Gully, which enters the Kowmung about 200m north of the Christys Junction on the same side. Look for the mine shaft 100m away from the Kowmung and about 10m above the river level. It may be overgrown.

Firewood is scarce at the camp-site, so bring a stove. Use water from Christys Ck (boiled).

If you like fishing, Rainbow Trout may be caught in the Kowmung right at the Christys Ck junction, and since they are introduced you will be doing the native species a favour.

The next day's climb out (via the same route) can be easily managed by taking a few breaks on the way up, say at the top of each "step". Have lunch at the same spot - on Bullhead Mountain. With an 8.30am start you should be back at the car-park by 3pm.

Grade: Day 1. Medium, 10.5km, 930m descent.
Day 2. Medium/Hard, 10.5km, 930m asc.
Very steep and rough in places (5m of rope useful in lowering packs down the rock fall of Cambage Spire.
Total Distance: 21km.
No Public Transport.Best in Autumn/Spring.
Maps 68,69 and CMA Kanangra and Yerranderie.   George Daniel

BUSH ROCK
Much bush rock for sale has been illegally procured from the natural public lands around Sydney. This illegal removal has had an enormous adverse environmental impact, resulting in loss of habitat for reptiles and invertebrates, altered fire regimes and vegetation loss. Boycott this product at all cost. Alternatives for landscaping include sleepers, treated pine logs and cut stone.

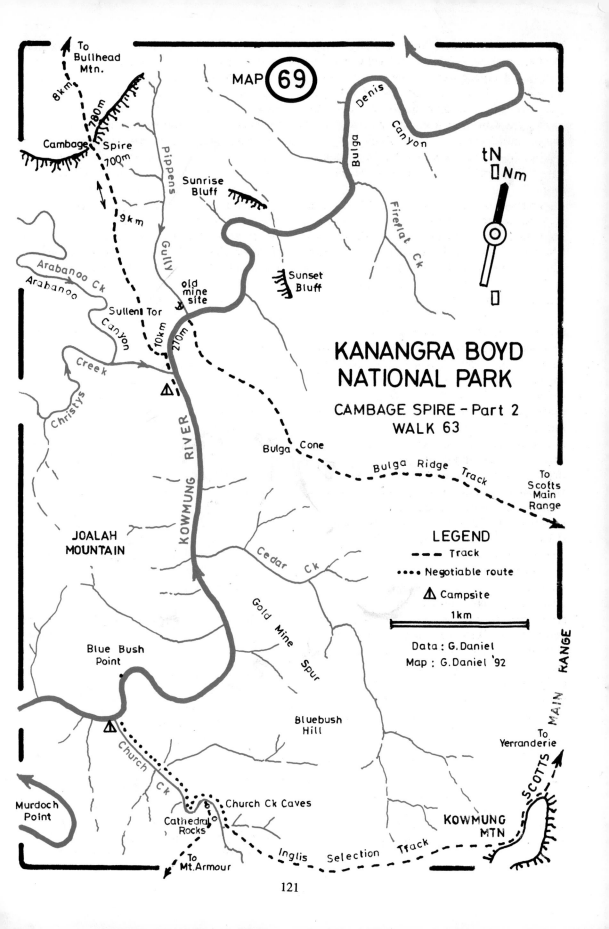

To Bullhead Mtn.

8km

780m

Cambage Spire 700m

700m

9km

Pippens

Gully

Sunrise Bluff

Arabanoo Ck

Arabanoo

Sullent Tor

Canyon

Christys

Creek

10km

old mine site

210m

Sunset Bluff

MAP 69

Bulga

Denis

Canyon

Fireflat Ck

tN
Nm

KANANGRA BOYD
NATIONAL PARK

CAMBAGE SPIRE – Part 2
WALK 63

Bulga Cone

Bulga Ridge Track

To Scotts Main Range

JOALAH
MOUNTAIN

KOWMUNG RIVER

Cedar Ck

Gold Mine Spur

LEGEND

– – – Track
. . . . Negotiable route
⚠ Campsite

1km

Data : G.Daniel
Map : G.Daniel '92

Blue Bush Point

Bluebush Hill

SCOTTS   MAIN   RANGE

Church Ck

To Yerranderie

Murdoch Point

Church Ck Caves

Cathedral Rocks

Inglis Selection Track

KOWMUNG MTN

To Mt.Armour

121

63. KANANGRA BOYD N.P.: KANANGRA WALLS ROAD - KOWMUNG RIVER VIA THE UNI ROVER TRAIL

After you have done some other walks in the Kanangra area (for experience), this long but pleasant two-day trip to the Kowmung River is suggested.

The starting point is near Kanangra Walls - 2km past the bridge and camp-sites at Boyd River crossing. (For directions to Boyd River Crossing **see Walk 61**).

Look for the fire trail off to the right just past a quarry on the left. Drive along the fire trail for 1.5km to a trail fork, clearing and sign-board. The sign-board reads "Uni Rover Trail to Kowmung River 18km". Leave your car here. An 8.30am start to the walk is suggested. The track was once marked with aluminium markers but only a few remain. However, the track is generally well defined.

The first few kilometres are along a partly overgrown timber-cutters vehicle track. This track bears SW then SSW. It continues as a well defined track past swamp areas to the first highlight of the trip, a prominent rock outcrop beside the track - Lost Rock. This is the suggested spot for morning tea. From here, there are extensive views over the Kanangra Wilderness including the Boyd Range - which is your way to the Kowmung River.

Press on past muddy Upper Wooglemai Creek then up Mt Goondel, 3.5km from the sign-board at the start. It is then a steady slog (generally down though) to Mt Savage - marked by a 60cm high cairn. Try to be here for lunch.

Continue on the track over Hobnail Hill and on to Mt Lannigan. Hereabouts the track gets a little thin, and is easy to lose, so check your direction with a compass. The bearing is generally SE. Stick with this bearing until the track becomes clearer again.

Soon after, you should arrive at Birdcall Lookout, where there are great views to the SW. Navigation is easier now - the route is down a narrow unambiguous ridge generally bearing south - Lannigans Spur. Follow this spur all the way to the river. Flat topped Mt Colong (pronounced Coolong) looms ahead most of the way. At about 300m from the river the track bears SE, (not south as shown on the Yerranderie topo).

You arrive near a sharp bend in the river where there are some of the best swimming holes on the Kowmung. You should arrive about 2.45pm. The water is good. Camp here on one of the numerous sandy camp-sites.

[The track continues on the northern side of the river for 300m upstream to a crossing point, where Lannigans Creek meets the Kowmung River - worth a look. The track on the other side of the river goes up Lannigans Creek to Colong Caves, 5km further on.]

Return the same way. Start early and take a few breaks going up Lannigans Spur. It is a long climb out. You will probably take an hour longer for the return trip. Have morning tea at Birdcall Lookout, lunch at Mt Savage and afternoon tea at Lost Rock.

Grade: Day 1. Medium. 18km, 920m descent on track.

Day 2. Medium/hard. 18km, 920m asc on track.

Total Distance: 36km.

Best in Autumn or Spring.

No Public Transport.

Maps   70-72   and   CMA   Kanangra, Yerranderie.

George Daniel and Helen Fastovsky

BACKPACKS:

For one day walks choose a daypack with a capacity of about 20 litres. You need space for a jumper, rainwear, water bottles, lunch, camera etc. Side pockets for water bottles (used frequently) are handy. A waist belt is a marginal advantage.

For two-day and longer walks a useful capacity is 65-70 litres. Internal frame jobs are best. Side pockets are handy for frequently used water bottles and/or a metho container (if carrying a stove). Side pockets of synthetic fabrics slip through scrub easily. A separate compartment for your sleeping bag and/or tent at the bottom is also handy. Look for a light weight nylon (water proofed) or part Cordura pack at about 1.0kg (an equivalent canvas or all Cordura pack could be 2.4kg).

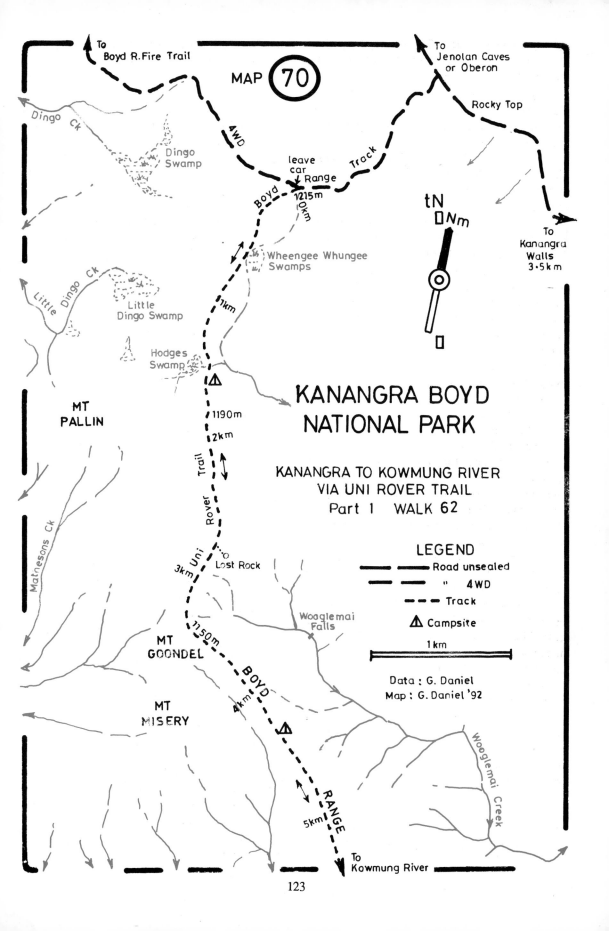

MAP 70

To Boyd R.Fire Trail

To Jenolan Caves or Oberon

Rocky Top

4WD Range Track

Boyd

Dingo Ck

Dingo Swamp

leave car
1215m
0km

tN
□Nm

□

To Kanangra Walls 3·5km

Wheengee Whungee Swamps

Little Dingo Ck

Little Dingo Swamp

1km

Hodges Swamp

⚠

MT PALLIN

1190m

2km

KANANGRA BOYD NATIONAL PARK

KANANGRA TO KOWMUNG RIVER VIA UNI ROVER TRAIL
Part 1   WALK 62

Uni Rover Trail

Lost Rock

3km

Woogiemai Falls

LEGEND
— — — Road unsealed
– – – "   4WD
- - - Track
⚠ Campsite

1km

Data : G. Daniel
Map : G. Daniel '92

MT GOONDEL

1150m

BOYD

MT MISERY

Mathesons Ck

4km

⚠

Woogiemai Creek

RANGE

5km

To Kowmung River

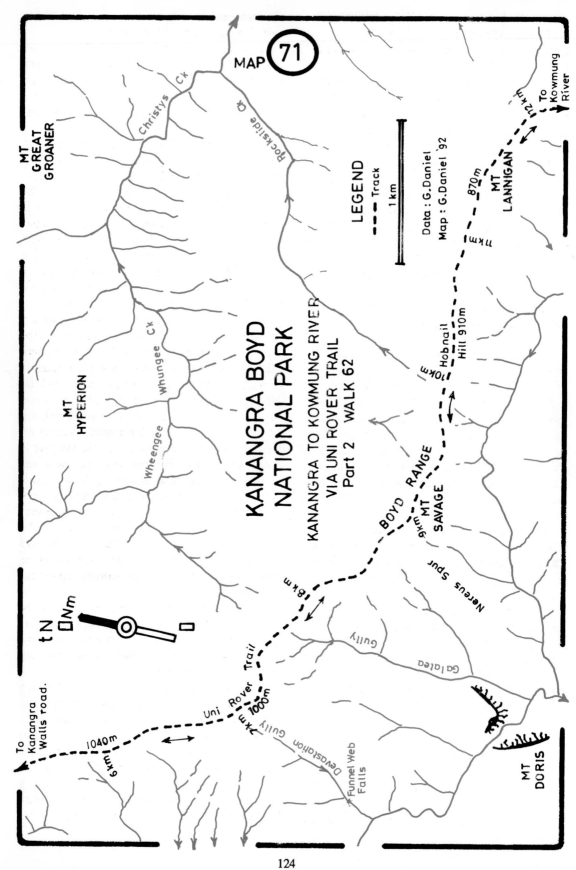

MAP **71**

MT GREAT GROANER

Christys Ck

Rockslide Ck

LEGEND

Track

1 km

Data : G.Daniel
Map : G.Daniel '92

To Kowmung River

12 km

MT LANNIGAN

870 m

11 km

Whungee Ck

MT HYPERION

Wheengee Ck

KANANGRA BOYD NATIONAL PARK

KANANGRA TO KOWMUNG RIVER
VIA UNI ROVER TRAIL
Part 2   WALK 62

Hobnail Hill 910 m

10 km

BOYD RANGE

MT SAVAGE

9 km

Nereus Spur

↑N
□Nm   □   □

8 km

Galatea Gully

Uni Rover Trail

To Kanangra Walls road.

1040 m

6 km

1000 m

7 km

Devastation Gully

Funnel Web Falls

MT DORIS

64. BLUE MTNS & KANANGRA BOYD N.Ps: BATSH CAMP - COLONG CAVES - LANNIGANS CREEK - KOWMUNG RIVER VIA THE UNI ROVER TRAIL

Colong Caves on Caves Creek is part of a rugged limestone karst area in the Middle Kowmung wilderness. It is a beautiful area - about as pristine and remote as you can get.

The Batsh Camp to Colong Caves and return section of this walk may be done as a one-day walk, however the complete two-day walk is recommended because of the long drive from Sydney (257km, 4.5hrs). By getting away early from Sydney, and starting off from Batsh Camp (also known as Bats Camp) at 10am you should reach Mossy Camp near the Kowmung River by 3pm. If travelling to Batsh Camp for the first time it is recommended that you don't drive there at night as the navigation is difficult. Leave the side-trips to Colong Caves and Mount Moogan for the return trip.

To reach Batsh Camp take the road from Oberon heading south at Ross St beside the Westpac Bank. Set the tripmeter to zero. At 0.4km turn left at a sign to Jenolan Caves - Kanangra Walls and Prison Camp. At 4.8km, turn right at a sign to Shooters Hill and Prison Camp. At 32.4km turn left off the Goulburn road onto a gravel road. This road goes to Mount Werong and Yerranderie. At 38km, at the Prison Camp turn off, keep left. At 42.2km, at a road junction (right to Goulburn), keep left.

The Batsh Camp sign is at 72 km. At the end of a prominent descent, just after a creek crossing (Back Swamps Creek) turn left and drive in 1.5 km. The camp-site is named after Batsch, a gold miner who worked the area. Park here.

From Batsh Camp, walk down the fire trail east for 300m to a sign-board indicating "Uni Rover Trail" on the left at a creek crossing. There is a 4WD barrier across the start of the trail. Cross the creek and follow this 4WD trail. After 1.8km, the track nears Mount Moogan. Then at 2.5km the trail ends on a small knoll.

The track down Acetylene Spur to Lannigans Creek starts off NE and is extremely steep toward the end. Limestone outcrops are visible on the way down.

At Lannigans Creek, turn left. If the creek is dry enough walk/rockhop along it. Lannigans Creek is especially beautiful. It is in pristine condition and has the usual trimmings of Hakea bush, lawyer vine and black snakes.

Take the side tracks around pools and other difficult spots. Have lunch at Carkeneller Creek junction (4.8km from the start). It comes in from the west. It is rocky and often dry, but there is a side track, which if taken, could cause you to miss sight of it.

Continue on for 3.2km to Mossy Camp, with good grassy, level camp-sites on both sides of the creek. Leave packs and walk downstream for five minutes around three slight bends to the Kowmung River. Collect water there if there is none near the camp (Lannigans Creek sometimes goes under rubble hereabouts though still flowing). At the Kowmung, note the track emerging from other side and see Lannigans Spur to the right - The Uni Rover Trail continues via it to Kanangra Walls (**see Walk 63**).

Next day, an 8.30am start is suggested. Return the same way along Lannigans Creek to the Acetylene Spur track junction. Leave packs here and walk upstream for 40m to a creek junction - Caves Creek on the left and Lannigans Creek on the right. Beware of stinging trees in areas adjacent to the creeks. Follow Caves Creek for 200m (4 mins) and look for a small clearing on the right. It has a fire place on it. (No camping is permitted in this limestone belt, i.e. near the caves). Take the track leading up to the caves entrance arch. The cave entrance has several large stalagmites (broken) and stalactites. A three metre lip bars the way into the cave but it can be circumvented by walking a little to the left. Do not go in beyond the daylight area as entry to the cave system requires a permit, suitable equipment and experience.

Several attempts have been made to mine the limestone at Colong Caves, but through the efforts of Conservation groups such as NPA, the cave system has remained un-mined and an important asset to the National Park.

Return to Lannigans Creek and on the way notice the water bubbling out through the limestone from the cave system at creek level. Walk back downstream and climb Acetylene Spur (270m), which takes about 45 minutes. Have lunch at the top where the track meets the fire trail.

On to the Mount Moogan diversion, starting 750m away at the nearest approach of the fire

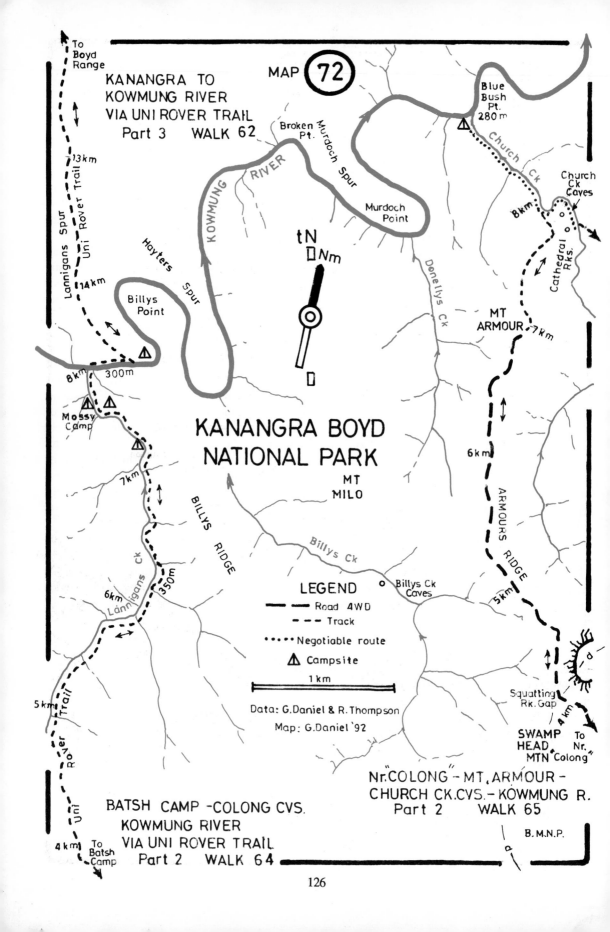

To
Boyd
Range

13km

Lannigans Spur

Uni Rover Trail

14km

KANANGRA TO
KOWMUNG RIVER
VIA UNI ROVER TRAIL
Part 3   WALK 62

MAP 72

Broken Pt.

Murdoch Spur

KOWMUNG RIVER

Murdoch Point

Blue Bush Pt. 280 m

Church Ck

8km

Church Ck Caves

Cathedral Rks.

Hayters Spur

Billys Point

tN
Nm

Donellys Ck

MT ARMOUR 7km

8km   300m

7km

Mossy Camp

KANANGRA BOYD
NATIONAL PARK

MT MILO

6km

ARMOURS RIDGE

BILLYS RIDGE

Lannigans Ck

350m

6km

Billys Ck

Billys Ck Caves

5km

LEGEND

───── Road 4WD
- - - - Track
• • • • Negotiable route
△ Campsite

|————| 1 km

Data: G.Daniel & R.Thompson
Map: G.Daniel '92

Squatting Rk. Gap

4 km

SWAMP HEAD MTN

To Nr. "Colong"

Nr."COLONG"- MT. ARMOUR -
CHURCH CK. CVS.- KOWMUNG R.
Part 2   WALK 65

B. M.N.P.

5 km

Uni Rover Trail

4 km To Batsh Camp

BATSH CAMP -COLONG CVS.
KOWMUNG RIVER
VIA UNI ROVER TRAIL
Part 2   WALK 64

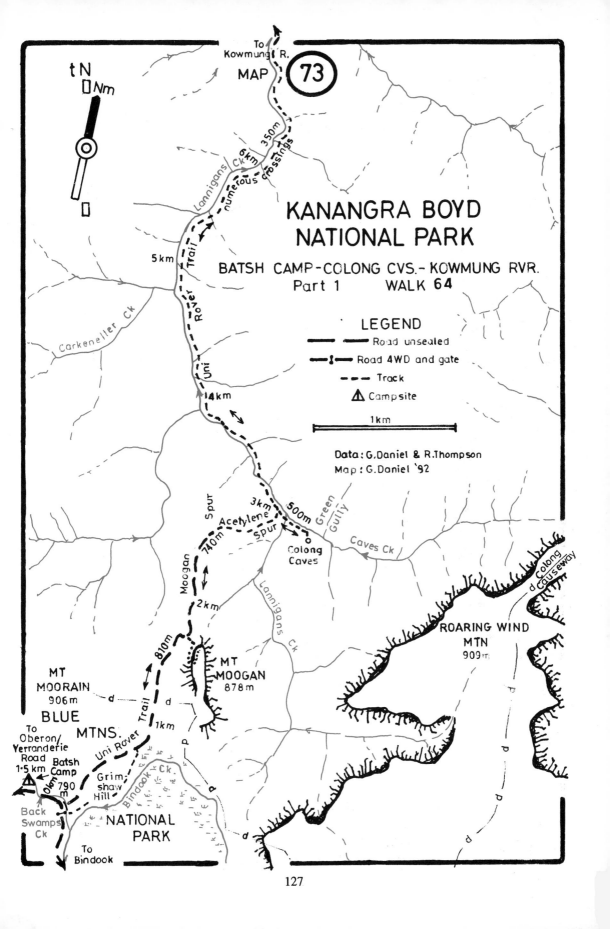

tN
◻ Nm

To
Kowmung R.
MAP (73)

350m
6km
numerous crossings
Lannigans Ck

KANANGRA BOYD
NATIONAL PARK

BATSH CAMP-COLONG CVS.- KOWMUNG RVR.
Part 1   WALK 64

5km
Uni Rover Trail
Carkeneller Ck

LEGEND
━━━━━━ Road unsealed
━┫━┫━ Road 4WD and gate
╴╴╴╴ Track
⚠ Campsite

14km

1km

Data: G. Daniel & R. Thompson
Map: G. Daniel '92

Spur
3km
Acetylene
Spur
500m
Green Gully
Caves Ck
740m
Moogan
Colong
Caves
2km
Lannigans Ck

ROARING WIND
MTN
909m
Colong Causeway

810m

MT
MOORAIN
906m   d
BLUE
MTNS.
To
Oberon/
Yerranderie
Road
1·5 km
Batsh
Camp
790m
Uni Rover Trail
1km
Grim
shaw
Hill
Bindook Ck
⚠
Back
Swamps
Ck
NATIONAL PARK
To
Bindook

MT
MOOGAN
878m

trail. Follow an indistinct track to the rock face, then contour around to the right about 150m where you will find an access ramp to the top. Once on top, follow the cliff edge around to a point above where the track meets the rock face. Landmarks visible include Crafts Wall and Kings Tableland. Return to the fire trail, turn west and retrace steps to Batsh Camp.

Grade: Day 1. Medium, 9km, 100m asc.

Day 2. Medium/Hard, 10km , 600m asc.

Total Distance: 19km.

Best in Autumn and Spring.

No public transport.

Maps 73,72 and CMA Bindook, Yerranderie.

Richard Thompson and George Daniel

65. BLUE MOUNTAINS N.P.:
OBERON STOCK ROUTE - MT ARMOUR - CHURCH CREEK - KOWMUNG RIVER

Compared with other routes, the walk to Kowmung River via Church Creek is comparatively easy. However, a long drive through Oberon and Mount Werong is required (5hrs from Sydney) including a considerable distance on gravel roads - very rough in places. The long drive allows a relatively easy walk to a beautiful remote area.

The start of the walk is reached by driving through Oberon and Shooters Hill following signs to Mount Werong and Yerranderie (**see Walk 64** for details). From the Batsh Camp turn-off, continue on along the Oberon Stock Route. After 2.5km at a road fork, bear left, then 10.4km further on after descending from Blackall Rocks ford the Jooriland River. Continue on a further 1.9km and ford Colong Creek.

Beyond Colong Creek (900m), turn left onto a fire trail not far from Colong Homestead ruins (15.7km from the Batsh Camp turn-off). Drive along for 2km to a trail junction and leave the car (a dwelling can be seen on the left across a ford).

Walk along the right branch trail NNW for 100m and pass through a locked gate. Follow the trail on the eastern side of the upper reaches of Colong Creek. Continue on a track via a bridge across Egans Swamp and pick up the trail on the other side. It follows the western side of the creek/swamp and eventually passes below Colong Point (4km from the start). After another 1km there is a trail junction. Keep on straight ahead

(WNW) - the right branch follows the Tonalli valley to Yerranderie. After 1km you reach a small clearing on the left near a swamp, which makes a pleasant spot for lunch.

After lunch, continue along the main trail. There are open views to the north towards Kanangra Walls. On the right look for the distinct feature of Chiddy Obelisk. At Mount Armour the road descends sharply to the right of the main ridge before ending abruptly. A track continues on, traversing back across the ridge-line before descending to a large clearing on Church Creek just downstream from a large limestone formation (karst). There are extensive limestone caves but these can only be entered with a permit (and experience).

No camping is permitted within the karst area itself. However, a short walk down Church Creek (often dry) leads to the Kowmung River and a superb camping site. The return trip is by the same route.

Grade: Day 1. Medium, 10km, 40m asc.

Day 2, Medium, 11km, 440m asc.

Total Distance: 20km (caves excursion 1km).

Best In Autumn and Spring.

No Public Transport.

Maps 74,72 and CMA Bindook, Yerranderie

Richard Thompson

TENTS

A good compromise for protection, weight, space and price is the two person, ridged, wall tent of rip-stop nylon with floor, insect screens and window (not recommended for snow country). Such tents weigh about 1.6kg and come with no fly. Substitute light weight poles and stakes (of aluminium alloy for those supplied). Rubber solution painted along stitching may be necessary.

By comparison high-tech tents may cost much more and weigh more.

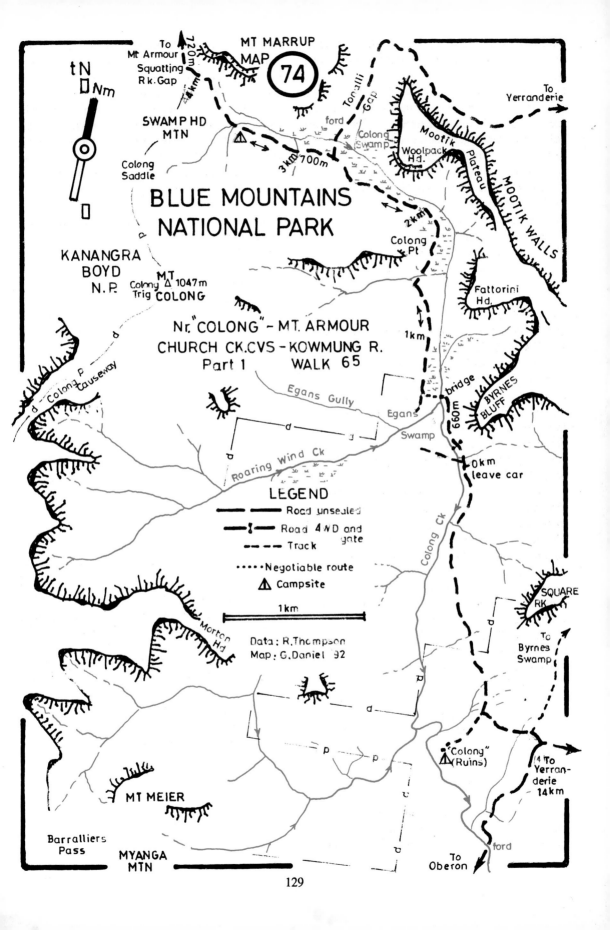

To Mt Armour
Squatting Rk.Gap

720m

To
Yerranderie

SWAMP HD
MTN

ford

Tonalli Gap

Colong Swamp

Mootik Hd.

Woolpack Hd.

Mootik Plateau

MOOTIK WALLS

Colong Saddle

3km 700m

BLUE MOUNTAINS
NATIONAL PARK

2km

Colong Pt

Fattorini Hd.

KANANGRA
BOYD
N.P.

MT
COLONG △ 1047m
Colong
Trig

1km

Nr."COLONG" - MT. ARMOUR
CHURCH CK.CVS - KOWMUNG R.
Part 1   WALK 65

Egans Gully

bridge

BYRNES BLUFF

Colong Causeway

Egans Swamp

660m

Roaring Wind Ck

0km
leave car

Colong Ck

LEGEND
━━━━ Road unsealed
━●━ Road 4WD and gate
━ ━ ━ Track
• • • • Negotiable route
⚠ Campsite

SQUARE RK

To
Byrnes Swamp

|—— 1km ——|

Data: R.Thompson
Map: G.Daniel '92

Morton Hd.

"Colong"
⚠(Ruins)

To
Yerran-
derie
14km

MT MEIER

Barralliers
Pass

MYANGA
MTN

ford

To
Oberon

66. BLUE MOUNTAINS AND NATTAI N.Ps.: KATOOMBA TO MITTAGONG VIA MOUNT COOKEM, SCOTTS MAIN RANGE, YERRANDERIE AND BELOON PASS

The classic walk from Katoomba to Mittagong is a great challenge. There are two major rivers to cross and gruelling climbs up Mt Cookem and Beloon Pass. The rewards, however, are great with panoramas and the experience of remoteness. **Clearly this walk is for experienced bushwalkers only, proficient in bush navigating.** The route does not require a Sydney Water permit, but before your intended trip, phone Sydney Water at Guildford (02)681-0345 to enquire as to the depth of the Coxs River at Kelpie Point - near the walk crossing point.

Day 1: Start off from Katoomba station. Make an early start. Walk (or catch a taxi) to the car-park above the Golden Stairs via Katoomba St, Katoomba Falls Rd, Cliff Drive, Violet St, Oak St, Cliff Drive (again) and Glenraphael Drive (the road along Narrow Neck). Continue along the gravel road and go around a gate 700m on.

After 8.3km from the start you reach Narrow Neck where there are interesting rock formations and great views over Megalong Valley. On Bushwalkers Hill pass a Fire Tower on the right and a rain gauge on the left at 12km. Look for Waratahs (in Spring) and Gang-gang Cockatoos. One km further on at a road bend (east to south) there is a blocked water pipe protruding from a soak. It is a few metres away from the left hand side of the road at a clearing with a camp-fire place. Collect 3 litres of water from the soak for the camp and next day's "march". At Clear Hill, after admiring the views, look for and take the track at the western side of road which goes down a ladder in a cleft heading south to the top of Taros Ladder. Spikes and rungs are your way down (about 8m) - not a "big deal" but if you have a rope (10m of clothes line cord will do) you could lower your pack down with it.

Once down, follow the track along Little Cedar Gap and over Mount Debert to Medlow Gap (2.5km) - where there is a 3-way service road junction, a helipad, a sign-board and a water-hole (often dry). You have come 17.4km. Camp here.

Day 2: Aim for a 7am start. Head off west. Go around a gate and along a service road toward Kelpie Point. Note a fork in the road at 19.5km - keep left. At 22.5km, at a slight bend in the road (Jamison 463495) there is a cairn marking a track on the left side of the road, slightly down from the roadside. Take this track down to the Coxs River.

You are now going through a Sydney Water "corridor" in which no camping is allowed. The usual depth of the Coxs River at the crossing point is about 0.6m (do not try to cross if more than 1m deep). The river here has a rocky bottom, which is usually slippery. Wear Volleys or joggers and take a pole to assist balance. [Remember to undo the buckles of your pack before crossing].

Once across, follow the eastern bank in a northerly direction to where the river bends to the east. At the most northerly point of this river bend (Jamison 471499) - look for an old Water Board sign on a tree. Behind this tree, the track winds up a spur to Mt Cookem which should take about 1.5 hours to climb. A cairn marks the place where the track meets a road - there are great views nearby from the cliff edge (if you can still stand). Continue on the road which leads to Yerranderie via Scotts Main Range. [The suggested water collection spot along Scotts Main Range is at New Yards, but the location of 13 man-made water-holes is also provided for emergency use, but boil the water first. These water-hole locations also assist with position fixing].

At 28.2km, you pass within 100m of Kowmung Lookout, however there is no track to it. Next at 29.3km, note road (with gate) branching off east. Further along at 32.2km, the Old Cedar Road branches off east and 200m further still, there is a house ruin on the right.

The first of the 13 water-holes on Scotts Main Range appears at 32.8km on the western side of the road. Water-hole No.2 is also on the western side of road at 34.4km. A turn-off, 200m on, leads to New Yards (a Church owned property). Seek permission to obtain water from their tanks 300m in from the Scotts Main Range road. Carry enough water (3 litres per person) for the camp 5.4km further on and the walk the next day. Pass No.3 water-hole at 37.5km (eastern side) and No. 4 at 39.4km (western side).

At 39.7km, divert 300m from Scotts Main Range Road via a western branch road to Bran Jan house ruin - named after an aborigine who lived there [This road continues on to the Kowmung River]. Camp at the Bran Jan house ruin near a road junction. There are camp-sites

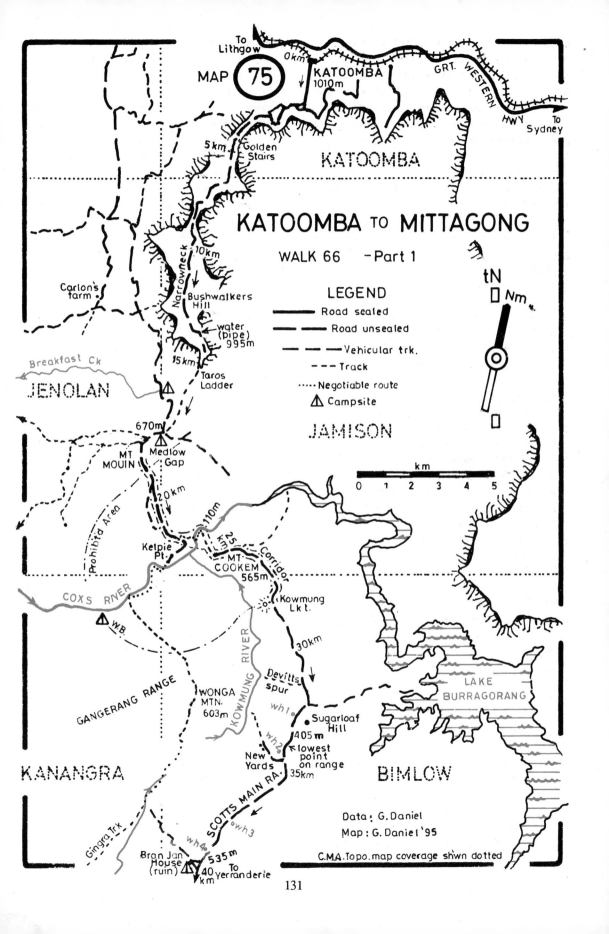

MAP **75**

To Lithgow   0km   KATOOMBA
1010m   GRT. WESTERN HWY   To Sydney

KATOOMBA

5km   Golden Stairs

KATOOMBA TO MITTAGONG

WALK 66   – Part 1

LEGEND
— Road sealed
– – Road unsealed
– · – Vehicular trk.
- - - Track
·········· Negotiable route
⚠ Campsite

tN
Nm

Carlon's farm

Narrowneck

10km   Bushwalkers Hill

water (pipe) 995m

15km

Taros Ladder

Breakfast Ck

JENOLAN   ⚠

JAMISON

km
0 1 2 3 4 5

670m   ⚠

MT MOUIN   Medlow Gap

20km

110m

Kelpie Pt.

25km

MT COOKEM 565m   Corridor

Prohibited Area

Kowmung Lkt.

COXS RIVER   ⚠ W.B.

30km

GANGERANG RANGE

KOWMUNG RIVER

WONGA MTN. 603m

Devitts spur   LAKE BURRAGORANG

wh1   Sugarloaf Hill 405m

wh2   lowest point on range

New Yards   35km

KANANGRA   SCOTTS MAIN RA.   BIMLOW

wh3

wh4

Gingra Trk.

Bran Jan House (ruin)   ⚠ 535m   40km   To Yerranderie

Data: G.Daniel
Map: G.Daniel '95
C.M.A.Topo.map coverage sh'wn dotted

along the road side if you do not make Bran Jan by nightfall.

Day 3: Even though this is a relatively easy day, a 7am start is suggested. Return to the Scotts Main Range Road via the road that heads SE. Spot water-hole No.5 at 41.1km and No. 6 at 44km, both on the eastern side.

If you are doing the walk in Spring, fields of different coloured flowers make welcome sights. Just past Bull Island Saddle at 49.5km is water-hole No.7 on the northern side. Soon after, at 49.9km is a rain gauge on the southern side of the road. Water-hole No.8 pin-points you at 51.2km. Then at 51.7km you are on Mt Feld (no sign-board). Just past the turn off to Denis Ridge, there is a grassy area with shady trees on the western side of the road which makes a good lunch spot. Water-hole No.9 rises out of the haze at 52.7km on the southern side. At 55km, a track branches off on the western side which leads down Bulga Ridge to the Kowmung River. Water-hole No. 10 is on the eastern side at this point. Then just as you are dozing off you come to a sharp bend in the road at 56.6km. The direction change is from south to east. At this bend on the southern side is the Inglis Selection track to Church Creek Caves - press on. Cross Butchers Creek (a few centimetres deep) at 58km. Good water.

It all starts to happen now. Water-hole No.11 is at 58.5km (northern side) and water-hole No.12 at 60km (on southern side). Byrnes Gap appears at 60.1km with imposing Gander Head NE and Rodwell Head SW. There is a house with water tanks here. Water-hole No.13 is at 60.4km on the eastern side. Yerranderie beckons - do not run. Its peak looms ahead. Just before you cross the Tonalli River look for a "common" on the eastern side - a large grassy area with a rock pile at one side. This is often populated by hundreds of kangaroos. The Tonalli River crossing is at 63.7km (a few cm deep) - note a camp-site on the western side, via a short vehicle track in - although it is suggested you press on up the hill to Yerranderie. See the old post office (now a guest lodge). Val Lhuede (pronounced Loo-ee-dee) owns Yerranderie and has a phone. An aircraft can be arranged if you need to fly out to Camden or Katoomba (total cost is about $65). Enquire at the Guest Lodge.

Yerranderie Peak lies to the south - walk on up the hill further, then cross the airstrip via a road to an excellent grassy camping area at the rear of the Old Court House. Grassy areas, good shade trees, tank water and toilets are available here. With a 7am start you could expect to arrive here at 3pm.

Day 4: Get another early start (7am). Leave Yerranderie and head east across Basin Creek at 68.7km. Then at old Twin Peaks (69.6km) note turn off to the south at a gate which is the stock route road to Oberon. Press on east - ignore a minor road turn off to the north at 71.7km. A Water Board locked gate has to be negotiated at 73.4km. Wind down the long road, ignore minor turn offs at 75.1km and 76.2km. You are on the Sheepwalk Drive. There is a good morning tea break spot at Byrnes Creek. Next, note a side road with a gate on the right at 77.9km. Then at 78.8km at the end of a "straight", look for and take an insignificant vehicle track to the left at a quarry. There are spectacular views of the upper Burragorang Valley from further along this track and you can see to the east a gap in the cliffs of the Wanganderry Tableland - Beloon Pass. The track winds down SE, across the Jooriland River (usually a few cm deep) to the Wollondilly River.

The Wollondilly is usually 0.5m deep here. It is rocky and slippery. Take a pole and wear Volleys or joggers. Follow the road on the other side, NE, SE and then NE to a minor vehicle track heading east, signposted Beloon Pass (GR Nattai 529131) at 84.9km. Take it and at another minor junction just after a creek crossing (at 85.2km), take the northern trail. It climbs gradually for 500m to a sharp bend where the road changes direction from ENE to north, where there is a second sign indicating Beloon Pass (GR Nattai 536133). Leave the fire trail here and follow the faint track heading ESE, cross a minor gully, then continue on along an even fainter track up a ridgeline towards the cliff and Beloon Pass. The ascent of 590m is rocky, very rough and steep. In general, the route follows a "ridge" and there are a few markers along the way. There are great views of the upper Wollondilly from the top.

After a break, take the track which heads east to a usually dry water course. Follow it via a track on its right hand side to where another dry watercourse joins from the north. Turn east down along the watercourse. Collect water from a rock hole 50m down from the watercourse junction, 3L per person. Soon after, the track re-commences on the northern side of Travis Gully. Follow it down

KANANGRA

Gingra Trk

KANANGRA
BOYD
NATIONAL
PARK

Roots
Rdg

Denis Rdg

BLUE
MOUNTAINS
NATIONAL
PARK

SCOTS MAIN RANGE

Bull T. Saddle

wh7
wh8

50 km rain gge

MT FELD
650m

wh9

Bulga
Rdg
55km wh10
       692m

Inglis Selection Trk

560m wh11

wh12 Byrnes Gap
60km wh13
      624m

539m

65km 614m

YERRANDERIE

440m

70km

BLUE
MOUNTAINS
NATIONAL
PARK

To
Oberon

BINDOOK

JOORILAND

C.M.A. Topo. map coverage
shown dotted.

To
Kowmung
River
Bran Jan
House (ruin)

535m
40km

To Mt Cookem

wh5

wh6

45km

Butchers   Ck

BLUE
BREAKS

TONALLI RIVER

Basin   Ck

tN
□ Nm
□

gate

75km 1,160m

270m

Corridor

80km

110m

RIVER
RIVER

WOLLONDILLY

To
Bonnum Pic

MAP 76

KATOOMBA to MITTAGONG

WALK 66 - Part 2

LEGEND

——————— Road unsealed
— — — — Vehicular trk
- - - - - Track
········· Negotiable route
△ Campsite

km
0 1 2 3 4 5

Data: G.Daniel
Map: G.Daniel '95

BIMLOW

LAKE
BURRAGORANG

NATTAI

Beloon
Pass
600m

85km

Vineyard
Flat

140m
90km

Colleys
Flat

To
Mittagong

133

to join an old vehicle track, then continue on to Vineyard Flat at 89.8km - the overnight campsite. Nattai River water should be avoided.

Day 5: Once again, start off by 7am. Follow the vehicle track south from Vineyard Flat, cross the Nattai River, then again at 90.7km and at 91.7km. It is great walking here, and it is soft underfoot too. There are views of West and East Nattai Walls (sandstone cliffs). Cross again at 92.9km and 93.6km. You may find the ruins of a shack on a grassy flat opposite Allum Flat. Follow the fire trail heading SE for 2km past a private access road on the right then after another 600m there is a yellow arrow marker indicating where you turn off the fire trail. [From this point to Mittagong, markers are blue]. Follow the very old vehicle track towards the Nattai River. Where the trail becomes indistinct at a swampy area head towards the southern bank of the Nattai and follow a rock ledge until the trail picks up again.

Follow the river past Round Flat and continue on, crossing the river three times. The track then leaves the western side of the Nattai at 101.3km and crosses a dry swamp basin to the west of a large hill, suitable for a lunch break, before rejoining the Nattai after crossing Wanganderry Creek, which comes in from the south. The Nattai turns from a westerly to northerly flow here. On the southern side of the river make your way along a track, then a dry river bed. Cross the river to Emmetts Flat and a ruin. After 500m there is a good picnic/camp-site opposite Macarthurs Flat, where the river again changes direction from north to west. (Starlights Track joins here). Continue on the eastern side of the river along a marked trail toward Rocky Water-holes Creek. Where markers disappear, stay close to the river. After 4.5km from opposite Macarthurs Flat look for Rocky Water-holes Creek entering from the east. It is indistinct. If you find it, collect water for the camp. Cross the Nattai River to its western side and look for a camp-site. Water is also available from Needle Creek, which comes in from the west, about 1km further up the Nattai.

Day 6: Get an early start (7am yet again) - follow the marked track toward Mittagong. This involves five crossings before Jellore Creek, which comes in from the west at 111.5km. You then cross the Nattai six more times to Flora Gully at 114.8km. Stockyards Creek comes in from the east at 115.3km. From the eastern side of the river, the marked track heads SE up to an old road. Have lunch under the trees here. Follow this road south for 1.4km to Drapers Creek (ignore two branch trails to the right). [Drapers Creek is the last camp-site before Mittagong.]

Go past a camp-site, then at a bend in the trail in a clearing, find the marked track which heads off SE up over a spur, then about 500m further on you pick up an old road. Continue on this road a further 500m, then take some indistinct earthen steps on the right side of the road down to the Nattai. Follow the marked track beside the Nattai then cross to the western side near Box Vale Creek. Recross to the northern side, cross Box Vale Creek, round the Box Vale Spur, then cross to the western side. Continue on to Nattai Creek junction. Cross Nattai Creek, then at a track junction, there are markers indicating the way to 40 Foot Falls and the Box Vale Track. Keep on SE following the Nattai along the track, and cross Gibbergunyah Creek, then walk up the steep embankment of the Mittagong by-pass. Turn right and go under the bridge over Gibbergunyah Creek and follow a fire trail SSE for 800m and cross over a tributary of Gibbergunyah Creek. Immediately after, turn left and follow a track for 500m to where it meets a fire trail. Turn left for 400m, then take a track branching off to the right heading SSW to Lake Alexandra via a wooden bridge. From the southern tip of Lake Alexandra follow Queen St to the Hume Highway. Cross over to the Clock Tower. The lane opposite takes you to the station. If all goes well, you could expect to be at Mittagong station by 6pm.

If you miss the last train for the day, camp the night at the Caravan Park 1.4km NE along the Hume Highway near the swimming pool.

Grade: Day 1. Easy/Med, 18km, 340m desc.
Day 2. Medium, 23km, 585m asc.
Day 3. Medium, 26km, 296m asc.
Day 4. Medium/Hard, 24km, 600m asc.
Day 5. Easy/Medium, 18km, 90m asc.
Day 6. Medium, 22km, 380m asc.
Total distance: 132km.
Best in Autumn and Spring. Winter day light hours too few.
Public Transport: Train to Katoomba and from Mittagong.
Maps 75-78, 60, 66 and CMA Jamison, Bimlow, Yerranderie, Nattai, Hilltop and Mittagong.   George Daniel

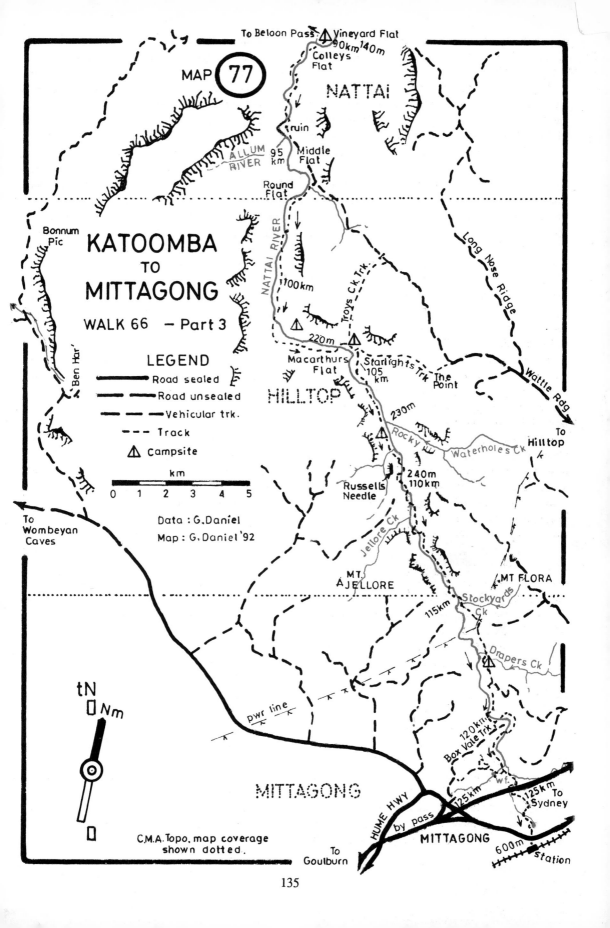

MAP 77

To Beloon Pass ⚠ Vineyard Flat
90km 140m
Colleys
Flat

NATTAI

ruin

95 km   Middle Flat

ALLUM RIVER

Round Flat

KATOOMBA
TO
MITTAGONG

WALK 66 — Part 3

LEGEND

——— Road sealed
– – – Road unsealed
- - - Vehicular trk.
· · · Track
⚠ Campsite

km
0 1 2 3 4 5

Data : G. Daniel
Map : G. Daniel '92

Bonnum Pic

Ben Har'

NATTAI RIVER

100km

⚠

220m   ⚠

Troys Ck Trk.

Macarthurs Flat

Starlights Trk
105 km   The Point

HILLTOP

230m

Rocky Ck

Waterholes Ck

To Hilltop

Wattle Rdg

Long Nose Ridge

To Wombeyan Caves

⚠ 240m
110km

Russells Needle

Jellore Ck

MT. JELLORE

MT FLORA

Stockyards Ck

115km

Drapers Ck

⚠

tN
□ Nm
◎
□

pwr line

MITTAGONG

120km
Box Vale Trk.

125km
To Sydney

w.f.

HUME HWY
by pass

125km

MITTAGONG

600m station

C.M.A. Topo. map coverage
shown dotted.

To Goulburn

135

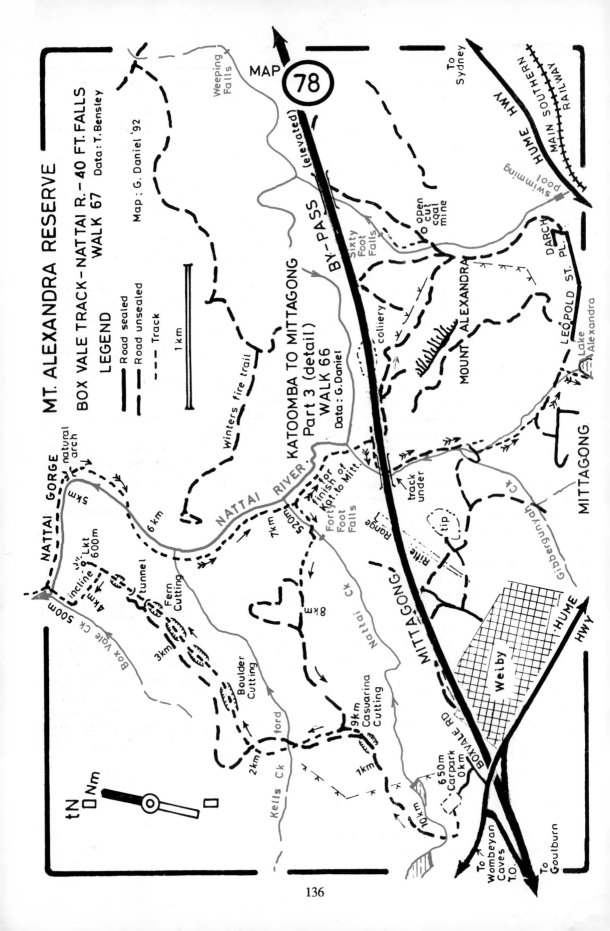

MT. ALEXANDRA RESERVE

BOX VALE TRACK – NATTAI R. – 40 FT. FALLS
WALK 67   Data: T. Bensley

Map: G. Daniel '92

LEGEND

—— Road sealed
━ ━ Road unsealed
- - - Track

1 km

KATOOMBA TO MITTAGONG
Part 3 (detail)
WALK 66   Data: G. Daniel

MAP 78

To Sydney

HUME HWY

MAIN SOUTHERN RAILWAY

swimming pool

open cut coal mine

Sixty Foot Falls

BY-PASS (elevated)

colliery

MOUNT ALEXANDRA

LEOPOLD ST. PL.

DARCH

Lake Alexandra

MITTAGONG

Weeping Falls

Winters fire trail

NATTAI GORGE

natural arch

5km

Lkt 600m

tunnel

incline

Fern Cutting

6 km

7 km

520m

Finish for Kat. to Mitt.
Forty Foot Falls

Range

track under

tip

Rifle

Gibbergunyah Ck

MITTAGONG

Box Vale Ck 500m

4km

3km

Boulder Cutting

ford

2km

Kells Ck

8 km

Nattai Ck

Casuarina Cutting
9 km

1km

10km

650m
Carpark 0km

BOXVALE RD

Welby

HUME HWY

To Wombeyan Caves T.O.

To Goulburn

NATTAI RIVER

Nm
†N

136

SOUTH-WEST SECTOR

67. MT ALEXANDRA RESERVE: BOX VALE TRACK - NATTAI RIVER - 40 FOOT FALLS

The Box Vale Railway was built in 1888 to transport coal from the mine on Box Vale Creek to the Southern Railway Line just south of Mittagong. The mine operated until 1896 during which time about 1000 tons of coal per annum was mined.

This walk incorporates the Box Vale Walking Track along the railway formation from the Old Hume Highway to a lookout over the Nattai River. The walk also includes a return loop, which is rough in places and involves river crossings, along a section of the Nattai River.

From Sydney, leave the F5 freeway at the Mittagong exit (Aylmerton interchange). Travel through Mittagong and at the town centre (clock tower), veer right along the old Hume Highway toward Berrima and Goulburn. Pass under the Mittagong by-pass, then immediately turn right into Box Vale Road. A sign indicates the Box Vale Track. There is a parking area with good water and toilets at the trackhead, 200m in off the Hume Highway.

Head off WSW along the Box Vale Track. Cross Nattai Creek and as the track rises, note a large dam from vantage points beside the track. Continue on through Casuarina Cutting then note the fire trail branching off to the right (which is the return route from 40 Foot Falls). The track crosses Kells Creek then passes through Boulder and Fern Cuttings (with abundant beautiful tree ferns), through a tunnel, then on for 500m to a lookout which provides extensive views of rugged mountainous country along the Nattai Valley.

Walk back about 100m to the signposted "Box Cart loading area". Look for a packed rock "incline" construction indicated by a yellow marker on the western side of the trail. The incline drops 160m to Box Vale Creek, a tributary of the Nattai. This incline is steep and care should be taken when descending on the loose surface. At the bottom, note the basalt creek bed.

Take the track on the eastern side of the creek for about 100m to the Nattai River. Do not drink water from the Nattai - it is heavily polluted by a garbage tip, Mittagong sewage treatment works and effluent from a mushroom farm.

Cross over the Nattai River at the Box Vale Creek junction (yellow marker) and walk upstream on the northern bank. There are blue markers which indicate the Mittagong to Katoomba route. At a river bend, the track goes through a beautiful natural arch which has formed in a large sandstone rock. Cross the river about 500m on and proceed on the western bank. Cross Kells Creek and walk for another 1km to Nattai Creek. Turn right up Nattai Creek on the eastern bank (yellow marker) and follow the track (which crosses the creek on rock platforms) to the 40 Foot Falls track junction at a large ant hill. Walk to the falls and scramble into a large cool cave behind the waterfall.

Return to the main track. The track from here is well marked and constructed. It leads up via a steel ladder and steps to a fire trail. Walk west along the trail for 1.1km to a picnic table, then turn left back along the Box Vale Track to the car-park.

Grade: Medium, 160m asc.

Distance: 10km.

Suitable all seasons but best in Spring.

No public transport.

Map 78 and CMA Mittagong.

Brochure: Dept of Lands "Box Vale Walking Track" available at the Mittagong Tourist Office.

Trevor Bensley

Box Vale Track .... Editors' Note

The Mt Alexandra Reserve of 1000 hectares, NW of Mittagong, was dedicated in 1984. Following a public meeting, a committee was formed to oversee the construction of the Box Vale Track. Trevor Bensley was elected Chairman. Trevor was principal of Toombong Special School for State Wards and Juvenile Offenders. His pupils assisted in building the track over a two-year period.

68. BUNGONIA S.R.A. AND MORTON N.P.: BUNGONIA LOOKDOWN - MT AYRE - SHOALHAVEN RIVER - BUNGONIA GORGE - BARBERS CREEK

On the edge of the Ettrema wilderness is Bungonia Gorge - the deepest limestone gorge in Australia. This two-day walk takes you into this remarkable canyon, and along a pleasant stretch of the Shoalhaven River to a good camp-site near Barbers Creek at the base of Long Point. There are great spots for swimming in the Shoalhaven River at many points along the way.

The trip from Sydney to Bungonia SRA (the walk starting point) takes about 3hrs (190km). Turn left off the Hume Highway at South Marulan and drive to the small town of Bungonia then on to the SRA. At Bungonia SRA there is a pleasant camping area with showers, toilets and a communal kitchen. It is situated on a plateau above the Shoalhaven River and contains many interesting short walks to lookouts and limestone caves.

On arrival, register at the Ranger's Office, pay the entry fee and lodge your walk plan. Leave your car at the adjacent car-park (as the security here is better than at the lookdown car-park).

Walk NE for 1.7km along the road to Bungonia Lookdown. The Lookdown faces due north over the Marulan limestone mining operation on the other side of Bungonia Creek - try imagining how the view was before quarrying began. You can also see where your walk will take you along the Shoalhaven.

The track down to the river heads SE from the Lookdown and is signposted. The route is via Mt Ayre (white markers). The red trail is shorter and steeper but is dangerous due to falling rocks. Warning signs are at track junctions. It is 900m to Mt Ayre, then 1.1km to another excellent lookout which gives great views down the Shoalhaven valley. From here the track descends steeply to the river. The track leads over a small knoll near the end of the descent above the confluence of Bungonia Creek and the Shoalhaven River. Turn left and head up Bungonia Creek for about 200m, where you will find a suitable grassy spot for a lunch break.

After lunch leave packs and follow the track on the northern side of the creek upstream. There are signs warning of danger from rocks falling from blasting operations at the quarry above.

Blasting times (not weekends) and warning signals are specified.

After 2.7km from the Shoalhaven you reach the boulders of the "block-up". Pick your way around, over or under the boulders to a relatively flat part of the canyon floor. Take a break - you may see a Lyrebird in flight or rock climbers on the canyon walks.

Return along Bungonia Creek, regain packs, then take the track on the western side of the Shoalhaven. The track follows the river downstream but moves away from the bank on occasions to avoid Casuarina thickets. Just before Barbers Creek, the track moves up several metres off the flat then crosses Barbers Creek. Collect water for the night's camp and the next day's walk, then follow the track past a turn-off on the left which leads up Long Point to King Pin Mountain and Long Point Lookout. Continue on to the good camp-sites beside the Shoalhaven at the base of Kin Pin Mountain - where the river course changes from north to NW.

Next morning leave packs and walk downstream by the river to where the river starts to curve around Rainbow Ridge. Grassy flats provide pleasant walking for about 1km from the camp-site.

Regain packs and head back towards Bungonia Creek, then take the track back up to Bungonia Lookdown via Mt Ayre. Have lunch at the lookout near the top on the way. Finally, walk back the 1.7km to the car.

Grade: Day 1. Medium/Hard, 13km, 90m ascent, with steep grades and very rough walking in the canyon.

Day 2. Medium, 10km, 460m ascent, steep grades.

Total Distance: 23km.

Suits all seasons.   No public transport

Map 79 and CMA Caoura.

George Daniel and Pam Robinson

NPA WALKS PROGRAM
NPA provides a regular walks program for its members. Over 400 walks are available in the Sydney region each year. They range from easy one day strolls to week-long wilderness walks. Many walks are suitable for family groups.

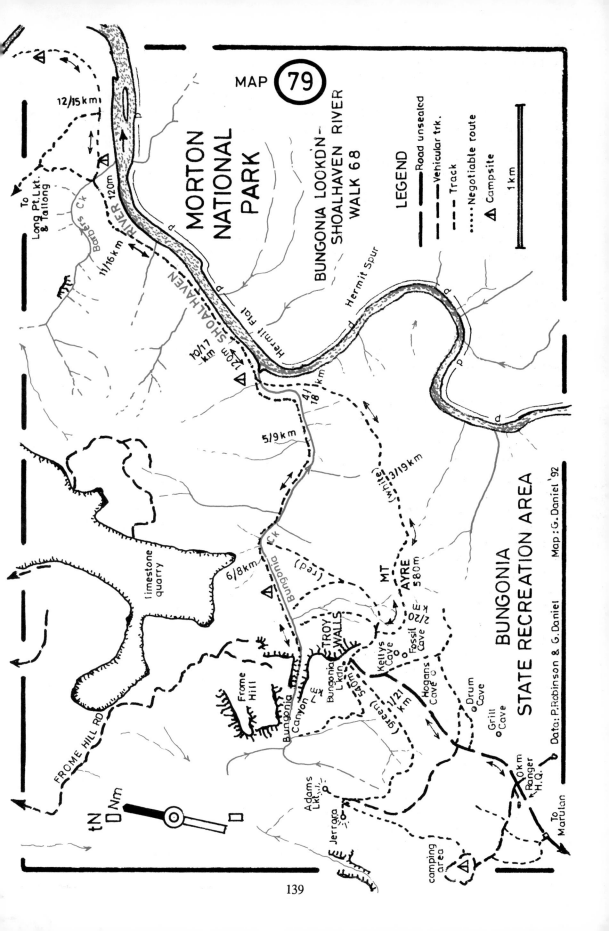

MAP 79

MORTON NATIONAL PARK

BUNGONIA LOOKD'N–
SHOALHAVEN RIVER
WALK 68

LEGEND

Road unsealed
Vehicular trk.
Track
Negotiable route
△ Campsite

1 km

BUNGONIA
STATE RECREATION AREA

Data: P. Robinson & G. Daniel   Map: G. Daniel '92

SHOALHAVEN RIVER

Barbers Ck

To
Long Pt.Lkt.
& Tallong

12/15 km

11/16 km   120m

120m L/Hd
km

Hermit Spur

Hermit Flat

4/
18 km

5/9 km

(white)
3/19 km

MT
AYRE
580m

2/20
km

6/8 km

limestone quarry

Bungonia Ck
(red)

FROME HILL RD

Frome Hill

Bungonia
Canyon

TROY
WALLS

Bungonia
Lkd'n

540m

1/21
km

(green)

Kellys Cave

Fossil
Cave

Hogans
Cave

Drum
Cave

Grill
Cave

Ranger
H.Q.

0 km

To
Marulan

Adams
Lkt.

Jerrara

camping
area

tN
Nm

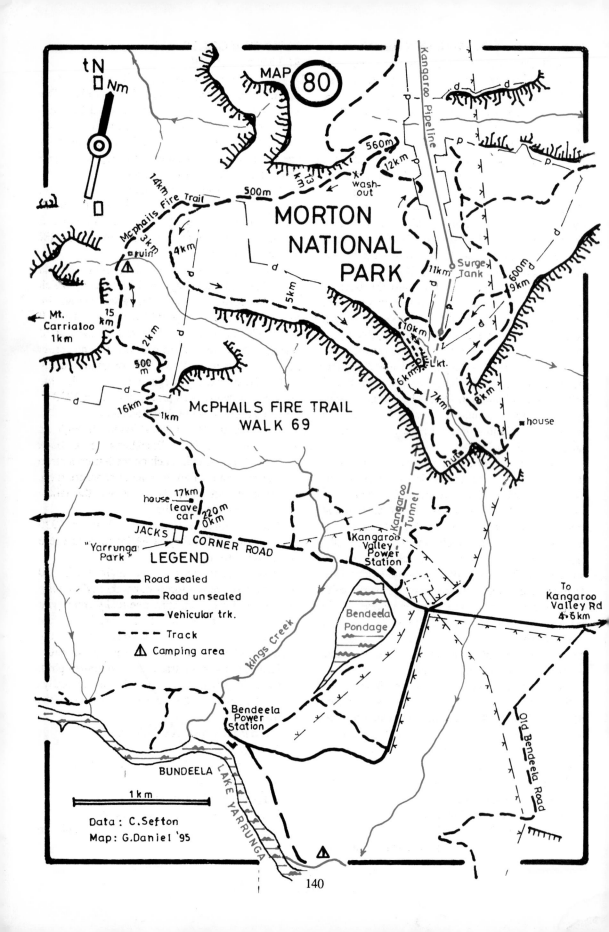

MAP 80

MORTON
NATIONAL
PARK

Kangaroo Pipeline

McPhails Fire Trail

← Mt.
Carrialoo
1km

McPHAILS FIRE TRAIL
WALK 69

Surge Tank

Kangaroo
Tunnel

house
leave car

JACKS   CORNER ROAD

"Yarrunga
Park"   LEGEND

Kangaroo
Valley
Power
Station

To
Kangaroo
Valley Rd
4·5 km

——— Road sealed
– – – Road unsealed
– – Vehicular trk.
- - - Track
△ Camping area

Kings Creek

Bendeela
Pondage

Old Bendeela Road

Bendeela
Power
Station

1 km

Data : C.Sefton
Map : G.Daniel '95

BUNDEELA

LAKE YARRUNGA

69. MORTON N. P.: McPHAILS FIRE TRAIL

McPhails Fire Trail winds through magnificent forests with huge Turpentines and stands of Coachwoods and Red Cedar to a lookout on an escarpment edge where there are excellent views of Lake Yarrunga and the Ettrema wilderness in Morton National Park.

From the main Kangaroo Valley Road, turn west onto Jacks Corner Road, 500m north of Hampton Bridge. The road is signposted "Bendeela Picnic Area". Drive to Bendeela Pondage then for a further 1.4km (50m before "Yarranga Park"). McPhails Fire Trail can be seen on the right (north) leading up a hill. Park the car in the paddock adjacent to the trail.

Follow the trail up the hill, past the base of Mount Carrialoo. The trail then swings right (NE). Continue on this section of the trail over a partially cleared saddle. Proceed about 600m past this clearing and at a junction take the track which branches right (SW) - 3.5 km from the start. This track is located under the main escarpment and follows a bench through forested areas past small clearings and an abandoned house for 4km to a major transmission line. Leeches can be a problem on this section.

Follow the transmission line road to the top of the escarpment then take the first road to the left (after 1.5km) which crosses the Kangaroo pipeline. One hundred metres past the pipeline the road crosses a small creek and 200m further on at a road bend, take the track which heads off SW from near a fence across a creek and through some scrub. The track meets a wider track which follows the route of an underground cable (indicated by marker posts) to the edge of the escarpment - a great place for a late lunch. There are magnificent views of Mt Carrialoo, Mt Moollatoo and Lake Yarrunga to the west and Kangaroo Valley to the south east.

Return to the main trail and continue on for 2.1km to a trail junction - left branch sign-posted McPhails Fire Trail. Take this trail which follows a creek down from the escarpment to rejoin the outward route after 1.6km. Finally, walk back across the saddle, past Mt Carrialoo to the car.

Grade: Medium, 350m asc.**Distance:** 18km.
No Public Transport.
Best in Spring and Autumn.
Map 80 and CMA Bundanoon.

Caryll Sefton and Terry Whatman

70. WODI-WODI TRACK, STANWELL PARK

This is a 6.5km circuit walk in the scenic amphitheatre of the Stanwell Creek Valley. The Wodi-Wodi track, which commences at Stanwell Park railway station was constructed by Wollongong City Council on lands acquired by the Department of Planning for regional open space. The track is clearly marked.

From Stanwell Park station, head down through leafy streets to Stanwell Park Beach. If the weather is favourable, you could enjoy a swim. The hang gliders soaring off Bald Hill provide a spectacle.

After a break, walk south along the beach and view Stanwell Park Lagoon. The lagoon, which supports abundant bird life, was formed by deposits of sand closing off the flow of Stanwell Creek. Continue on up a steep hill on sections of Kalaroo Ave and Murrawal Street and cross Lawrence Hargrave Drive (the original railway route). Next, walk through a tunnel under the railway line which was probably built in 1920 to provide access for railway maintenance.

Continue up the Bullock Track through an almost pure stand of Blackbutts to a track junction. Take the side-track on the left up a steep but not strenuous climb to a lookout where there are excellent views of the coast and the tallest railway viaduct in Australia.

The eight-arched viaduct was built in 1920 across Stanwell Creek. The 69.5m high structure is still in use today.

Retrace your steps to the main track and continue through rainforest down through a gully to Stanwell Creek - an attractive rocky creek with moss-covered boulders. If the creek is low enough, rock-hop 300m downstream to the railway viaduct which was seen from the lookout.

Return to the main track, then continue uphill, past the steep branch track on the left to Kellys Falls. Continue on the main track (right) to the railway station.

Grade: Easy/Medium, 310m asc.
Distance: 6.5km.
Public Transport: Train to Stanwell Park.
Suits all seasons.
Map 81 and CMA Appin.
Pamphlet - Wollongong City Council

Pam Robinson

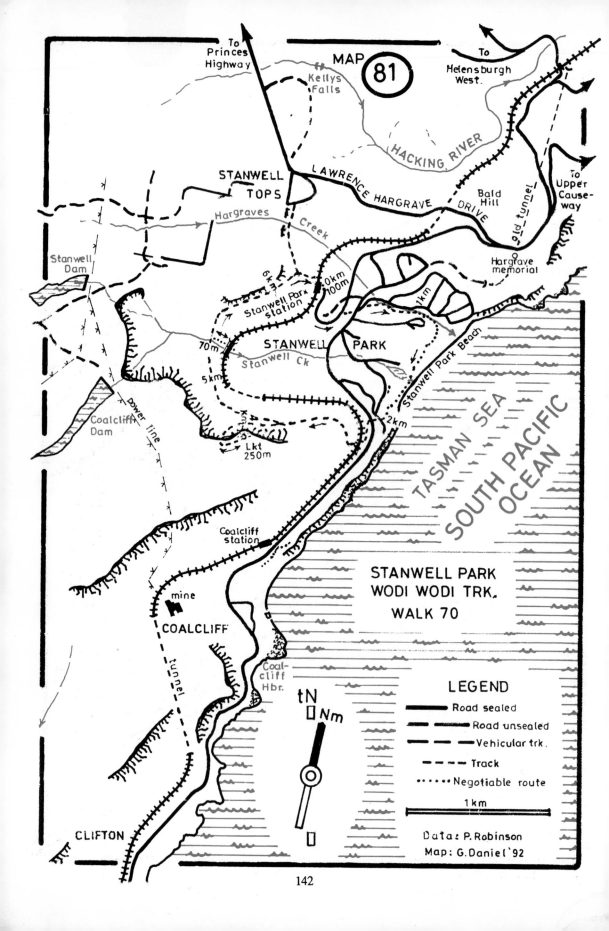

MAP **81**

To Princes Highway

Kellys Falls

To Helensburgh West.

HACKING RIVER

STANWELL TOPS

LAWRENCE HARGRAVE DRIVE

Bald Hill

old tunnel

To Upper Causeway

Hargraves Creek

Stanwell Dam

Stanwell Park Station

6 km

Hargrave memorial

0km 100m

1 km

STANWELL PARK

Stanwell Park Beach

70m

Stanwell Ck

5 km

Power line

Coalcliff Dam

Lkt 250m

2km

TASMAN SEA

SOUTH PACIFIC OCEAN

Coalcliff station

mine

COALCLIFF

tunnel

Coalcliff Hbr.

STANWELL PARK
WODI WODI TRK.
WALK 70

tN
Nm

CLIFTON

Data: P. Robinson
Map: G. Daniel '92

LEGEND

———— Road sealed
—‑—‑— Road unsealed
— — — Vehicular trk.
- - - - Track
· · · · · Negotiable route

|———— 1 km ————|

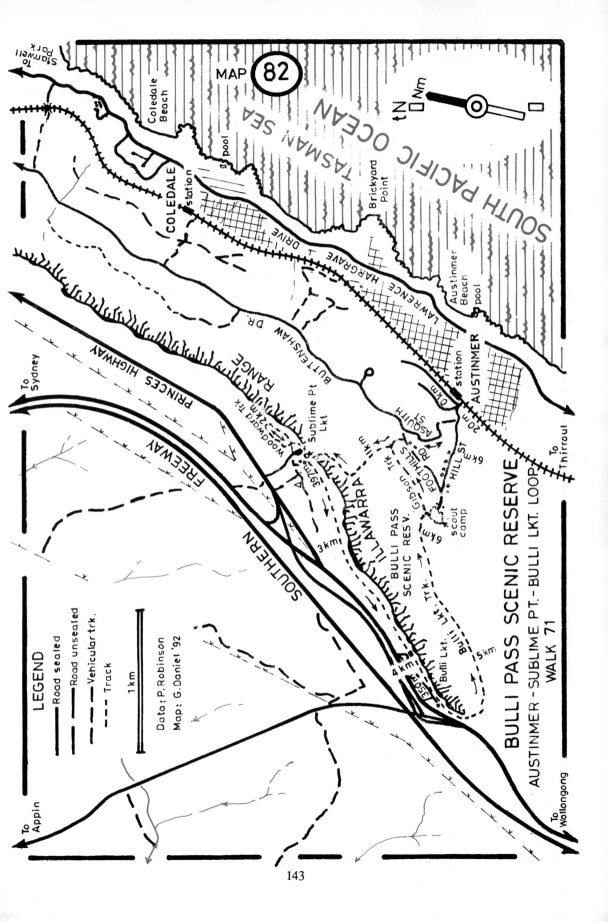

MAP 82

SOUTH PACIFIC OCEAN

TASMAN SEA

To Stanwell Park

Coledale Beach

St pool

COLEDALE station

LAWRENCE HARGRAVE DRIVE

Brickyard Point

Austinmer Beach pool

AUSTINMER station

ASQUITH ST

SOUTH HILL ST

HILL ST

FOOTHILLS RD

Gibson Trk

FOOTHILLS TRK

scout camp

0km
20m
6km
6km

To Thirroul

BUTTENSHAW DR

ILLAWARRA RANGE

Sublime Pt Lkt

Woodward trk 22m

392m

3km

4km
5km

BULLI PASS SCENIC RES.

Bulli Lkt. Trk.

Bulli Lkt. Trk.

355T

PRINCES HIGHWAY

SOUTHERN FREEWAY

To Sydney

To Appin

To Wollongong

BULLI PASS SCENIC RESERVE

AUSTINMER - SUBLIME PT. - BULLI LKT. LOOP
WALK 71

LEGEND
Road sealed
Road unsealed
Vehicular trk.
Track

1 km

Data: P. Robinson
Map: G. Daniel '92

71. BULLI PASS S.R.: AUSTINMER - SUBLIME POINT - BULLI LOOKOUT CIRCUIT

The Illawarra Escarpment near Wollongong comprises majestic cliffs, scenic amphitheatres and forested talus slopes. West of Austinmer is a good circuit walk which features extensive coastal and escarpment views, a beautiful swamp, and rainforest. Doug Gibson, after whom part of the circuit was named, formed the Illawarra Bird Observers' Club. Steps and ladders are involved on two legs of the walk but they are neither daunting nor difficult.

From Austinmer station, walk up Balfour and Asquith Streets to the southern end of Buttenshaw Drive. There is parking space here and at the northern end of Foothills Road. Walk into the bush where a sign indicates "The Sublime Point Track". Walk up 80 plus steps to the bench where the circuit begins.

At the track junction, continue straight ahead on the Sublime Point Track. The climb to the top takes about an hour with several rests to catch your breath and admire the views of the coast which unfold through the trees. The track ascends steeply through pleasant mixed bush, and steps and ladders assist the climb. On reaching Sublime Point Lookout, take the circular Woodward track (800m) to the north. It leads though woodland and heath on the escarpment top and provides further views of sheer sandstone cliffs and the coastal plain north and south of Austinmer.

After a break follow the track (sign-posted) south to Bulli Lookout for more views. [There are toilets and a cafe at both Sublime Point and Bulli Lookouts.] At Bulli Lookout, descend through Turpentines, then closed forest with a pleasant rainforest canopy to a Scout camp, then complete the circuit via the Doug Gibson Track through dense forest on the upper bench of the escarpment. This track crosses a pretty rainforested creek, then passes an attractive swamp filled with bulrushes and surrounded by Cabbage Tree Palms and Red Cedars with a view to Sublime Point. Finally, return down the steps to the car or station.

Grade: Easy/Medium, 390m asc.
Distance: 8km.
Suits all seasons.
Public transport: Train to Austinmer.
Map 82 and CMA Bulli.   Pam Robinson

72. ILLAWARRA ESCARPMENT S.R.A.: MT KEIRA RING AND SUMMIT TRACKS

Mt Keira is a skillion-shaped land mass which juts east from the Illawarra Range. This walk suggestion includes the ring track as well as side-trips to Robertsons Lookout and the Mt Keira Summit via Dave Walsh's Track.

Start the walk at Byarong Park on Mt Keira Road where there are picnic facilities and parking.

Take the track near the gateway to the Guides Camp. After 100m, turn right along the Ring Track through a forest of hybrid Blue Gums. The track leads east for 500m, crosses Mt Keira Road to Geordies Flat, then swings north and climbs to a higher bench. On the eastern side of the mountain you pass through sections of subtropical rainforest with Stinging Trees, Red Cedars, Native Tamarinds and Sassafrass as well as large areas of Lantana (an introduced weed). You then cross under a power-line and continue right (west) at a track junction to again meet Mt Keira Rd.

Cross over and take the branch-track on the right to Robertsons Lookout (2km return). This diversion takes you through Eucalypt forest near the escarpment edge to a lookout with fine rainforest views.

Return to the Ring Track, turn right and walk for 500m to a track junction. Take the signposted Dave Walsh's Track on the left which leads up to the Mt Keira summit. The track crosses Mt Keira Rd (yet again) then starts climbing firstly through rainforest, then through forests dominated by Turpentines, Stringybarks and Silvertop Ash. Near the top you emerge on to an exposed ridge-line where there are wonderful views.

On the summit, turn right and walk the short distance to Five Islands Lookout which offers spectacular views of Mt Kembla, Mt Nebo, Lake Illawarra as well as the Five Islands (islets off the coast dedicated as nature reserves).

Return down Dave Walsh's track to the Ring Track. Turn left and complete the circuit to Byarong Park (1km).

Grade: Easy, 150m asc.   **Distance:** 8km.
No public transport.   Suitable any season.
Map 83 and CMA Wollongong.
Pamphlets: Mt Keira Ring Track and Dave Walsh's Track by NP&WS.
Pam Robinson and John Clarke

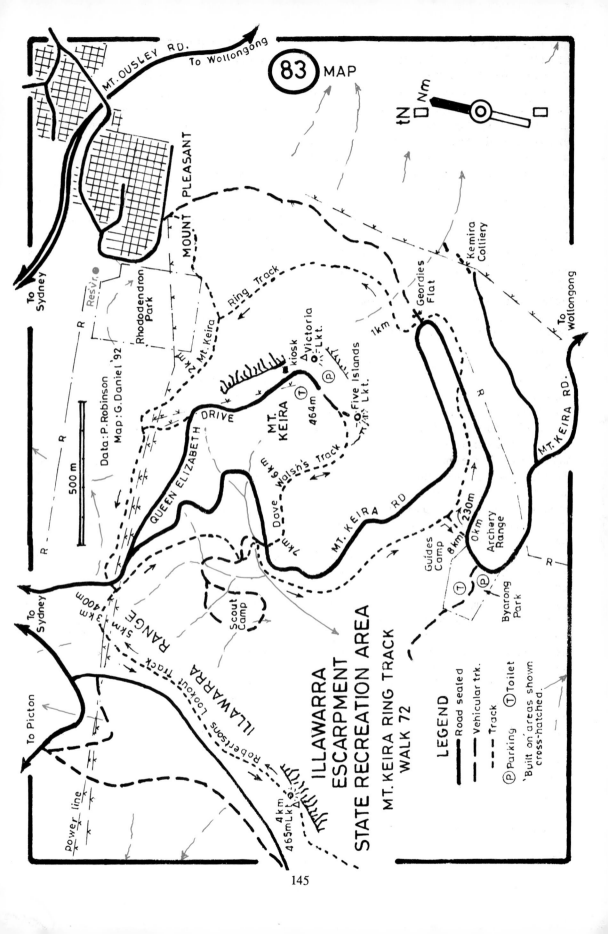

ILLAWARRA ESCARPMENT
STATE RECREATION AREA

MT. KEIRA RING TRACK
WALK 72

83 MAP

tN
Nm

MT. OUSLEY RD.
To Wollongong

To Sydney

MOUNT PLEASANT

Resvr.

Rhododendron Park

Ring Track

2km Mt. Keira

kiosk

Victoria Lkt.

MT. KEIRA
464m

Five Islands Lkt.

6km Dave Walsh's Track

QUEEN ELIZABETH DRIVE

7km

Data: P. Robinson
Map: G. Daniel '92

500 m

MT. KEIRA RD.

Geordies Flat

1km

Kemira Colliery

To Wollongong

MT. KEIRA RD.

R

230m

0km

Archery Range

8km

Guides Camp

Byarong Park

Scout Camp

To Sydney

ILLAWARRA RANGE

5km 3km 400m

Robertsons Lookout Track

Power line

To Picton

To Sydney

4km
465m Lkt.

LEGEND

Road sealed
Vehicular trk.
Track
P Parking   T Toilet
Built on areas shown
cross-hatched.

145

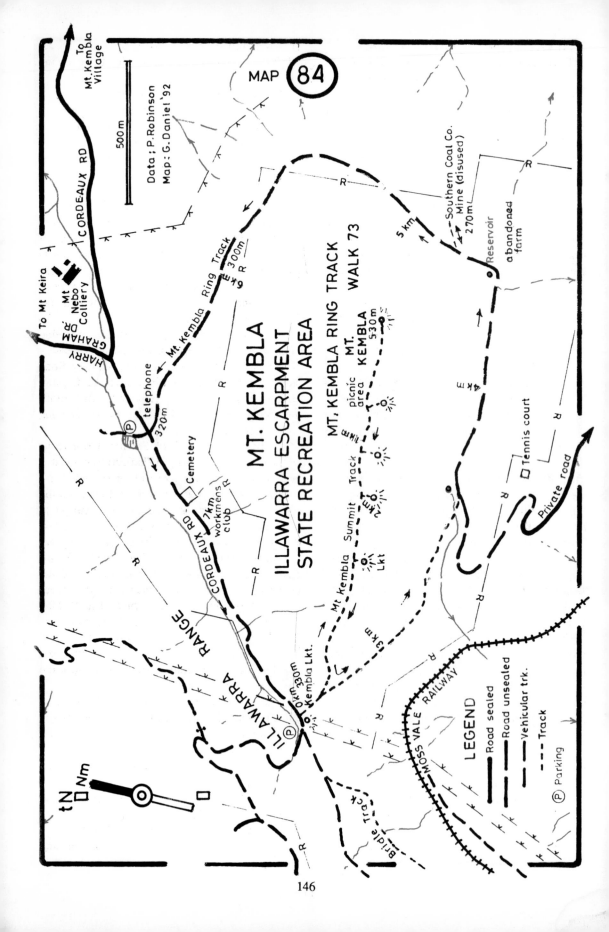

MAP 84

Data: P.Robinson
Map: G.Daniel '92

500 m

To Mt.Kembla Village

CORDEAUX RD

To Mt Keira

GRAHAM DR.

HARRY

Mt Nebo Colliery

telephone

320 m

Mt. Kembla Ring Track

6 km

300 m

R

R

5 km

Southern Coal Co. Mine (disused)

270 m

R

Reservoir

abandoned farm

4 km

MT. KEMBLA
ILLAWARRA ESCARPMENT
STATE RECREATION AREA

MT. KEMBLA RING TRACK
WALK 73

MT. KEMBLA
530 m

picnic area

Cemetery

7 km

workmens club

R

R

R

CORDEAUX RD

ILLAWARRA RANGE

Mt Kembla Summit Track

2 km

1 km

Lkt

3 km

0 km 330 m
Kembla Lkt.

R

R

Tennis court

Private road

R

MOSS VALE RAILWAY

Bridle Track

LEGEND

Road sealed

Road unsealed

Vehicular trk.

Track

P Parking

N
Nm

146

73. ILLAWARRA ESCARPMENT S.R.A.: MT KEMBLA RING & SUMMIT TRACKS

The Mount Kembla area is steeped in history associated with coal mining. This walk takes you to a number of sites associated with mines in the Mt Kembla area as well as through lush rainforest, Eucalypt forest and summit-top heath. There are also wonderful lookout points which provide extensive coastal and escarpment views.

Start the walk from Mt Kembla Lookout on a saddle between Mt Kembla and the main escarpment. Access is from the village of Mt Kembla via Cordeaux Rd and up past the Nebo Colliery turn-off or from Mt Keira via Harry Graham Drive. There is a large tower and a parking area at the lookout.

Initially, head off east through a forest of Gully Gum, River Peppermint and Coast White Box for 100m, then at a sign-posted track junction, take the left branch to the Mt Kembla Summit (3.2km return).

As the track rises steadily up the western side of Mt Kembla you pass though a mixed forest of Eucalypts and rainforest trees. Boulders along the way provide good vantage spots. The summit is composed of Hawkesbury sandstone and supports Silver Top Ash, Black She-oak and tea trees. There is a visitors' book at the summit and there are excellent views over the Dapto coastal plain, Lake Illawarra and the Port Kembla area. After admiring the views, return down the Summit Track and turn left onto the Ring Track.

The Ring Track descends steeply via stone steps into cool rainforest with Red Cedar, Brown Beech and Cabbage Tree Palms. After 1km, the track passes a disused dam, once used to supply water for pit ponies for the Mt Kembla colliery.

The track continues on through an abandoned farm site with thickets of introduced Coral Trees then swings north. Take the short side-track on the right to the disused Southern Coal Company mine. The mine was worked for only three years (1887-1890) because of the poor quality coal.

Return to the Ring Track which swings around the northern side of Mt Kembla for 1.9km through a pure stand of Blue Gums to Cordeaux Road. Turn left and walk 300m where you will see a cemetery on the left. Some of the graves date from the Mt Kembla Mine Disaster of 1902 in which 94 men died.

Finally, walk SW 1km along Cordeaux Rd, past the miners Workmens' Club (built in 1880's) and Windy Gully to Kembla Lookout and the car.

Grade: Easy/Medium, 320m asc.
Distance: 8km.
Suitable all year.   No public transport.
Map 84 and CMA Wollongong.

Pam Robinson

74. PORT KEMBLA - WINDANG ISLAND

Just to the south of the large industrial development of Port Kembla is the 7km sweep of Perkins Beach. From its southern end, just across from the Lake Illawarra entrance, is Windang Island, from which there are great views north and south along the coast and inland towards the Illawarra Escarpment.

Start off from the car-park near the swimming pool at the northern end of Port Kembla Beach - access is from Five Islands Road, Military Road and Olympic Boulevard, Port Kembla. Explore Hill 60, which has fine views and fortifications which date from World War II, before heading south along Perkins Beach.

Walk the full length of Perkins Beach to its southern end at Windang (6.7km). At low tide it is possible to swim/wade across the entrance to Lake Illawarra (alternatively cross the entrance via the road bridge) and walk out along the sandspit to Windang Island. You can walk around it in less than half an hour and the views from its top are excellent - especially of the Five Islands off Port Kembla, the entrance to Lake Illawarra and the escarpment beyond. The views to the south include Shellharbour, Bass Point, The Saddle, Saddleback Mountain and Barren Grounds Nature Reserve. To the west Blackbutt Forest shows out against the settled areas. You can also often see the fluoro-coloured windsurfers in action near the entrance and out to sea.

Return the same way or walk to Shellharbour Road at Lake Illawarra and catch a bus for the return trip to Port Kembla.

Grade: Easy/Medium, 10m asc.
Distance: 16km return, 10km with car shuttle.
Suits all seasons.
Public Transport: Train to Port Kembla and bus from Lake Illawarra.
Map 85 and Wollongong Street Directory.

Pam Robinson

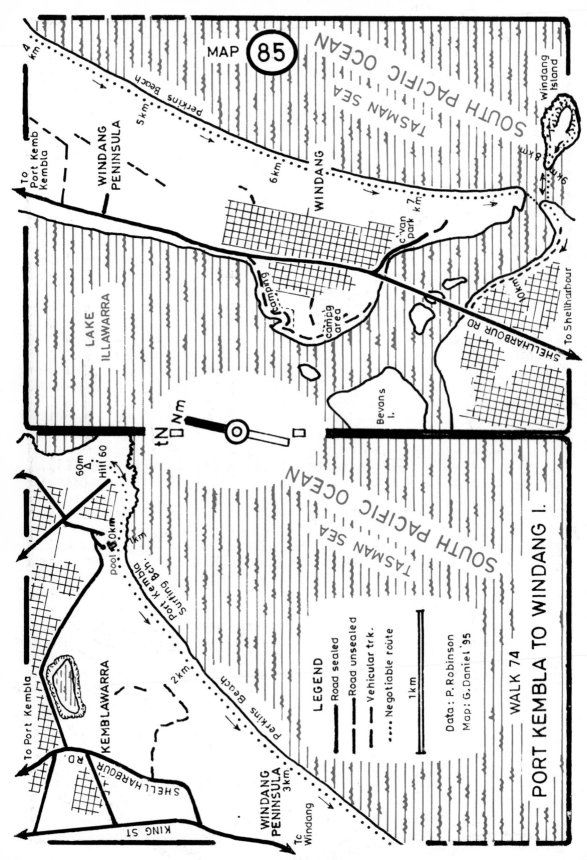

MAP 85

SOUTH PACIFIC OCEAN

TASMAN SEA

Windang Island

Perkins Beach

4 km

5 km

6 km

7 km

8 km

9 km

10 km

To Port Kemb Kembla

WINDANG PENINSULA

WINDANG

c'van park

camping

camp'g area

SHELLHARBOUR RD

To Shellharbour

LAKE ILLAWARRA

Bevans I.

N

SOUTH PACIFIC OCEAN

TASMAN SEA

60m
Hill 60

pool 0km

1km

2km

3km

Port Kembla Surfing Bch.

Perkins Beach

To Port Kembla

KEMBLAWARRA

KING ST

SHELLHARBOUR RD

WINDANG PENINSULA

To Windang

LEGEND
Road sealed
Road unsealed
Vehicular trk.
Negotiable route

1km

Data : P. Robinson
Map: G. Daniel '95

WALK 74

PORT KEMBLA TO WINDANG I.

148

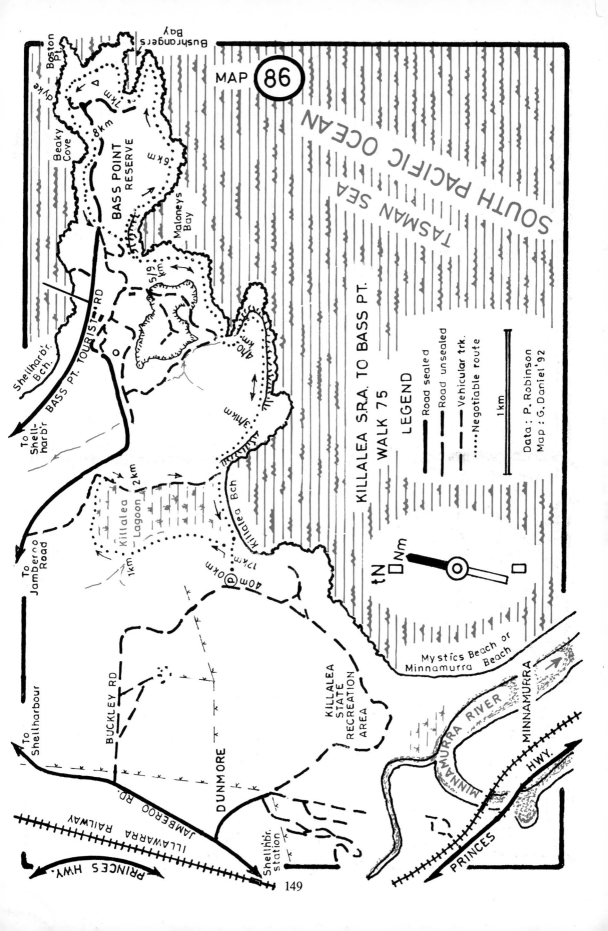

MAP 86

SOUTH PACIFIC OCEAN

TASMAN SEA

KILLALEA S.R.A. TO BASS PT.

WALK 75

LEGEND

Road sealed
Road unsealed
Vehicular trk.
Negotiable route

1 km

Data : P. Robinson
Map : G. Daniel '92

Bushrangers Bay
Boston Pt.
dyke
Beaky Cove
BASS POINT RESERVE
1km
.8 km
.6 km
Maloneys Bay
5/9 km
Shellharb'r Bch.
BASS PT. TOURIST RD.
To Shellharbour
4/10 km
3½km
Killalea Lagoon 2km
Killalea
1km
Killalea Bch
1½km
4om
To Jamberoo Road
To Shellharbour
BUCKLEY RD.
DUNMORE
JAMBEROO RD.
Shellhb'r. station
KILLALEA STATE RECREATION AREA
Mystics Beach or Minnamurra Beach
MINNAMURRA RIVER
MINNAMURRA
PRINCES HWY.
ILLAWARRA RAILWAY
PRINCES HWY.

N Nm

75. KILLALEA S.R.A. AND BASS POINT RESERVE: KILLALEA BEACH - BASS PT

Bass Point is a prominent vegetated peninsula with many interesting rock pools, beautiful marbled pink and black rocks, quiet beaches and interesting littoral rainforest and Banksia and Tea-Tree heathland.

From Shellharbour, drive south 1.5km along the Jamberoo Road and turn off left into Buckley Road to Killalea State Recreation Area. Park in the parking area on the hill, where there are views of Stack Island, Minnamurra Headland and beyond.

Follow the track down to Killalea Beach, then walk inland (NW) to circumambulate Killalea Lagoon. Take binoculars to assist in identifying the numerous species of waterbirds on the lagoon.

Though trackless at this point, it is possible to walk around the coastline to Maloneys Bay then on past a small dyke to Bushrangers Bay, one of the State's few marine reserves which is excellent for swimming, snorkelling and scuba diving.

Next, continue around the coast to Boston Pt and the Boston Memorial which commemorates the loss of four Australian lives in a rescue of 62 American sailors from the "Cities Service Boston" which struck rocks off the point in 1943.

Head west past a large volcanic dyke at a picnic area to Beaky Bay, then on to the Middy or Red Sands Beach. Take the railed stairway here, head south on a track to Bass Point Road.

Take a diversion here east along the road to view a rainforest community that has grown on the sand dunes perched on the rocky headland. Unfortunately the road has been routed right through the rainforest and has resulted in considerable disturbance and weed infestation. The most common tree is the large Plum Pine, whilst other rainforest species include Lillypilly, Red-fruited Olive Plum, a native Celtis and a Small-leaf Fig.

Return to where the track from the Middy meets the road, pass under the Bass Point Reserve entrance gates, then head south along a road to Maloneys Bay. Finally, walk back along the coast to Killalea Beach and up to the car-park.

Grade: Easy/Medium, 50m asc, trackless sections and rock-hopping. **Distance:** 13km.
No public transport.   Suits all seasons.
Map 86 and CMA Albion Park.

Pam Robinson

76. KIAMA - MINNAMURRA VIA THE COAST

The coastline between Kiama and Minnamurra provides easy walking. There are scenic ocean beaches and rugged headlands formed by volcanic activity.

From Kiama station, walk up to Blowhole Point. Admire the Blowhole and the rugged point, then head off west along the coastline toward Kiama Harbour. There are high cliffs with interesting pink and green coloured rocks. Next walk over Pheasant Point, then along Bombo Beach to Bombo Point - another area worth exploring. From the southern end, follow the road around the headland and down into the quarry, and marvel at the massive columns of basalt exposed by the quarrying. Walk back around to the western side of the headland then climb to the top for 360° views.

Return from the headland and follow the cycleway by the railway line then walk along Cliff Drive past Cathedral Rocks, then head down and walk along Boyds Beach.

Next, walk over and around Minnamurra Headland where there are beautiful views of the Minnamurra River estuary and sandspit, Stack Island and Cathedral Rocks. There is a fine little beach below for swimming.

Finally, walk via Charles Ave, and North Street to Minnamurra station.

Grade: Easy, 30m asc.
Distance: 8km.
Public Transport: Train to Kiama and from Minnamurra.
Ideal in Summer.
Map 87 and CMA Kiama.

Pam Robinson

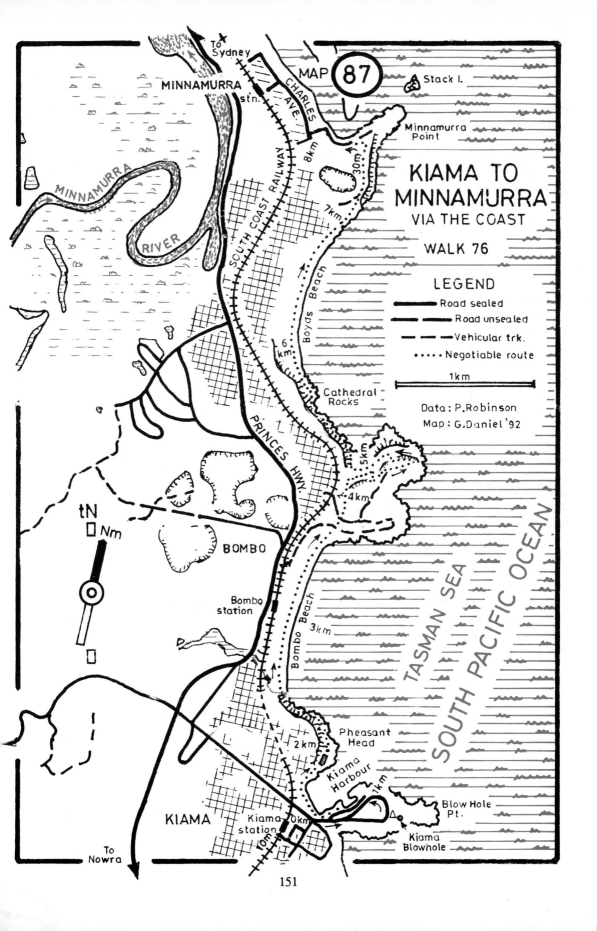

To Sydney

MINNAMURRA
stn.

CHARLES AVE.

MAP 87

Stack I.

Minnamurra Point

Minnamurra RIVER

SOUTH COAST RAILWAY

8km

30m

7km

Boyds Beach

6 km

Cathedral Rocks

5km

4km

PRINCES HWY

BOMBO

Bombo station

Bombo Beach

3km

Pheasant Head

2km

Kiama Harbour

1km

KIAMA

Kiama station

0km

To Nowra

Blow Hole Pt.

Kiama Blowhole

KIAMA TO MINNAMURRA
VIA THE COAST

WALK 76

LEGEND

— Road sealed
— Road unsealed
– – Vehicular trk.
···· Negotiable route

1km

Data: P. Robinson
Map: G. Daniel '92

TASMAN SEA

SOUTH PACIFIC OCEAN

tN

Nm

77. BUDDEROO N.P.: CARRINGTON FALLS - MISSINGHAM STEPS

Budderoo National Park contains an extensive undulating plateau about 600m above sea level and vertical cliffs of clean quartz sandstone, over 100m high, which form the northern side of the Kangaroo Valley. At Carrington Falls the Kangaroo River plunges 50m off the plateau into a secluded, shady valley. Missingham Steps provides (moderately difficult) access to this beautiful area below the cliff-line.

Turn off the Illawarra Highway, 2km east of Robertson and drive about 5km along the Jamberoo/Nowra Road. Take the Carrington Falls Road on the right and park the car at the car-park above Carrington Falls (signposted).

Firstly, view Carrington Falls from the lookouts, then cross the Kangaroo River to the Nellies Glen picnic area. At a trail fork, take the right branch to Nellies Water-hole - a delightful, fern-fringed pool dominated by a low waterfall. On the western bank upstream of the waterfall is an old sapphire field (a paddock pock-marked with shallow pits, giving the impression of a World War I battlefield).

Having visited Nellies Water-hole, return to the trail fork at Nellies Glen picnic area and take the left branch which is partly obstructed by an earth mound.

Walk down this track to a fork. Take the left branch marked with a "To the Gorge" sign and continue until the trail dips down into a valley and then up again to a fenced paddock.

Continue along the fence line, taking steps to avoid a wet area where the trail crosses a hanging swamp. Now begin to look out for a much narrower trail on the left. It is near a root ball of a fallen tree on one side of the trail. Take the side-track and turn right at the next fork as advised. The track now narrows considerably and after swinging to the left it eventually peters out atop of the steep descent into the "Missingham Steps" gorge.

Take a breather, the descent into the gorge is an extremely steep one - in fact, in places it is almost vertical, although hand and footholds are plentiful (so the climb down is not as daunting as it appears to be from the top).

Having made the descent you will find yourself in a different world - not one of Gum Trees and Banksias but one of Coachwoods, Tree Ferns, moss cushions and ferny grottoes. A tiny stream enters the gorge from the right and trickles almost silently off towards its eventual junction with the Kangaroo River. In so doing it has cut its way down to the very base of the river cliff line so that where it breaks out of the Missingham Steps gorge it is some 30m below the level of Budderoo Plateau.

Missingham owned a local saw mill. Last century he cut steps into the gorge that now bears his name so that his employees and their families could negotiate the steeper parts of the gorge down to the river for a picnic. Today few of the steps remain. Many have found resting places in odd positions, the rock in which they had been cut having fallen away from the cliff wall. Thus, you will find solitary steps leading nowhere - cut into the faces of what are now stream bed boulders.

With many steps no longer in place, there are points along the length of the stream gorge where the going becomes a little awkward. At one point you need to negotiate a 2m drop. Where the gorge breaks through the cliff-line, progress is easier. There is no marked track but tagged trees indicate the easiest route down through rainforest.

At the valley bottom, cross the river and view the smooth, white cliff-face opposite - an outcrop of coal shale. Look for fossil Glossopteris leaves preserved in pieces of talus at the cliff bottom and crystalline calcite geodes in some of the rock slabs beside the river. The geodes (or vugs) are infilled with black, brown and white calcite crystals.

A short rock-hop downstream takes you to the junction of the river with a tributary joining it from the NW - Diharowal Creek. This stream is also confined between cliffs which come down almost to the waters edge. Up this stream there is an attractive line of falls and cascades.

Further upstream the tributary is blocked by enormous sandstone blocks which have fallen from the upper cliff-line near an attractive pool. This blockage marks the end of the walk. After a break, return by the same route.

Grade: Medium, 310m asc.

Distance: 8km.

Suits all seasons.

No public transport.

Map 88 and CMA Robertson, Kangaroo Valley.

Jim Chapman

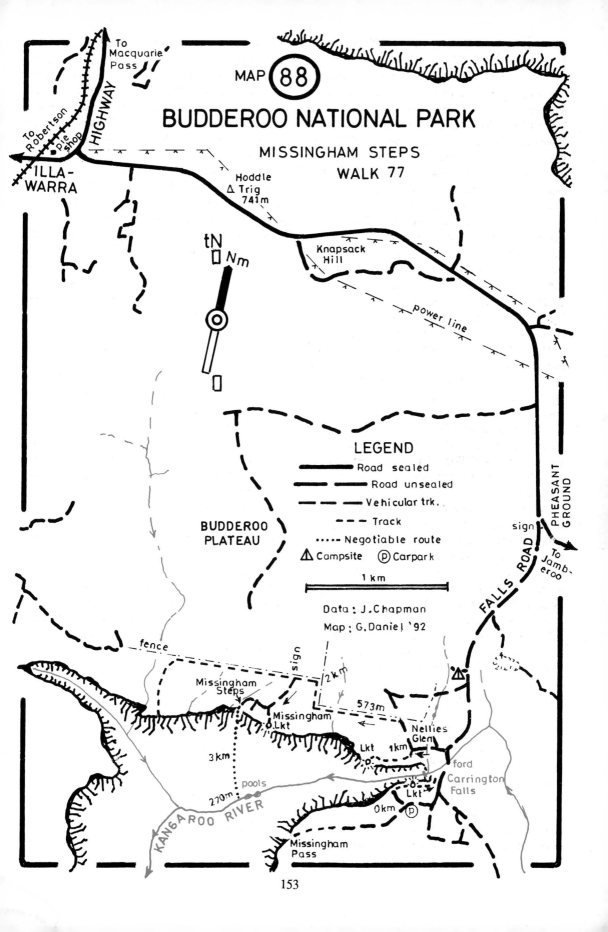

MAP ⑧⑧

BUDDEROO NATIONAL PARK

MISSINGHAM STEPS
WALK 77

To Macquarie Pass

To Robertson

Pie shop

HIGHWAY

ILLA-WARRA

Hoddle △ Trig 741m

tN

□ Nm

Knapsack Hill

power line

BUDDEROO PLATEAU

LEGEND

Road sealed
Road unsealed
Vehicular trk.
Track
Negotiable route
△ Campsite ⓟ Carpark

1 km

Data: J.Chapman
Map: G.Daniel '92

FALLS ROAD

PHEASANT GROUND

sign

To Jamberoo

fence

sign

2km

Missingham Steps

Missingham Lkt

573m

Nellies Glen

Lkt

1km

3km

ford

Carrington Falls

pools

270m

Lkt

KANGAROO RIVER

0km ⓟ

Missingham Pass

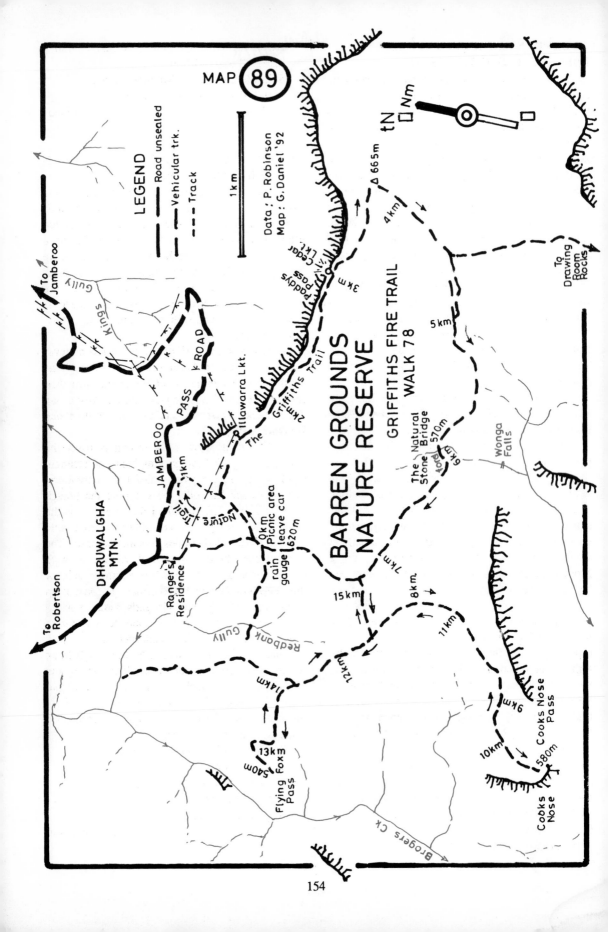

MAP (89)

LEGEND
— Road unsealed
— Vehicular trk.
--- Track

1 km

Data : P. Robinson
Map : G. Daniel '92

To Jamberoo

Kings Gully

JAMBEROO PASS ROAD

Illawarra Lkt.

Paddys Pass

Cedar Lkt.

The Griffiths Trail

3 km

△ 665m

4 km

To Drawing Room Rocks

5 km

BARREN GROUNDS
NATURE RESERVE

GRIFFITHS FIRE TRAIL
WALK 78

The Natural Stone Bridge
570m

Wonga Falls

6 km

DHRUWALGHA MTN.

To Robertson

Nature Trail

11 km

Ranger's Residence

0 km
Picnic area
leave car
620m

rain gauge

Redbank Gully

7 km

15 km

8 km

11 km

9 km

10 km

12 km

14 km

13 km
540m

Flying Fox Pass

Cooks Nose Pass

580m

Cooks Nose

Brogers Ck.

154

78. BARREN GROUNDS NATURE RESERVE: GRIFFITHS TRAIL

Barren Grounds is a star-shaped plateau with sheer escarpment sides and a narrow neck access. One of the important reasons for reserving this area is that it provides habitat for the rare Bristle Bird and Ground Parrot. Within the nature reserve is a bird observatory managed by the Royal Australian Ornithological Union. Nature reserves are dedicated primarily for nature conservation purposes, and unlike national parks, less emphasis is placed on recreational opportunities. None the less, in this nature reserve, there is a nature trail and a walking track system to some splendid lookouts. Be sure to stick to the tracks.

To reach the walk starting point, travel south from Wollongong through Albion Park towards Jamberoo. Turn right where a sign indicates "Minnamurra Falls". Travel on past the Minnamurra Falls turn-off and up Jamberoo Pass. Take the sharp turn-off left to Barren Grounds Nature Reserve (signposted).

Alternatively, turn east off the Illawarra Highway at the Robertson Pie Shop (2km east of Robertson) towards Jamberoo Pass.

Drive in past the Warden's residence to a parking area and picnic ground (1km).

The Griffiths trail is a circular walk of 8km with a crescent shaped 1km nature trail leading off. It is worth the diversion because it leads across a swamp area, down off the edge of the escarpment and along through some rainforest which is unusual as it is on a north-facing slope. Mosses, ferns, rocks, lichens and a waterfall can be seen along the way.

Back on the main trail, turn left through heath country. Barren Grounds is 70% heath and 30% forest and has a varied display of wildflowers, especially in Spring and Summer. After 500m turn left along a track to Illawarra lookout for fine views of Kiama, Lake Illawarra and beyond. Resume the main track and follow the trail to Cedar Lookout, then past the branch trail to Drawing Room Rocks and on to Stone Bridge.

After 1.1km at a track junction, either continue ahead for 700m back to the car-park, or turn left to Cooks Nose (5km return) for spectacular views of the Kangaroo and Broger Valleys and/or Flying Fox Pass (4km return), for fine wilderness views.

Grade: Easy/Medium, 50m asc.

Distance: Griffiths trail plus nature trail - 8km; All trails - 17km.

Suits all seasons.   No public transport.

Map 89 and CMA Kangaroo Valley.

Pam Robinson

79. SADDLEBACK MOUNTAIN - BARREN GROUNDS VIA HODDLES TRACK

In the 1830s, Robert Hoddle surveyed a route from the coast at Kiama to the Barren Grounds and on to Goulburn. The walking track named after him now stretches from Saddleback Mountain Lookout near Kiama, along the saddle and up through the largest sub-tropical rainforest remnant in southern NSW to the top of the escarpment at Barren Grounds. The track is clearly marked, although there are some rough, steep pinches.

Leave the Princes Highway at the Kiama turn-off (Gipps Street). From the Post Office, head south along Manning Street for about 1km then turn right into Saddleback Road. Drive up Saddleback Road for 6.5km to Saddleback Lookout and park the car.

Head off in a westerly direction from the Lookout car-park through grassland and remnant patches of sub-tropical rainforest containing Sassafrass and Lillypilly trees. Ignore the branch track on the left which leads down to the Foxground Road. After the saddle, cross a stile and enter Barren Grounds Nature Reserve. The track leads through beautiful rainforest with Coachwoods and lianas on the southern side of the steep rock face of Mt Noorinan. The last steep climb up onto Barren Grounds takes you to vegetation of a very different nature with Grass Trees, Banksias and other heath species.

Once on the escarpment take the rough track which leads off SW for about 300m along the cliff-edge. Have lunch on the large rocks and enjoy the beautiful views of Foxground Valley, the ocean, Saddleback Mountain and Jamberoo Valley. Return the same way.

Grade: Easy/Medium, 240m asc.

Distance: 6km.

No public transport.

Suits all seasons.

Map 90 and CMA Kiama.

Pam Robinson

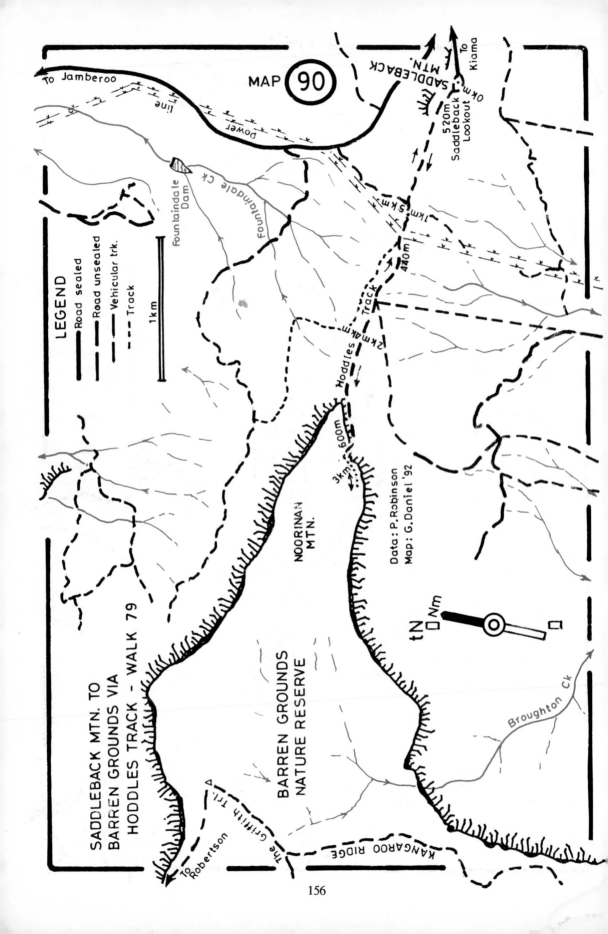

MAP 90

SADDLEBACK MTN. TO
BARREN GROUNDS VIA
HODDLES TRACK – WALK 79

LEGEND
Road sealed
Road unsealed
Vehicular trk.
Track
1km

To Jamberoo
Power line
Fountaindale Dam
Fountaindale Ck

To Kiama
To SADDLEBACK MTN.
0km
520m Saddleback Lookout
1km
5km
440m
2km
Hoddles Track
600m
3km

NOORINAN MTN.

BARREN GROUNDS
NATURE RESERVE

Broughton Ck

The Griffith Trl.
To Robertson
KANGAROO RIDGE

Data: P.Robinson
Map: G.Daniel '92

Nm
Nt

156

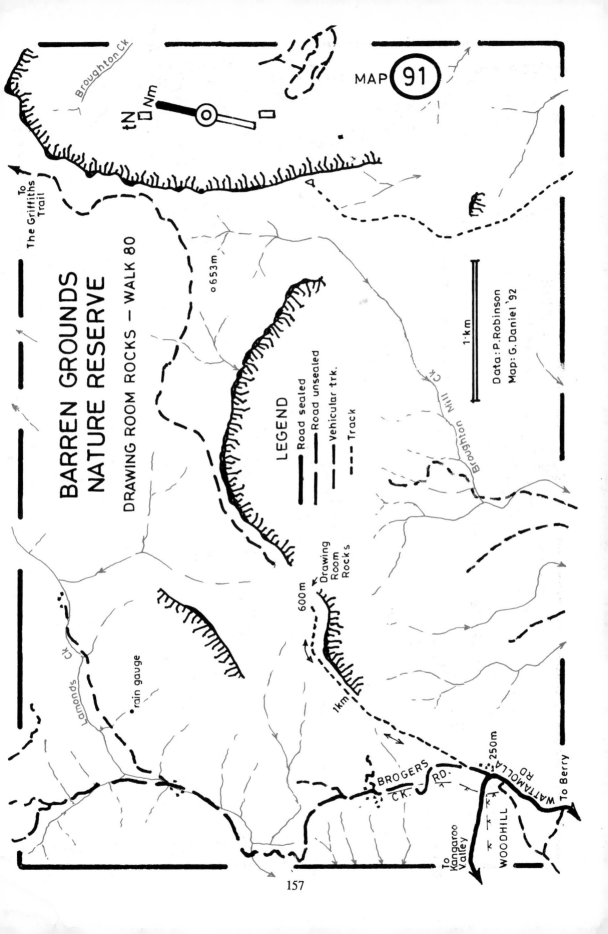

BARREN GROUNDS
NATURE RESERVE

DRAWING ROOM ROCKS — WALK 80

MAP 91

LEGEND

Road sealed
Road unsealed
Vehicular trk.
Track

tN   Nm

Data: P. Robinson
Map: G. Daniel '92

1·km

To The Griffiths Trail

Broughton Ck

o 653m

Drawing Room Rocks

600 m

Lamonds Ck

rain gauge

Broughton Hill Ck

1km

250m

BROGERS CK.

WATTAMOLLA RD

WOODHILL

To Berry

To Kangaroo Valley

80. BARREN GROUNDS NATURE RESERVE: WATTAMOLLA ROAD, WOODHILL - DRAWING ROOM ROCKS

Drawing Room Rocks, high on the Illawarra Escarpment on the edge of Barren Grounds Nature Reserve, offers wonderful views of the Kangaroo and lower Shoalhaven Valleys. From the top you can admire these views as you sit on eroded sandstone rocks shaped like tables and chairs.

From Sydney, head south down the Princes Highway towards Berry. Immediately before the town, cross the bridge over Broughton Mill Creek and turn sharp right into Wattamolla Road, just before Apex Park.

Travel seven winding kilometres to a sharp bend on a saddle to Woodhill where the road descends into Kangaroo Valley. There is a branch road heading north and an area to park at this point. Leave the car here.

The track leads NNE up a ridge through varied vegetation and sandstone escarpment to the top of Barren Grounds. Walk along through heathland to Drawing Room Rocks. The ascent of 350m takes about 1hr. The distance is 1.7km.

The rock formations resulted from softer sandstone eroding below hard ironstone cappings. Enjoy the views then return the same way.

Grade: Easy/Medium, 360m asc.
Distance: 3.5km.
Suits all seasons.
No public transport.
Map 91 and CMA Kangaroo Valley.

Pam Robinson

81. SEVEN MILE BEACH NATIONAL PARK

Seven Mile Beach National Park protects a narrow strip of forested lands along an 8km stretch of coastline between Gerroa and Shoalhaven Heads on the South Coast. The land systems within this small national park are coastal sand-ridges and a large wetland known as Coomonderry Swamp. The NPA played the leading role in having this area dedicated as a National Park.

The park is 140km south of Sydney. Leave the Princes Highway at Werri Beach and take the road through Gerringong and Gerroa toward Shoalhaven Heads. Turn left to the signposted Seven Mile Beach N.P. picnic area near the middle of Seven Mile Beach.

Enjoy a surf and walk along the beach or through the forest on service trails as far as desired before returning to the picnic area. It is interesting to note the succession of vegetation communities from Spinifex grass on the coastal fore-dunes to tall Bangalay and Blackbutt forest further inland. Intermediate communities include Coast Wattle and Coast Tree heaths with stands of Coast Banksia. If time permits, inspect Coomonderry Swamp, a fine wetland and waterbird habitat fringed by Teatree thickets, Swamp Mahogany and Swamp Oak on the western side of the Gerringong - Bomaderry Road.

This walk can be combined with walk 82 (Coolangatta Mountain) to make a full day's outing.

Grade: Easy, 10m asc.
Distance: 5-10km.
Suits all seasons.
No public transport.
Map 92 and CMA Berry, Gerroa.

Pam Robinson

82. COOLANGATTA MOUNTAIN

Coolangatta Mountain is a 304m high peak comprised of shale, sandstone and tuffs on the South Coast near Shoalhaven Heads. From the summit, there are wonderful views of the lower Shoalhaven River Valley.

Access is through Coolangatta Historic Village, which is on the Berry - Bomaderry Road at Shoalhaven Heads (2.5hrs drive from Sydney). It is well worth a look around.

Ask at the desk for permission to do the walk. The proprietors are friendly.

The walk is a fairly steep one up through Spotted Gums and Burrawangs to the top, taking about an hour (2km). There are excellent views of the Shoalhaven delta, Coomonderry Swamp, Gerroa, Seven Mile Beach and Shoalhaven Heads. A convict dam and the Berry family cemetery can be visited on the way back to the car.

Grade: Easy/Medium, 300m asc.
Distance: 4km.
Suits all seasons.
No public transport.
Map 93 and CMA Berry, Gerroa.

Pam Robinson

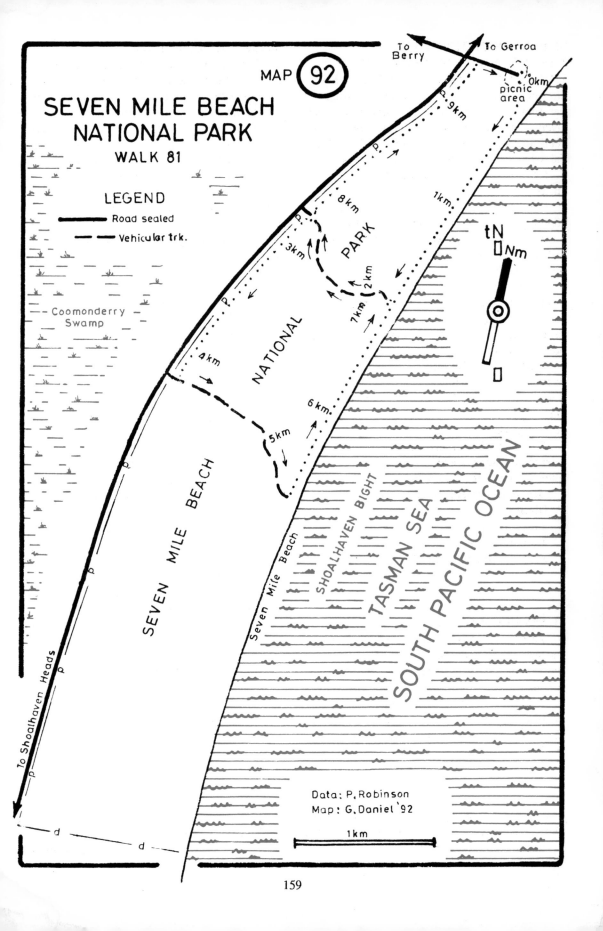

MAP (92)

SEVEN MILE BEACH
NATIONAL PARK
WALK 81

LEGEND

——— Road sealed

- - - Vehicular trk.

To Berry

To Gerroa

0km
picnic area

9km

8km

1km

NATIONAL PARK

3km

2km

7km

tN
Nm

4km

6km

5km

Coomonderry Swamp

SEVEN MILE BEACH

Seven Mile Beach

SHOALHAVEN BIGHT

TASMAN SEA

SOUTH PACIFIC OCEAN

To Shoalhaven Heads

Data: P. Robinson
Map: G. Daniel '92

1km

159

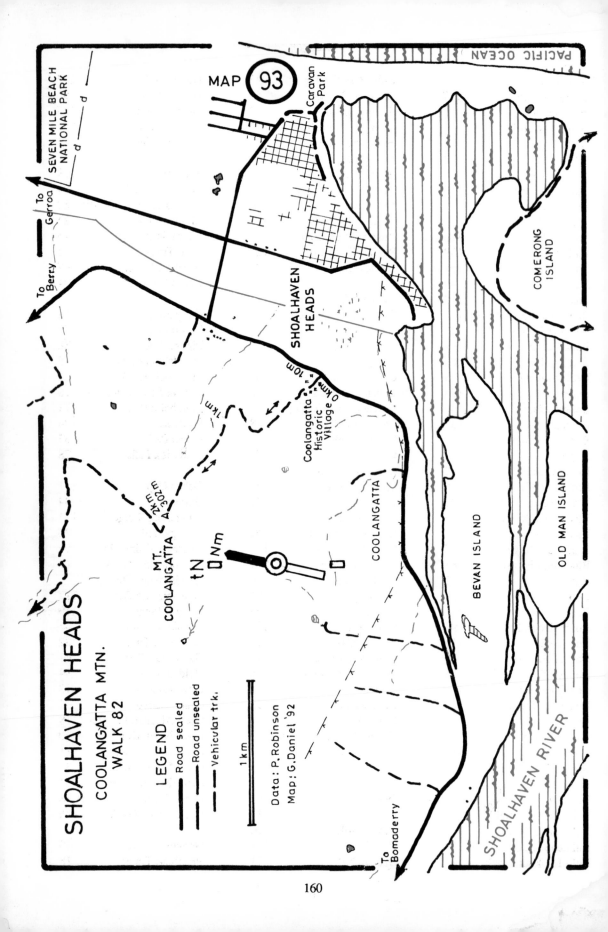

SHOALHAVEN HEADS
COOLANGATTA MTN.
WALK 82

LEGEND
— Road sealed
— Road unsealed
- - - Vehicular trk.

1 km

Data: P. Robinson
Map: G. Daniel '92

MT. COOLANGATTA
A 302 m

tN

MAP 93

SEVEN MILE BEACH NATIONAL PARK

PACIFIC OCEAN

Caravan Park

To Gerroa

To Berry

SHOALHAVEN HEADS

Coolangatta Historic Village

COOLANGATTA

COMERONG ISLAND

BEVAN ISLAND

OLD MAN ISLAND

SHOALHAVEN RIVER

To Bomaderry

160

INDEX

NOTES